06/07

# Newcastle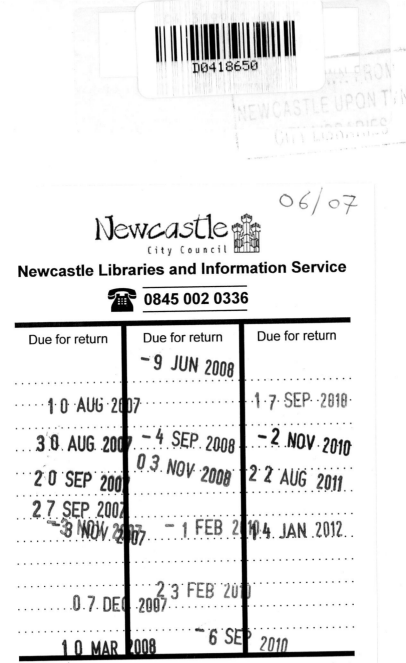
### City Council

## Newcastle Libraries and Information Service

☎ **0845 002 0336**

| Due for return | Due for return | Due for return |
|---|---|---|
| | ⁻9 JUN 2008 | |
| 1 0 AUG 2007 | | 1 7 SEP 2010 |
| 3 0 AUG 2007 | ⁻4 SEP 2008 | ⁻2 NOV 2010 |
| 2 0 SEP 2007 | 0 3 NOV 2008 | 2 2 AUG 2011 |
| 2 7 SEP 2007 | | |
| ⁻3 NOV 2007 | ⁻ 1 FEB 2010 | 4 JAN 2012 |
| | | |
| 0 7 DEC 2007 | 2 3 FEB 2010 | |
| 1 0 MAR 2008 | ⁻6 SEP 2010 | |

Please return this item to any of Newcastle's Libraries by the last
date shown above. If not requested by another customer the loan
can be renewed, you can do this by phone, post or in person.
**Charges may be made for late returns.**

'Willetts's gloriously readable biography paints a picture of a life which, for all its disappointments, was richly lived. I finished the book rather regretting never having had the opportunity to have stood Maclaren-Ross a drink.'
**Mail on Sunday**

'A fascinating trawl through Soho's bohemia.'
**Independent on Sunday**

'*Fear and Loathing in Fitzrovia* is an amusing and ultimately tragic account of the post-war bohemian Julian Maclaren-Ross whose self-destruction was emblematic of an age of fire.'
**Anthony Daniels, *Sunday Telegraph*,**
**'Summer Books Recommendations'**

'[One of] three wonderful English literary biographies.'
**Washington Post Book World**

'The legendarily catastrophic life of Julian Maclaren-Ross has tempted biographers before. But the task of pursuing him, like the Hound of Heaven, through the sordid backstreets, rented basements and sodden saloon bars of his progress has always proved too much of a challenge. It is an extraordinary story of profligacy and waste which has been told, up until now, only in a million awed anecdotes... I have to take my hat off to Paul Willetts for his sheer industry in following his subject to places where few literary biographers need to tread.'
**Philip Hensher, *Spectator***

'Exhilaratingly depressing.'
**Times**

'Historical profiling of a high order, richly and racily done.'
**Literary Review**

'Scrupulous and moving.'
**Buenos Aires Herald**

'*Fear and Loathing in Fitzrovia* vividly recreates the colourful life of this troubled charmer... an excellent biography.'
**Observer**

For Peter Krämer

# NORTH
# SOHO
# 999

**A True Story of
Gangs and Gun-Crime
in 1940s London**

**Paul Willetts**

dewi lewis publishing

First published in the UK in 2007 by
Dewi Lewis Publishing, 8 Broomfield Road
Heaton Moor, Stockport SK4 4ND
+44 (0)161 442 9450

www.dewilewispublishing.com

Copyright © 2007
For the text: Paul Willetts
For this edition: Dewi Lewis Publishing

ISBN: 978-1-904587-45-3

Design & artwork production by Dewi Lewis Publishing

Printed and bound in Great Britain by
Biddles Ltd, King's Lynn

2    4    6    8    10    9    7    5    3    1

First Edition

# Foreword

The figure of the trigger-happy young gangster, wreaking blood-spattered havoc on Britain's city streets, tends to be portrayed as a contemporary phenomenon. In the immediate aftermath of the Second World War, however, the country was stalked by a similar menace. Skim through any national newspapers of that era and you'll see item after item about shootings, armed robberies and hijackings, many of them committed by ruthless young gangsters. Of the innumerable gun-crimes perpetrated between May 1945 and the end of that decade, none generated more intense press coverage than the murder at the heart of *North Soho 999*, a murder that came to be regarded as the climax of the post-war crimewave.

What could have been just another shooting attained extra significance through its intrinsic drama and through the subsequent police investigation which was replete with the twists and turns of a detective novel. Like the killing of the Merseyside toddler James Bulger forty-six years later, the crime also owed some of its notoriety to a single, haunting photograph, reproduced countless times in newspapers and magazines.

Though the murder in question is now largely forgotten, it ranks among the most significant British crimes of the twentieth-century. Besides sparking an investigation on an unprecedented scale, it inspired one of Britain's most commercially successful movies, spawned the country's first hit television cop show and brought together several of the most celebrated and brilliant crime-fighters of the era, men whose lives would be transformed by what happened.

I was researching an altogether different book when I first read a cursory account of the events depicted in *North Soho 999*. Over the next few months my interest in the subject gradually supplanted my interest in the book I'd planned to write. I found myself drawn to the story because it offered a corrective to popular misconceptions about late 1940s London, misconceptions fostered by the gentility of so many of the English movies of that period. I was equally intrigued by the way that the story foreshadows current concerns about escalating violence, youth crime, social collapse and the widespread availability of guns. Mind you, for all its surprising topicality, the story remains as evocative of its era as the crimes of Jack the Ripper are evocative of the teeming, fog-shrouded Victorian slums.

In constructing my book, I've plundered the voluminous police files devoted to the case. These contain detailed witness statements, photographs and even plans of the scene of the crime. I've gleaned valuable supplementary material by interviewing former Metropolitan Police officers who were serving at the time of the murder. I have, in addition, used a wide range of other sources, police files dovetailing with reportage, memoirs, newsreels, architects' drawings and other documents culled from collections as diverse as the BT Group Archives and the Metropolitan Police Historical Collection. Extensive notes on the sources are included at the back of the book.

Sometimes *North Soho 999* may read like a novel, but it remains a work of non-fiction. None of the dialogue is invented. This has, instead, been lifted from witness statements and published accounts of the crime, specified in the notes. The same is true of the thoughts ascribed to the participants in the story. Unlike the dialogue, these are not indicated by quotation-marks. In most cases they are nonetheless exact transcriptions. To suit the context in which they feature, the tense of several of them has been altered. For the same reason first-person sentences have occasionally been changed to the third-person and others have been paraphrased.

At certain points in the book, there are what may appear to be suspiciously detailed portraits of locations where the action takes place. Such descriptions—anything from the layout of a building to the view from a window—are the product of research, not creative embellishment. Of course I was often tempted to use my imagination to fill tantalising gaps in the available material. Had I done so, I knew that I'd have compromised the story and diminished its inherent power. No matter how scrupulous any description is, though, objectivity represents an elusive ideal. The writer can't help but imprint his or her outlook, personality and interests on what's being described. Still, I hope I've conveyed an accurate picture of this extraordinary story which, in contrast to most true-life stories, possesses the shapeliness and resonance of fiction.

# I

# BLOOD
# ON THE
# CROSSROADS

J ust before 2:30pm on Tuesday 29 April 1947, three men clutching
revolvers entered a shop in central London. The shop, which they
intended to rob, was a combined jeweller's and pawnbroker's called
Jay's. It occupied a narrow, single-storey building with two entrances, one
of them through an adjacent yard, the other on Tottenham Street. Jay's was
at the end of a row of small shops and other businesses. On that side of the
street, there was a greasy spoon café, a hairdresser's, a scrap metal dealer's
and a shoe repairer's. Opposite there was a fish and chip shop, a timber
merchant's and a cheap restaurant, popular with the writers, artists and
students who flocked to this area, regarded in those days as being an
extension of Soho.

During the immediate post-war years, Soho was, thanks to its large
French, Italian, Jewish, and Greek communities, famed for its lively,
cosmopolitan ambience, an ambience found nowhere else in London. Most
of the area's main streets possessed a distinctive character. Old Compton
Street was known for its aromatic shops that stocked what were then
regarded as exotic foods: fresh herbs, macaroni, rollmops, pickled anchovies,
root ginger and nutmeg. Wardour Street—'the only street in the world
that's shady on both sides'—was synonymous with the film industry.
Neighbouring Dean Street was noted for its tiny preview cinemas and for
the Rehearsal Rooms where anyone from opera singers to zoot-suited black
musicians performing tired imitations of the Ink Spots could be heard
ploughing through their repertoires. Every day except Sunday, Rupert
Street was where fruit, vegetables and flowers could be bought from road-
side stalls. Poland Street was the preserve of sweatshops manufacturing
clothes. Greek Street was renowned for its restaurants, all hamstrung by the
government-imposed five shilling limit on the cost of a meal and the
unavailability of key ingredients, among them olive oil and parmesan.
Berwick Street was where predominantly Russian, Polish and Jewish
market traders sold a dizzying array of goods that encompassed fish,
stockings, paraffin and cloth. Archer Street was the informal musicians'
employment agency where a loud, gossiping throng convened each
afternoon. And Charlotte Street was associated with the bohemianism that
permeated the pubs, restaurants and cafés of what was dubbed 'North Soho'.

Only about fifty yards separated Jay's from where Tottenham Street
bisected Charlotte Street. Though the lunchtime rush had died down by
the time the armed gang entered the shop, there were still plenty of people
around the crossroads, some of them walking past, others loitering in the
street. None of them seem to have paid much attention to the three
intruders.

About a minute later, a muffled gunshot was audible from inside Jay's.

Unperturbed by the noise, which sounded similar to a car backfiring or the tailgate of a lorry being slammed shut, the people in the street carried on with what they were doing.

A few seconds after that, a customer emerged from the front entrance to Jay's. Like a rugby player evading a tackle, he instantly stepped to his right. He then stood outside the greasy spoon café next-door and watched the gunmen exit the shop. They were wearing raincoats, flat-caps with the brims pulled down and scarves tied over the bottom halves of their faces. Backing across the pavement, they kept their revolvers trained on the shop's staff who had gathered in the doorway.

The gang's getaway car, a black four-door Vauxhall Saloon, paintwork gleaming in the warm sunshine, was parked in front of Jay's. One of the gunmen hurried round the bonnet and climbed into the driver's seat. The other two scrambled through the near-side doors. As they did so, a delivery van rattled past. It slowed down and came to an abrupt halt in the middle of Tottenham Street. Lorries were already parked on both sides, so the gang's intended escape-route was blocked. The driver didn't even have the option of mounting the kerb and going round the blockage because there were too many pedestrians in the way.

Instead of reversing and trying a different route, the driver yelled something, then leapt out of the car. He was accompanied by the other masked men, still brandishing their revolvers. Coats billowing behind them, the gang sprinted towards Charlotte Street.

There were shouts of 'Stop, thief!' and 'Police! Police! Stop them!' These reverberated between the low, shabby buildings on either side, the façades of which were coated with soot from innumerable chimneys.

To the left of the gunmen, a dilapidated, chest-high picket-fence enclosing a bomb-site flickered past. Audible in the distance was the stutter of a motorbike engine. The noise rose in volume as the gang approached the crossroads, which was dominated by the New Scala Theatre, an Edwardian replica of La Scala Opera House in Milan. Moments before they reached there, a powerful red motorbike appeared from the righthand side. Its rider, Alec de Antiquis, was a thickset, handsome Anglo-Italian in his mid-thirties. He wore a leather jerkin, gauntlets and goggles, along with a helmet that concealed his wavy black hair, cut short at the sides and neck. On his back he was carrying a heavily loaded khaki rucksack. When he saw the masked gunmen running along Tottenham Street, he decided to intervene. It was a split-second decision that would have dramatic repercussions.

In a bid to prevent the gunmen from escaping, Antiquis switched off the motorbike's engine and steered it on a collision course with them.

Standing upright on one pedal and braking with his other foot, he swerved into the path of the three fugitives. As he dismounted, he had a gun pointed at his face, the most conspicuous facet of which was a pencil-moustache, trimmed into a neat circumflex. Motionless, he said nothing to provoke the gunman who didn't say anything either. The gunman squeezed the trigger. Prefaced by a soft click, not dissimilar to a dry twig snapping underfoot, a gunshot echoed around the street. The revolver recoiled in the gunman's hand.

Rivulets of blood flowed from Antiquis's well-defined hairline and down the lefthand side of his closely shaven cheek. He then collapsed, his weighty bike toppling over. It landed on his back with sufficient force to knock the air out of his lungs.

Several women who had witnessed the shooting let out piercing screams. Other nearby pedestrians responded by dodging into doorways or diving to the ground like soldiers under fire. All those bodies on the pavement created the fleeting illusion that upwards of a dozen people had been wounded in the mayhem.

The gunman who had just shot the motorcyclist skirted his victim, turned onto Charlotte Street and headed in the direction of Euston Road. At the same time his accomplices resumed their sprint down Tottenham Street.

Robert Delap, employed by the shoe-repairer two doors down from Jay's, charged into the street, cobbler's hammer in hand. He threw it at the fleeing gunmen but it missed them. Heels beating a brisk rhythm, they ran along the pavement, past a row of houses. The larger of the gunmen overtook his partner-in-crime. A three or four yard gap between them quickly opened up. The smaller man was having trouble breathing through the white scarf tied across his face. He wrenched it down with his spare hand, exposing his features to the frightened gaze of passers-by.

Directly ahead, Charles Grimshaw—a surveyor who had travelled into the West End from the north London suburbs—was deep in conversation with a friend. They were standing at the mouth of Charlotte Mews. Grimshaw looked up to find two armed fugitives bearing down on him. When the first of the gunmen dashed past, Grimshaw ducked behind a parked car. He waited till the next gunman drew level with him, then thrust out his right leg in a strange goose-stepping movement. The gunman tripped over the outstretched leg. Before hitting the ground, he let go of his revolver. It bounced across the pavement and settled just out of reach. He was poised to retrieve it when Grimshaw jumped on his back. The writhing gunman struggled in vain to shake off his much bigger, stronger adversary. Meanwhile his accomplice glanced round in time to see the conclusion of the wrestling-match. The accomplice went back to help the other gunman who remained pinned to the ground, chin pressed against the rough surface of a paving-slab.

Taking a well-aimed kick, the taller of the gunmen made jarring contact with Grimshaw's skull. The impact flung Grimshaw off balance, enabling the man beneath him to push him over, stand up and retrieve the revolver from the gutter. With the gun pointed at Grimshaw, the man bellowed, 'Keep off!'

But there was no danger of Grimshaw disobeying. Dazed and unable to move, the surveyor sat on the pavement like a defeated boxer listening to the referee's slow count.

The two fugitives continued running down Tottenham Street. Skin basted with sweat, the smaller of the gunmen hesitated on the corner of Whitfield Street. He paused long enough to check whether anyone was following them. Satisfied that they were not being pursued, he pocketed his revolver and attempted to catch up with the other gunman who was rapidly pulling away from him. At the junction with Tottenham Court Road, along which double-decker trolley-buses routinely whirred, the front-runner veered left. His accomplice went the same way. They passed a chemist's and a blitzed church. Within seconds, they had both crossed the busy road and vanished into the crowd.

❖

At least a couple of dozen witnesses were hovering near the crossroads where Antiquis had been shot. They included Alfred Stock, the grey-haired, sixty-two-year-old Managing Director of Jay's. Pupils bulging behind thick glasses, blood pouring from a gash on the crown of his head, he had just stumbled out of his shop. Robert Delap, who was standing in the street, asked him if he was alright. He assured Delap that he wasn't too badly hurt. Delap then went to the assistance of the wounded motorcyclist. So did Abraham Buckner, the customer who had left Jay's seconds before the gunmen.

Antiquis was lying face down on the pavement, head resting on the worn kerb, body partially concealed beneath his motorbike. The heavy, Indian-built machine, its engine still radiating heat, had to be lifted off him. It was then wheeled away.

A steady flow of blood had matted Antiquis's hair, soaked his clothes and formed a puddle in the dry gutter. Despite the wound that he had sustained, he was still breathing. Through bloodied lips, he mumbled, 'They have shot me... Stop them... I did my best.'

Together with Delap, Buckner tried to make Antiquis comfortable while they waited for help to arrive. Delap peeled off his own jacket, rolled it into a makeshift pillow and manoeuvred it under the wounded man's head.

By then someone had dialled '999', the well-publicised emergency number introduced in London almost a decade earlier. The call went from the automatic telephone exchange on nearby Howland Street to the switchboard at New Scotland Yard, headquarters of the Metropolitan Police.

New Scotland Yard, generally abbreviated to 'the Yard', consisted of two colossal buildings. The older of these, spanning nine floors, was a turreted, late Victorian edifice, designed by Norman Shaw. Into his decorative redbrick design, he'd been contractually obliged to use granite quarried by convicts at His Majesty's Prison Dartmoor. Next to what was dubbed the 'Shaw Building', there was a more recent extension. Both buildings towered over the Westminster Bridge stretch of Victoria Embankment.

Staffed by Post Office employees, all of them women, the Yard's switchboard dealt with about 2,000 calls every hour. The women, who wore padded headphones that squeezed their hair out of shape, sat at a long metal counter with two banks of colour-coded switches. Rising from the counter was a wall of sockets and single-pin plugs.

Switchboard operators were trained to take no more than five seconds to transfer a call. First, they had to ask the person on the other end which service was required: police, fire brigade, or ambulance. Police *and*

*New Scotland Yard, seen from Westminster Bridge. (Copyright: Metropolitan Police Historical Collection)*

*The switchboard at New Scotland Yard.*
*(Copyright: Metropolitan Police Historical Collection)*

ambulance, in this case.

999 calls were put through to the Information Room. Situated in a semi-basement within the section of the Shaw Building, misleadingly named the Back Hall, this provided what journalists were fond of characterising as 'the nerve centre of the battle against crime.' Always alive with urgent but measured conversations, counter-pointed by the crackle of a typewriter, it was a large room which little daylight penetrated. On one side was another switchboard, usually tended by half-a-dozen male officers. From where they were sitting, these experienced officers could see the electric clock mounted on the wall above them. The call from North Soho came through just after 2:30pm, its arrival signalled by a flashing red light.

The first spare operator spoke to the person phoning from the scene of the crime. Operators in the Information Room were taught how to stay calm while coaxing relevant facts from panic-stricken callers. On this occasion the caller reported that there'd been gunfire and that there were

*The Information Room at New Scotland Yard. (Copyright: Metropolitan Police Historical Collection)*

several people lying on the ground, all of whom appeared to have been injured.

Before ringing off, the operator was expected to assure the caller that help was on its way. The operator then had to hurry over to the far side of the room where there were four big tables with street-maps on them. They were arranged in a square and divided by narrow aisles. All four maps had protective sheets of glass over them, reflecting the striplights above. The maps depicted the area under the jurisdiction of the Metropolitan Police, better known as the 'Met'. With the exclusion of the financial district under the control of the City of London Police, this area extended from Croydon in the south to Wood Green in the north, from Ealing in the west to Dagenham in the east. Altogether it covered 734 square miles.

Visitors often commented on how the Back Hall reminded them of a wartime RAF aircraft plotting room, as portrayed in numerous movies. But there were no glamorous young women here, just sober-looking men in uniform, faces puckered into expressions of concentration, the air around them scented with stale tobacco, hair-oil and sweat. Like gamblers playing in a casino, they leant over the tables and slid coloured wooden discs across the glass. These represented cars and motorbikes from the Traffic and Accident Group, river patrol boats, unmarked so-called 'Q cars', plus ordinary patrol cars, most of which were fitted with bulky two-way radios. Each of the Met's twenty-four divisional areas, identified by a letter of the alphabet, was allocated a patrol car, more commonly known as a 'wireless car'.

The operator who had taken this latest call had to pinpoint the intersection between Tottenham and Charlotte Streets on the appropriate map table. The map showed that the scene of the crime was close to the northern boundary of C Division.

Next the operator had to work out which of the available police vehicles was nearest to there. No more than three minutes after receiving a 999 call from anywhere in central London, the Met aimed to have a police vehicle at the scene of the crime. In most situations only a single car was sent, but the North Soho incident warranted two vehicles, one of which was a Q car. Information Room rules decreed that the vehicles were identified by placing red, bracelet-sized hoops over the counters representing them.

Both cars were assigned numbers, which had to be scribbled down and passed to an Announcer. He sat behind a fat silver microphone, through which he was responsible for sending a message giving basic information about the robbery and subsequent shooting. The chosen cars were instructed to head for 73-75 Charlotte Street.

❖

A short, twinkly-eyed forty-two-year-old man with plump cheeks, an angular nose and narrow, almost lipless mouth was beetling towards the Rathbone Place end of Charlotte Street. For business trips such as his current one, he wore a blue suit, dark tie and brown trilby. He was heading for the Fitzroy Tavern, a popular pub around two-hundred yards beyond the intersection with Tottenham Street. When he spotted the crowd gathered round the injured motorcyclist who was still lying on the pavement, he imagined somebody had been knocked down by a car. Since the victim of the apparent crash was already receiving attention, the man walking past didn't stop because he was a bit pressed for time. Besides, he saw no point in crossing over and joining the crowd. He would only have got in the way. It wasn't as if he had any medical expertise to offer. Nor did he possess the morbid curiosity that had driven so many people to stand round gawping at the motorcyclist. Gruesome sights were, after all, far from unusual for someone in this man's line of work.

Anyone forced to guess his occupation would, in all likelihood, have said that he was an accountant or perhaps a businessman. Yet Albert Pierrepoint was among Britain's most feared men, his name inextricably associated with violent death. For even the most hardened of criminals, few encounters were viewed with greater trepidation than 'a meeting with Mr Pierrepoint'.

Back in 1931 he had, against his mother's wishes, joined the family business, founded by his late father thirty years previously and continued by his uncle. Until he was eleven-years-old Pierrepoint had been unaware of the deadly career pursued by his father Harry and uncle Tom. He had only discovered their secret when he'd caught sight of a news-hoarding advertising *Thomson's Weekly News*. The hoarding had carried a photo of his father, juxtaposed with the headline 'MY TEN YEARS' EXPERIENCES BY HENRY A. PIERREPOINT RETIRED EXECUTIONER'. Through reading the weekly instalments of his father's reminiscences, over which he'd pored obsessively, Pierrepoint had conceived the ambition to take over his father's duties.

What had attracted him to the job, he claimed, was the prospect of distinguishing himself from his contemporaries, most of them destined for lives as anonymous drones in the Lancashire cotton-mills. At a time when few people owned cars or could afford more than occasional long-distance train journeys, the opportunity to travel also presented a powerful incentive. All of which explains why he had once began a school essay with the line, 'When I leave school I should like to be the Official Executioner...'

Death had appeared oddly glamorous to him at that age. Now he was well acquainted with the grim reality of it. Even so, he considered hanging to be the most humane and dignified way of dispatching criminals who had received death sentences. While several of his fellow hangmen took what he regarded as dubious pleasure in their work, savouring their role as society's avenging angels, he viewed himself as a mere cog in the legal mechanism—an outlook that helped him to reconcile his job with the Christian principles he espoused.

Like his father, he had risen to the rank of Number One Official Executioner for Great Britain and Ireland. Through a private arrangement, originally negotiated by his uncle, he even found himself performing executions on behalf of the independent Irish Republic, which had a tradition of employing British hangmen. To members of the police and prison service, Pierrepoint was known simply as the 'Number One'. For him, the job was a God-given vocation from which he derived great professional pride. Casting only the briefest of glances at any of the diners leaving the adjoining restaurants, escorted by wafts of foreign food, he would have been able to make a fairly accurate estimate of both the length of rope and the drop required to hang them.

In between carrying out his duties, Pierrepoint and his wife Anne, a gentle, mumsy blonde who had been working in a sweetshop when he'd first met her, ran a pub on the outskirts of Manchester. They'd only taken over the tenancy a few months previously, so they were still learning about their new business. Leaving Anne in charge, Pierrepoint had caught a train to Euston Station that morning. He'd been summoned to the War Office from where he was due to collect the sheaf of official documents necessary for his latest trip to Germany. Since V-E Day, he had been there—and to the British-controlled zone in Austria—several times. Much as he liked travelling, this wouldn't be the most congenial of trips. For a start he didn't feel safe in Germany, hence the Browning revolver that he carried in his trouser pocket whenever he went there. The uncongenial nature of the trip was reinforced by the knowledge that Germany still resembled a gigantic bomb-site. Yet Pierrepoint was unlikely to see much of it because he would be working long hours.

That Thursday he was due to execute the next group of convicted Nazi war criminals. He sometimes had to dispatch as many as twenty-six of them in the space of twenty-four hours. But he wasn't complaining because the assignment had enabled him to get down to London again. He'd always had a liking for the place. As a child growing up in Huddersfield, it had seemed exotic and tantalisingly distant, its romantic allure nourished by a visit to the Palace Theatre in Bradford where he'd heard the veteran music hall artiste Ella Shields sing a jaunty, crisply phrased rendition of the classic London song *Burlington Bertie*. He could still picture her standing centre-stage, wearing top-hat and tails and a starched white shirt-front, his view of her framed by crimson velvet and gold hanging tassels.

Ahead of his 3:00pm appointment over in Whitehall he had been wandering around Soho, reacquainting himself with the area, which he'd got to know well during the fifteen years since he had first visited London for a week's training in the hangman's craft. He was planning to see Charlie and Annie Allchild, the extrovert Jewish couple who ran the Fitzroy Tavern. He had been friends with them since the 1930s. The relationship was close enough for him to be regularly invited up to their spacious and comfortable flat above the pub where they lived with Sally, their ten-year-old daughter. Pierrepoint adored children, though he had none of his own. In a rasping, cigar-smoker's voice more accustomed to belting out *Danny Boy* and other maudlin numbers, he used to sing nursery rhymes to Sally.

Whenever he was in town he liked to pay the Allchilds a visit. At every opportunity he picked their brains about the practicalities of running a pub. Immediately he arrived in London, he was also in the habit of phoning a mutual friend and arranging to meet him in the Saloon Bar. That mutual friend was Bob Fabian, a Scotland Yard detective to whom he had been introduced by another of the Allchilds' customers. But there hadn't been much point in contacting Fabian that day because Pierrepoint only planned a flying visit to the Fitzroy.

❖

West End Central, C Division's headquarters, occupied a seven-storey Art Deco building on the section of Savile Row near the junction with Burlington Street. The building was next to one of the exclusive tailors' shops for which Savile Row was famous. Though the police station had only been open for six years, it had already been refurbished, its original interior having been gutted by a huge German parachute mine that had landed across the road. The explosion had killed three officers, injured twenty-two others and left a rubble-strewn bomb-site where the buildings opposite had been.

Around 2:35pm the Radio Officer at West End Central received a message from the Yard's Information Room about the Charlotte Street shooting. The Officer then dialled one of an array of extension numbers. It connected him to the Criminal Investigation Department where forty-two male detectives and three female Constables, the latter restricted to cases involving women and children, were based. When the Radio Officer explained what had just happened in North Soho, the detective who answered the call decided it was important enough to pass straight over to the 'guvnor', Divisional Detective Inspector Bob Higgins.

Ordinarily, DDI Higgins—highest ranked of the detectives at West End

Central—would still have been at lunch. That afternoon, however, he'd taken an early break, so he was back at his desk in the CID offices.

He suspected that many people identified detectives with the kind of characters created by Raymond Chandler and other hardboiled crime writers, yet he regarded himself and his colleagues as rather dull, unromantic fellows in comparison. Ensconced in his office, he was wading through the usual stack of letters, forms, reports and witness statements, an aspect of the job which he didn't

*Architect's drawing of West End Central.*
*(Copyright: Metropolitan Police Historical Collection)*

value all that highly. To his way of thinking, real police work was about going out and making arrests, not directing operations from a distance or maintaining a tidy desk. In any event, as he knew only too well, dealing with official bumf wasn't one of his strong points. That was partly a matter of temperament and partly because his schooling, which had finished when he was fifteen, had equipped him with no more than a shaky grasp of the principles of grammar and punctuation.

The thought that certain senior detectives, many of them contemporaries, had gained promotion simply by doing a good administrative job irritated him. Put those chair-polishers in a witness–box at the Old Bailey and he had no doubt that they'd behave like floundering amateurs.

With each step up the CID ladder, the quantity of paperwork landing on Higgins's desk had grown heavier. He'd only been doing his current job for eight months. Aged forty-three, he was the youngest of the Met's Divisional Detective Inspectors. Not that he looked young. His oblong face and hefty five feet ten inch frame had already acquired the drooping fleshiness associated with middle-age. His dark brown hair, slicked back to reveal a high forehead, was greying at the temples. And his thin Cupid's

*Prostitutes touting for customers in London.*

Bow lips were often pursed into a worried expression, indicative of the increased weight of responsibility he had been required to shoulder. Responsibility was, however, something he craved, though he realised that the best he could hope for was a position as a Chief Superintendent or CID Commander. For a man like him, who had worked his way through the ranks, he knew the very top grades in the police were seldom attainable. The knowledge that these were occupied almost exclusively by those who landed them either through distinction or influence in other spheres provided him with a niggling source of frustration and resentment.

Higgins was in charge of the day to day work of the CID across many of the busiest districts of central London. His prestigious parish, covering Mayfair, Piccadilly, Leicester Square and Soho, could scarcely have been more different from the tranquil Rutland village where he had grown up. Within the area's noisy, densely populated streets and squares, a cross-section of criminal life thrived. There were gangsters such as the cigar-chomping Jacob Comacho, self-proclaimed 'King of the Underworld', who went under the names of either 'Jack Spot' or 'Jack Comer'. There were male and female prostitutes whose ranks had been swelled by wartime recruits. There were the pimps—'ponces' or 'johnsons'—who charged them protection money: men whom Higgins labelled as 'scum'. There were gangs of shoplifters, known by crooks and police alike as 'hoisters', the most notorious of these being the 'Forty Thieves', an elegantly attired all-female gang that had originated in the south London slum district of Elephant and Castle. There were confidence tricksters, ranging from small-time 'tweedlers' to big-time operators who invested in long-term scams, sometimes involving the construction of fake business premises. There were the 'spotters' who haunted plush hotels where they earmarked likely victims for the big-time con artists. There were street bookmakers who profited from off-course gambling's illegality. There were the smash-and-grab gangs who would steal a car, drive up to a shop, break the window and scoop up the contents of the window-display before speeding off. There were pickpockets, known as 'whizzers' or 'dippers', typically working in teams of three. There were dealers in what Higgins viewed as the 'despicable business' of illegal drugs, mainly small quantities of heroin, cocaine and marijuana, dubbed 'Indian hemp', so-called 'joy smokes' selling for as much as seven shillings and sixpence—around £10 in 2007 currency. There were the 'snow birds', intent on recruiting new customers for the drug dealers. There were the organisers of unlicensed 'bottle party clubs', principally in cramped, dimly lit Mayfair flats where customers who wanted to carry on drinking and dancing after the pubs closed would hand over exorbitant sums for the privilege. There were 'broadsmen', card-sharps who set up stalls in the street and swindled passers-by. There were people who, for as little as £2, would supply one of the government's compulsory identity cards. There were 'screwsmen' who specialised in burglary. There were 'petermen', skilled in the art of safe-cracking. There were blackmailers targeting male homosexuals whose carnal appetites were illegal at that time. There were fences who dealt in stolen property. There were 'strong-arm boys', thugs who ran protection rackets. There were forgers dedicated to faking paintings and antiques. There were touts who enticed 'steamers'—unwary customers—into 'spielers', fly-by-night gambling clubs where they'd be cheated out of their money. And, of course, there were the blackmarketeers, the snappily dressed 'spivs' who exploited the continued rationing of food and most consumer goods.

A highly profitable trade in such everyday commodities as sugar, butter and tea, clothes, cosmetics, whisky, cigarettes and stolen or forged ration coupons had evolved during the Second World War. Most people, however honest, could not resist treating themselves to 'a little something on the side'. Night-time warehouse robberies had, in consequence, become routine. So had 'van dragging' which entailed nimble thieves jumping onto passing lorries and flinging some of the contents out of the back, goods facetiously described as having 'fallen off the back of a lorry'.

Alongside the established criminals, there was a new generation of crooks, frequently ex-servicemen, toughened up by the military. A high proportion of these crooks were drawn from the estimated 17,500 deserters still at large. Without the ration books needed to purchase most items of food, deserters were forced to turn to crime in order to survive. Large numbers of them could be found in Soho where cheap cafés served unrationed foods: anything from salami and horsemeat to pigeonmeat and even sparrow-meat.

Small wonder, then, that Higgins had, since being promoted to the rank of DDI, been faced by a crimewave that kept threatening to get out of control. Among the most alarming aspects of this trend were the increase in violent crimes, in offences involving firearms, and in those committed by the fourteen to twenty age group, 10,300 of whom were convicted members of criminal gangs. Unfortunately Higgins did not have enough officers at his disposal to slow down the crimewave, let alone halt it.

As the latest annual report had made clear, staffing in the Met was at its lowest level since 1887. Many of the CID officers who had volunteered for military service had been killed, and more than 300 of them were still stationed in Germany, Austria and Greece. Though the Met had launched a recruitment campaign in January 1946, this was being hampered by the paucity of housing in London. Not that recruitment would, in the short-term at least, have solved the CID's staffing problem, because a minimum of five years' training and experience was required to create a capable detective. In the light of all that, Higgins felt it was ludicrous that men in their early fifties, men who had just reached the peak of their efficiency should be permitted to retire on a full pension, valued at two-thirds of their final salary. Large numbers of them were handing in their notice and taking advantage of the increased pay on offer elsewhere.

The manpower shortage hadn't helped to quell the air of defeatism that pervaded the Met, which Higgins nevertheless considered the greatest police force in the world. His colleagues had taken to joking about how

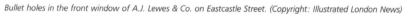

*Bullet holes in the front window of A.J. Lewes & Co. on Eastcastle Street. (Copyright: Illustrated London News)*

Britain may have won the war against Germany and her allies, but she was losing the war on the London underworld.

❖

As Pierrepoint neared the junction where Windmill Street joined Charlotte Street, the Fitzroy Tavern came into sight. Positioned on the far corner, it was a big, smoke-blackened, three-storey building with Dutch gables and a miniature onion dome. Next door was a bomb-site which made the Fitzroy stand out even more. Pierrepoint had been drinking there long enough to remember the four houses that used to occupy the bomb-site. One of these had had a spectacular grapevine growing up the front of it.

The pub's windows were almost opaque, their surfaces decorated by swirling, acid-etched patterns. From outside, it was hard to see much of what was going on inside. Entering the Fitzroy at lunchtime, customers were greeted by a soothing buzz of conversation from the incongruous array of people who drank there: locals, students, artists, writers, actors, politicians and eccentrics. They offered a startling contrast to the provincial clientele of Pierrepoint's own pub.

In keeping with most such establishments during that era, the Fitzroy was divided into a small, rough-and-ready Public Bar and a larger, comparatively smart Saloon Bar where Pierrepoint liked to go. At the far end of this L-shaped room was a coin-operated electric pianola. For a penny-a-time it hammered out a selection of familiar tunes at sufficient volume to mask the musical tinging of the cash-register.

Mementoes of both the First and Second World Wars adorned the walls of the Saloon Bar. Displays of cap badges, regimental insignia, and cigarette cards jostled for space with helmets, flags and framed propaganda posters emblazoned with rousing slogans: 'Women of Britain Say Go!', 'Help Serbia', 'Dig For Victory', and 'Save Us From The Hun!' More idio-syncratic still, the ceiling was normally covered in tightly wrapped packets of money, skewered by darts. These had been thrown by customers donating to the Allchilds' 'Pennies From Heaven' charity that funded day-trips for groups of up to 500 disadvantaged London children. Pierrepoint enjoyed lending a hand with these raucous events, for which the Allchilds also recruited other well-known helpers such as the revue star Ralph Reader.

On the wall above the counter was a large clock, its case made from half a beer barrel. It had stopped at 11:00am on Armistice Day 1918. Out of superstition, nobody had wound it since.

Pierrepoint was due at the War Office in less than thirty minutes, so he wasted no time in seeking out Charlie and Annie Allchild. Charlie was a bald, moustachioed East Ender with the physique of a snowman, his huge ball-like head balanced on an equally rotund body. He tended to wear dark trousers, a matching waistcoat, a tie, and a white shirt with the sleeves rolled up. Arcing across the front of his waistcoat, through which his stomach threatened to burst, there was usually a watch-chain. He had a gentle, humorous manner and a fondness for Cockney rhyming slang, the stairs to the beer cellar being habitually transformed into the 'apples and pears'.

His wife was a diminutive, portly woman in her early forties with wavy black hair cut into a servicable style. Like her husband, she had the ability to get on with most people but her friendliness was tempered by a no-nonsense attitude. She wore rimless, oval glasses that caught the light from the lanterns above the bar.

The Allchilds treated Pierrepoint to a drink on the house. Pumped up from the recently modernised cellar, his beer was dispensed through a new-fangled, pistol-like device which had already prompted a newspaper story headlined 'ANNIE—THE PISTOL-PACKING BARMAID'.

Speaking in a soft Yorkshire accent, Pierrepoint chatted with the Allchilds whom he hadn't seen for a while. How he could be so cheerful remained an enduring source of mystery to them. He and the Allchilds would have had plenty to talk about, though Pierrepoint was reluctant to say anything about his official duties. In all the years that the three of them had known each other, he'd only once alluded to the subject. He had admitted to Charlie that the black attaché case which he sometimes carried with him contained the tools of his trade.

So reticent was Pierrepoint about his official duties that he hadn't even mentioned them to his wife before their marriage three and a half years earlier. Not that she was under any illusion as to the nature of his frequent trips round the country. His reluctance to talk to her about them had, however, persisted. For him, the same rules of confidentiality between a priest and someone making a confession applied to the fleeting but intimate relationship between a hangman and condemned prisoner. All the same, plenty of people kept trying to get him to talk about specific hangings. The situation hadn't been helped by the inaccurate stories that had circulated in the press the previous year: stories about how he'd been chosen to execute Göring, Himmler and the other Nazi leaders. He had, courtesy of such unwanted publicity, received lucrative offers to go on lecture tours of America and to appear in variety shows in British theatres. Sharing the bill with comedians, magicians, plate-spinners, memory men and sentimental balladeers, he would have been expected to titillate the audience with a series of executioner's reminiscences. He'd always turned down such offers with the words 'I am not a showman.'

If he was going to get to the War Office on time, he couldn't spend more than a few minutes with the Allchilds. Knocking back his drink, he made for the exit. He then retraced his path down that side of Charlotte Street. North Soho's varied population was evident in the businesses lining the road between the Fitzroy and the junction with Tottenham Street. These included Aaron Zeidman's grocery; Raphael Massin Ltd, valet service; Schliephak & Stephenson, chemists; Giordano Ltd, wine merchants; Max Raznick, butchers; Rossi's restaurant; and Neophytis Vavlitis, Foreign Provisions.

The crowd that Pierrepoint had seen on his way to the pub was still milling round at the crossroads opposite the New Scala Theatre. And the injured man was still sprawled across the pavement awaiting the arrival of an ambulance. But Pierrepoint marched purposefully past without paying much attention to the commotion on the other side of the street.

❖

Two detectives from the Q car dispatched by the Yard's Information Room arrived at the crossroads where the incident had taken place. In their haste to get to the victim, they abandoned their new Austin Eight in the middle of the southbound carriageway of Charlotte Street.

Being CID men, neither of them were in uniform, though their choice of clothes, combined with their height and air of authority, rendered them instantly recognisable as police officers. The older of the detectives, dressed in a dark three-piece suit, crouched beside the wounded motorcyclist. Despite the afternoon warmth, Antiquis was shivering. The detective took off his own jacket and draped it over the wounded man's torso. In the meantime his colleague, who was wearing a pale, belted trenchcoat, bent over and carefully adjusted the position of Antiquis's head on the improvised pillow.

While the detectives were busy tending to him, Geoffrey Harrison—a news agency photographer—joined the crowd which had converged on Antiquis. Press photographers like him were reliant as much on luck as talent. To obtain a top-class, saleable picture, they had to be fortunate enough to be around at just the right moment. By an extraordinary coincidence, the type of coincidence that only happened once or twice in a news photographer's career, Harrison had been in North Soho at the time of the robbery. Lured into the street by the sound of the gunshot fired at Antiquis, he'd seen two of the gang running towards Tottenham Court Road. But he hadn't been quick enough to take a photograph of them. He compensated for that maddening failure by lining up a picture of the motionless body and stooping detectives. Just behind the detectives there was an old man with a walking-stick. Still swathed in winter clothes, he was talking to a much younger man. It wasn't hard to guess what they were discussing. The younger man had struck a casual pose, one hand in his trouser pocket, the other holding a cigarette to his lips. In contrast, the people further along the pavement wore disbelieving expressions. Everyone was so preoccupied by recent events, they didn't look at Harrison as he pressed the shutter-release button on his camera.

❖

When CID officers picked up the phone, they seldom knew what awaited them. For Higgins the unpredictability, the varied nature of police work in London was one of its biggest attractions. That same unpredictability was also one of its biggest drawbacks. Wedding anniversaries, birthday parties, family get-togethers and other arrangements were only ever a phone-call away from being swept aside. Yet his wife had always encouraged him to put his job first because she knew that was the one sure way to promotion and a better standard of living. Four months previously, Higgins's Christmas dinner with her and their children had been disrupted by a summons to take charge of a fresh murder investigation.

He was still at his desk at West End Central when his phone rang. He answered in a Midland accent that people often had trouble identifying, its

*Geoffrey Harrison's photograph of Alec de Antiquis lying at the scene of the shooting.*

soft rural cadences punctuated by hard vowels suggestive of smoke-wreathed industrial cities. Unlike many of the Met's senior officers, he had a shy, unassuming manner. On hearing a brisk account of the robbery and shooting, he was shaken out of his post-lunch doldrums.

At the Detective Training School in Hendon where he had been tutored in the rudiments of his job which he'd come to regard as a veritable mission in life, they had used Hans Gross's *Criminal Investigation* as their main textbook. Dubbed the 'Yard Man's Bible', this German volume—an English edition of which had first been published in 1924—stressed that each case should be approached with an open mind. Gross taught that officers who embarked on cases with preconceived theories ran the risk of disappearing down investigative cul-de-sacs. Rather than employ the evidence to construct a plausible account of the crime, they'd be looking for evidence to support their theories. Nevertheless it was tempting for Higgins to connect the North Soho shooting with an attempted murder that had occurred not far from Jay's about twelve hours earlier.

According to the report Higgins had received, Police Constable Meredith—part of the uniformed wing of C Division—had been patrolling Eastcastle Street at 3:00am or thereabouts when he had heard suspicious noises coming from the darkened entrance to A.J. Lewes & Co., a firm specialising in the manufacture of women's ball-gowns. When P.C. Meredith had approached the doorway, he'd been confronted by three men. Two of them had run away while the third member of the gang had hurled a box-opener or jemmy at him. Meredith had ducked just in time. The man who had thrown it had then run after the rest of the gang, turning to fire four shots at Meredith. These had missed their target, all but one of them piercing the shop window next to where the gang had been standing. Meredith had reported that the gang had escaped in a type of wooden-bodied car known as a 'shooting brake'.

Within a few minutes of learning about the more recent incident at Jay's, Higgins was speeding over to North Soho. CID officers of his rank routinely travelled in the back seats of squad cars, chauffeured by trained police drivers. The majority of squad cars were black, pre-war Wolseleys, fitted with leather upholstery, an illuminated 'POLICE' sign on the roof, plus an alarm-bell that made a distinctive pulsing noise.

Police drivers, who were taught to stick to the main roads whenever possible, could rarely resist an opportunity to show off their abilities by speeding to the scene of a crime. Yet Higgins had great confidence in those abilities, in their knack of combining safety with high speed.

Like it or not, drivers had to slow down as they approached Oxford Circus where a constable with a white armband was invariably on 'point duty'—directing the traffic. Point duty was one of several boring and lonely aspects of the job that new recruits were powerless to avoid, the tedium only broken by enquiries from passers-by and the occasional careless driver to admonish.

The obvious route from West End Central to North Soho led down Oxford Street towards the Lyons Corner House restaurant at the far end. Along with so many other seemingly innocuous locations, it held ugly memories for Higgins. Two years earlier, a deranged man named Jack Tratsart had invited five members of his own family to afternoon tea there. Without warning he had pulled out a revolver and shot three of them across the table, wounding his younger brother and killing his father and one of his sisters. Instead of fleeing the scene of the crime, Tratsart had waited for Higgins to arrive, then meekly surrendered.

In the afternoons Oxford Street played host to a shuffling procession of cowed-looking sandwich-board men in frayed overcoats. The crowded pavements were also dotted with spivs in wide-shouldered, double-breasted suits, their favourite pitches being outside the big department stores: Bourne & Holingsworth, Selfridges, Marshall & Snelgrove, John Lewis, and D.H. Evans, all on the lefthand side of the road. From open suitcases, the spivs sold items such as nylons, combs, hairgrips and elastic, items often unavailable in the shops. Higgins could have instructed his driver to pull over while he tried to arrest one of these characters, but he was in far too much of a hurry to waste time on small-fry like them.

❖

The Red Lion was a bow-fronted, nineteenth-century pub located near the House of Commons. Dark panelling with decorative glass insets sheathed its two tiny ground-floor bars. Members of Parliament who had sloped out of debates were often to be found there. On account of its proximity to Scotland Yard, it was also the regular lunchtime rendezvous for crime correspondents from the national newspapers and London's citywide evening papers, all based in the environs of Fleet Street.

That afternoon, a group of five such reporters had decamped from the Yard's Press Room to the Red Lion, where they were drinking half-pints of beer and munching cold sausages. Like the detectives featured in their stories, the uniformly male crime reporters didn't see much of their wives and children, yet they'd flourish snapshots of them at the faintest provocation. Despite the fierce competition for fresh stories and interesting new angles on continuing ones, there was obvious camaraderie among the so-called 'crime boys' whose conversation was dominated by shop-talk.

Lately they'd covered numerous violent crimes, contributing to the

*Passers-by milling round at the scene of the crime, photographed from outside the New Scala Restaurant.*

fear that Britain was in danger of sliding into anarchy. Headlines such as '6 AXE AND GUN BANDITS HOLD-UP COUPLE, AGED 70' had become a recurrent feature of their papers' front-pages. Firearms had played a pivotal role in most of these stories. During the past few months alone, there had been four fatal shootings in London and the surrounding area. A Jamaican serviceman had been killed outside a café in Bloomsbury, prompting a rooftop chase across Cartwright Gardens. A courting couple had been executed in their parked car on the edge of Epping Forest. And a prostitute had been gunned down outside the Blue Lagoon nightclub in Soho. On top of all that, there had been a series of armed robberies in the West End. Such was the atmosphere of burgeoning lawlessness that two muggers had recently been prepared to shoot at a police inspector who had attempted to arrest them in Hyde Park.

The crime reporters' late lunchtime chat was curtailed by the arrival of a colleague who had volunteered to stay behind in the Press Room and man the phones. Their colleague dashed into the pub and told them about the shooting on Charlotte Street. Abandoning their half-pints, they hurried out of the Red Lion. They were soon waving down passing taxis.

❖

Higgins's car entered North Soho at about 2:45pm. Much as he liked this cosmopolitan area's shops and restaurants, he viewed immigrants with a condescension typical of his generation. In his eyes, they were a hot-headed bunch, prone to that most un-British of crimes, the *crime passionel*. Besides, he couldn't help associating Soho with the sordid life that went on just below the surface, with prostitution and other forms of exploitation. Events that afternoon had done nothing to dispel these negative associations.

The crowd that had assembled at the junction with Tottenham Street swiftly slid into view. So did the ambulance parked there, a bold red cross standing out against its white paintwork. Its crew had just lifted Antiquis onto a stretcher when Higgins approached them. He could see that the wounded man was probably beyond human aid. The ambulancemen manoeuvred Antiquis into the back of their vehicle, its rear doors closing on him with ominous finality.

It rapidly covered the short distance from the scene of the crime to Middlesex Hospital. Opened in 1935, this gargantuan six-storey concrete building loomed over the T-junction between Tottenham and Cleveland Streets. During the recent war, firewatchers had used its roof as a convenient vantage point for spotting where bombs and rockets had landed.

Once the driver had steered the ambulance into the turnaround space in front of the hospital's neo-classical façade, Antiquis was lifted out of the back of the vehicle. He was carried through the heavy doors—manned by uniformed doormen—and across the big, marble-floored foyer.

At 2:47pm the stretcher-bearers entered the Casualty Department where they found Dr John Lewis, a white-coated Surgical Officer. On being told that the motorcyclist had been shot, Lewis inspected the bullet wound. It was located in the gap between the tip of Antiquis's left eyebrow and the nearest part of his hairline. The wound comprised a moist, nasty-looking hole. Even though the bleeding had stopped, the other signs were not encouraging.

❖

Most weekends Higgins liked to escape from the pressures of his job by playing at his local golf club in suburban north London. Friends from outside the police force often tried to get him to talk about the more unsavoury aspects of his work, but he refused to be drawn.

During twenty-two years in the Met, Higgins had been present at the aftermath of many violent incidents. He was pragmatic enough to recognise this as an inescapable component of his chosen career. Even so, the sight of the wounded motorcyclist had left him shaken. It offered a terrifying reminder of how precarious life was, how a vigorous man could, with brutal suddenness, be reduced to little more than a pathetic bundle.

Where the shooting had occurred there was a ten-yard skid-mark that culminated in a pool of coagulating blood. The motorcyclist's discarded gauntlets, goggles and rucksack were lying next to it. There were bloodstains on the rucksack. If Higgins's mother could have seen what he could see then, she would have been appalled, not only by the crime but also by the sordid nature of his job. She had never wanted him to join the police. For one thing she didn't regard it as a respectable occupation for someone from a family like his. Admittedly, they were lower middle-class at best, yet his father had enjoyed the prestige of working for an aristocrat —Sir Charles Fitzwilliam, Master of the Horse for King George V. Social considerations aside, both his parents had been concerned that a career in the police wouldn't provide him with much financial security. In retrospect Higgins realised that they'd been right about that. His bank balance would have been a lot healthier if he had remained with the firm of auctioneers where he'd been employed when he had left school. But he was glad that he hadn't let his parents' well-meaning disapproval deter him from becoming a policeman. In no way did he regret his long years of service which, he believed, had given him a more eventful and demanding life than the one he might have had.

The circumstances of the Charlotte Street shooting were bound to ensure that the case was front-page news, the type of case where the press tracked the Met's every move, where the police had to work against the clock. Higgins knew from experience what these all-consuming investigations were like. Only five years previously he had been part of the team hunting a sadistic killer whom the press had dubbed the 'Blackout Ripper'. Like so many murderers, the culprit—Gordon Cummins, a young RAF trainee—had been apprehended because he'd made a single, careless mistake. At the scene of an attack, he had dropped his government-issue gas-mask, enabling the Met to trace him. By that stage he'd murdered at least four women, three of them prostitutes, a section of society that Higgins regarded with moralistic distaste. Of course there was a danger that this latest case might go the same way as the Cummins investigation, expanding to include fresh victims. Higgins sensed that the Charlotte Street gunmen had to be caught with the least possible delay. They'd already used violence to escape from one, possibly two tight spots, so he felt that they wouldn't worry about shooting their way out of trouble again.

Higgins, who had the unmistakable straight-backed posture of a long-serving police officer, walked over to where the robbery had occurred. He couldn't miss the shop because there was a large advertisement for it painted across the side of the adjoining block: 'JAY'S SECOND-HAND JEWELS AND SILVER'.

Among the crowd still hanging round outside, there were plenty of witnesses to the robbery and shooting. From them or from the two detectives already at the scene of the crime, Higgins learned that the robbers had intended to escape in the car now parked, doors wide open, in front of the shop's main entrance. It was a black Vauxhall Fourteen, a model distinguished by its v-shaped radiator grille. Whoever owned the car must have treasured it because it was in immaculate condition. Its carriagework and chromium were so highly polished that Higgins was able to see his reflection in it, stretched and distorted as if he was looking at himself in a fairground mirror. Even its black and white number-plates were free from the normal grime. Its registration number—KPK 524— revealed two things: that the vehicle was only six months old, and that it had been registered in Surrey. Yet Higgins had worked on enough robberies to know that the chances of the owner being implicated were minimal. In fact, there was more chance of Higgins sinking a hole-in-one next time he teed off at Grimsdyke Golf Club which, the way things were going, wouldn't be any time soon.

Getaway cars were usually stolen during the run-up to a robbery. But there was no evidence of forced entry on this vehicle: no broken windows, no trace of anyone having tampered with the locks, no marks on the bodywork to indicate that one of the doors had been levered open. Assuming the car had been stolen, the thief must have used a duplicate key or maybe a set of skeleton keys. By checking the registration number against the Met's list of missing vehicles, it would be easy to find out where and when the theft had occurred—both valuable leads.

There was a possibility that the gang might have left their 'dabs'— fingerprints—somewhere on the car's bodywork or interior before ditching it. When Higgins had first joined the police, fingerprinting hadn't been used all that often. By 1947, however, the technique was employed on a regular basis. It was even sophisticated enough to reveal when the occasional fingerprint had, by means of a gelatine mould, been planted to mislead investigators.

Higgins arranged with the detectives under his command for the car to

*The abandoned Vauxhall Fourteen getaway car. (Copyright: Crown Copyright)*

be towed to the Forensic Science Laboratory in Hendon. There it could be examined by Detective Superintendent Fred Cherrill, Head of Scotland Yard's Fingerprint Branch. First, though, an auxilliary steering-wheel had to be fetched. One of Higgins's subordinates, who was wearing gloves, then clamped this ingenious device onto the existing wheel. That way the car could be steered without smudging any prints left behind by the previous driver. Even if there was only a single, partial print on the entire car, Cherrill and his assistants would find it.

❖

The crime reporters from the Red Lion had taken only a few minutes to reach North Soho. They were soon joined by behatted, trenchcoated colleagues from other Fleet Street newspapers that had been tipped-off through furtive phone-calls. These tip-offs tended to emanate from CID officers who would, in exchange, expect favourable press coverage at some future date. Such inside-information sometimes enabled reporters to arrive at the scene of a crime ahead of the police.

When a story of the magnitude of the Charlotte Street shooting broke, the Fleet Street news editors liked to pair their crime correspondents with non-specialist reporters, entrusted with finding the telling background details that lend flavour to an article. Lindon Lang, News Editor on the *Daily Mail*, had teamed the ageing, well-connected crime correspondent, Syd Brock, with the wispy moustached, slightly younger Arthur Tietjen. Though Tietjen wasn't a specialist crime reporter, he'd spent in excess of two decades covering trials at the Old Bailey. And he was fascinated by the disreputable side of Soho. He and Brock—a sturdy man with greasy tendrils of black hair combed over his bald head—formed a potent duo. The sharp-eyed Tietjen quickly justified being assigned to the story. Arriving at the scene of the crime, he noticed the aptness of the film poster displayed across the road from the getaway car. The poster advertised *Odd Man Out*, a new film in which James Mason played a gunman on the run from the police.

For the crime correspondents, like their opposite numbers in the CID. the patient accumulation and checking of information was the cornerstone of their work. In search of witnesses to the robbery, they carried out interviews with the bewildered people in the shops and other businesses around Jay's. By adopting genial, often naïve personas, the reporters hoped to encourage interviewees to confide in them. Flattered by the prospect of appearing in print, several people pretended that they'd seen more than they had.

Besides visiting the shoe-repair shop where Robert Delap worked, three of the reporters also descended on Handy's, the Tottenham Street café next to Jay's. The reporters consisted of Len Hunter from the *Daily Express*, Reg Foster from the *News Chronicle* and Bill Jones from the *Daily Herald*. Over successive cups of tea and salmon sandwiches, necessary to sustain them through what promised to be a long day's work, they questioned Norman Barnett, the café's white-aproned, waistcoated owner who described the moment when he'd heard the gunshot that had struck the motorcyclist. He and the reporters were watched by Hilde Marchant, an eminent journalist from *Picture Post*, the high-circulation news magazine which had commissioned a feature on Fleet Street's crime correspondents. She was accompanied by the magazine's robust, working-class staff photographer, Bert Hardy, whose portfolio included some of the best-known pictures of London during the Blitz. He took an atmospheric black and white photo of Barnett. It showed the café owner perching on his wooden counter while the journalists fired questions at him.

Higgins could have named several high-ranking colleagues who felt that reporters had sometimes hindered their objectives and therefore refused to cooperate with them. But he didn't share this antipathy towards journalists. He did, however, disapprove of what he considered the less reputable sections of the press for their habit of 'exposing' vice by printing a great

*Poster for Odd Man Out, displayed across the road from Jay's.*
*(Copyright: London Films)*

many details about it. On the whole he had found the press courteous and helpful. Needless to say, there had been exceptions, crime reporters who refused to observe confidences and who had no intention of playing by the rules of the game. The way he saw it, though, the benefits of cooperating with the press outweighed the disadvantages. He had often found that newspaper stories could be used to flush out vital evidence or witnesses. Besides, for all his diffidence, Higgins had a taste for publicity. His name appeared in the newspapers with satisfying regularity. But there was no danger of all that press exposure going to his head because his wife and children were always teasing him about it.

Undaunted by his family's gentle mockery, Higgins kept a scrapbook containing press cuttings in which he had featured. The earliest of these dated back to New Year's Day 1926 when he had been an inexperienced constable, unfamiliar with scenes of violent death. That first cutting, culled from the *News of the World*, offered a slightly embellished account of how, while on point-duty near Mornington Crescent tube station one morning, he'd been approached by a young boy who had led him into the bedroom of an upstairs flat in Camden Town. There he had found the corpse of a seventeen-year-old girl, clad only in a flimsy nightdress. She'd been strangled with one of her silk stockings. Her boyfriend, a feckless street-musician with whom she had been having a tempestuous relationship, had eventually been hanged for her murder. The case was, Higgins believed, an invaluable introduction to the type of crime he had to solve years later.

Bob Fabian standing outside a Soho café.

❖

In view of the seriousness of what had just occurred, Higgins realised that he'd better contact his immediate superior. Under normal circumstances Tom Barrett—Detective Chief Superintendent of Number One District which covered all of London north of the river— would have been the next officer above Higgins in the chain of command. Barrett had plenty of experience with front-page cases like this. Less than a year earlier, he'd been in charge of the investigation that had led to the arrest and execution of Neville Heath, who had picked up a drunken woman in a Knightsbridge pub, taken her to the Panama Club in South Kensington, then back to a hotel in Notting Hill where he'd tortured, mutilated, and murdered her. But Barrett wasn't available to lead the Antiquis enquiry because he had gone on holiday with his wife. Detective Chief Inspector Bob Fabian from C1—the CID's Central Office—was filling in for him while he was away.

Fabian belonged to what crime correspondents, keen to invest their stories with spurious glamour, habitually described as the 'Murder Squad'. To Higgins and his fellow CID officers, however, this elite unit was known as the 'Glory Boys'. It consisted of a Chief-Superintendent, seven Superintendents, fourteen Chief Inspectors and a cadre of junior officers, available to assist police forces anywhere in the country and sometimes even their foreign counterparts.

All too often a detective would spend his career waiting for a spectacular murder case likely to make his name, only to have it snatched by these interlopers. Ambitious though Higgins was, he harboured no resentment towards Fabian. The two of them were long-standing friends. They'd never worked together in the same unit, but they had spent the majority of their careers stationed in the West End, their paths regularly crossing. They also used to see a lot of each other outside working-hours.

Despite his exalted rank and recurrent, flattering appearances in the newspapers, Fabian remained the same engaging, approachable character he had always been. Friends sometimes referred to him as 'Fun and Games' because of his penchant for risqué anecdotes and practical jokes involving sneezing powder or pins concealed in the cushion of a chair. Unusually for someone in his profession, where a fatalistic outlook seemed a prerequisite, he had the ability to see the humorous side of any situation, no matter how dire.

When Higgins got through to the Yard, he was informed that Fabian had popped out for a bite to eat.

❖

Britain had just emerged from one of the harshest winters of the twentieth-century. Even in London and the south of the country, the effects of the weather had been severe. Heavy snowfalls had led to the cancellation of bus services as well as the closure of many roads, airports and railway lines, stretches of the tube network included. The weather had served to exacerbate the problems caused by the Labour government's mishandled nationalisation of the coal industry, resulting in power cuts. To conserve fuel, the government had briefly banned the popular sport of greyhound racing, ordered cinemas to be shut during the day and taken the nascent BBC television service off the air. The power shortage had also prompted the popular Lyons Corner House restaurant chain to close all its branches from 9:00am until noon and from 2:00pm until 4:00pm. These measures had compounded the bleakness of post-war life and reinforced the impression that the country was on the verge of collapse.

Savouring the spring sunshine that offered such a welcome contrast to the previous month's freezing temperatures, Fabian had walked over to the Colonial Club which offered a pleasant, more convenient lunchtime alternative to the hurly-burly of the Fitzroy Tavern, his favourite watering-hole. Between Scotland Yard and his destination, there was about a mile of unkempt parkland, comprising St James's Park and Green Park, large sections of which had, during the war, been used for growing vegetables and grazing sheep.

The Colonial Club, popular with former officials from the Raj and other British outposts, was situated in an elegant townhouse at 47 Curzon Street. Unlike its neighbours, it straddled a broad alley that led through to Shepherd's Market. The longish walk from Scotland Yard stoking his appetite, Fabian sat in the upstairs dining-room. Beneath a dusty chandelier, waiters in white mess jackets served the club's customers.

Fabian was a square-jawed, muscular forty-five-year-old who had a reputation as the best dressed detective at the Yard. That reputation owed much to his well-cut, double-breasted suits, purchased from a pricey Savile Row tailor's shop. Peeping out of his breast pocket, there was usually a white display-handkerchief.

He had a battered, pug-nosed profile, the legacy of numerous games of rugby, along with twice-weekly sparring at the Polytechnic Boxing Club where he'd prepared for a successful title challenge at the Met's Boxing Championships. Both as a sportsman and a detective, he was renowned for his tenacity, for combining flair with patience. Nowadays, though, his sporting interests were confined to regular games of snooker and trips to the races.

His dark eyes were topped by barely discernible eyebrows and black, brilliantined hair, neatly parted on the lefthand side and combed away from his forehead. A creature of habit, his hair was washed and trimmed every ten days at a barber's on Whitcomb Street. He liked going there because the jovial staff told good stories, provided clean towels and shaved him with sharp razors. His features were nevertheless beginning to betray the rigours of working regular fifteen-hour days. Not only was his skin looking pale and puffy but he also had shadows under his eyes, the corners of them radiating a web of creases whenever he flashed one of his frequent smiles.

With the obligatory twenty-five years' and three months' service behind him, he could have handed in his warrant-card and retired from the police on a full pension. Like so many of his former colleagues, he could then have doubled or even trebled his income by taking a post as Head of Security for either some big company or plush West End hotel. Better still, he wouldn't have been expected to work such long hours, enabling him to devote more time to his beloved garden. In hotels such as the Savoy, the Dorchester and the Grosvenor House, there was always a demand for ex-CID men, familiar with the many ploys used by the confidence tricksters who preyed on the hotels' wealthy guests. But Fabian enjoyed his work too much to exchange it for mere convenience and financial gain. He felt that no more fascinating a life could be offered to any man. The fact that his job brought him into contact with dukes, dustmen, bishops and pickpockets was something he relished. He also loved the thrill of the chase and the fame that accompanied high-level CID work.

In contrast to his friend Bob Higgins who had been itching to join the police from an early age, Fabian had drifted into the Met. His parents had wanted him to follow in his father's footsteps by becoming a technical draughtsman. When he was twelve-years-old, they had sent him to Borough Polytechnic to learn the trade. He sometimes thought about the sacrifices his parents must have made to send him there and how poorly he'd rewarded them. Unimpressive though his student work had been, he'd found employment in a series of airless offices. Feeling as out of place there as a recluse at a holiday-camp, he had passed his days perched on high stools while he produced meticulous drawings of objects, viewed from above, from the side, and in section. People rather than objects were, however, what really interested him.

Frustrated by the sedentary nature of the job, he had brooded over his predicament and nurtured vague dreams of becoming a detective. In his imagination, clad in the same get-up as Sherlock Holmes, a deerstalker hat combined with a tweed cape, he had puffed on a Meerschaum pipe as he'd examined footprints through an oversized magnifying-glass. But his daydreams would never have come to even partial fruition if he hadn't arrived home one evening to find the hulking figure of Inspector Frederick Rolfe, a long-standing friend of his parents, having a cup of tea with them. He had been transfixed by the Inspector's tales of life in the Met, tales that hadn't quite matched his preconceptions. He had nevertheless sensed there was a good chance that a career in the police would suit his temperament better than any drawing office.

Without telling his parents, he had obtained Rolfe's help in applying to join the force, his application supplemented by the compulsory declaration that his parents and grandparents were English citizens. Following a rigorous medical and less than rigorous written test, he had been accepted for the Met's eight-week training course which included lessons in first-aid, military-style drill, as well as police powers and procedure. After he'd completed the course, he had found himself on night duty, working in tandem with a more experienced constable, pacing the back-streets of Mayfair at a regulation 2.5 m.p.h. This had proved the perfect antidote to his previous desk-bound existence.

Now that he was older, he didn't mind being behind a desk once in a while. He had spent most of that day sitting in Tom Barratt's well-padded chair in a quiet, generously proportioned office at Scotland Yard. The office was in the North Building, a ten-storey extension completed in 1939 but, until lately, occupied by military personnel. Pipe clenched between his jagged, yellowing teeth, Fabian had gone through Barratt's in-tray, every so often pausing to sign official forms with the scratchy-nibbed fountain pen that he had brought with him.

At around 2:50pm, one of the Colonial Club's staff told Fabian that there was a telephone-call for him. Fabian never went to lunch without leaving details of where he would be and how he could be contacted in an emergency. And that was clearly what this was. Over the years he had become accustomed to receiving urgent calls at inconvenient times. Still, the timing could have been worse, much worse. This could have been another of those three o'clock in morning calls when he was dragged out of bed and ordered to travel to some far-flung corner of the country where the local force needed help with a murder enquiry.

Fabian picked up the phone and found Bob Higgins on the other end of the line. Typically so calm and measured, Higgins spat out his words in excited, telegraphic bursts.

'A nasty job on Charlotte Street, sir!' he said. 'Some young fellows with guns held up Jay's, the jewellers. Battle in the shop. And a man shot outside. Trying to stop them as they ran away. He's going to die.'

In a nasal, south London–inflected voice that was higher pitched than his rugged looks suggested, Fabian replied, 'Get the Yard's Photographic Department out, Bob. Phone the fingerprint people—Superintendent Cherrill or Syd Birch... See if the Forensic Laboratory can help. Phone my car and send it down to Jay's for me. I'll come in by taxi.'

❖

Fabian didn't have to wait long before a taxi picked him up. Amid the excitement he had already forgotten about his lunch. The taxi whisked him through the West End which he claimed to know like the back of his hand. Many of the adjacent buildings were, courtesy of the Luftwaffe, punctuated by patches of overgrown rubble. Sturdy wooden beams had been used to buttress the exposed flanks of neighbouring shops. Other buildings were enmeshed in scaffolding. Above ground level there were scores of broken or boarded-up windows. For Fabian and every other Londoner, such sights had become commonplace. It must have been hard to imagine things ever getting back to normal, back to the way they had been before the war. One thing that *had* returned to normal, though, was the traffic which had become heavy by the standards of the period. Serious congestion was nevertheless such a rarity that it received newspaper coverage.

Soon Fabian's taxi was heading through the narrow streets of North Soho, an area he knew well, perhaps better than any other. He had first got to know its secrets when he was a young and, by his own admission, innocent detective. Exploiting the fact that he'd been sufficiently unknown to pass for an ordinary member of the public, he had been ordered to drift round the local cafés and basement clubs in the hope of picking up scraps of information from the 'old lags'—ex-convicts—who frequented them. Even in places like that, the gaolbirds tended to stick out, thanks to their strange, hobbled gait, indicative of years spent pacing cramped prison cells.

Through the windows of his taxi Fabian could see the crowd that had formed around the spot where the latest shooting had taken place. He had witnessed scenes of this kind many times before. There was, he told himself, nothing that could happen in the West End which would surprise him.

Near the scene of the crime, Fabian got out of the taxi. He then went over to his friend Bob Higgins who was shaken by events. However pressurised the situation, Fabian exuded reassuring poise and composure. It was something no amount of lectures and practical exercises at the Detective Training School could teach. Until an officer was confronted by a situation like this, there was no way of knowing how he would react. Fabian had first found himself in a comparable situation not long after he'd been accepted into the CID. Summoned to the Cochon Club, a notorious basement dive on Frith Street, haunt of the French gangsters who used to run the London vice trade, he had been faced by a chaotic scene. With the smell of cordite still hanging in the air, the corpse of Charles Baladda, nicknamed 'Charles the Acrobat', had lain on the floor amid upturned tables as well as broken billiard cues, glasses and bottles. Baladda had, it transpired, been shot by his bitter rival, Emile Berthier—'Mad Emile'. Refusing to be intimidated by the hostile stares of the remaining drinkers at the bar, Fabian had marched the key witness back to Vine Street Police Station.

On taking charge of his latest investigation, Fabian ordered a thorough

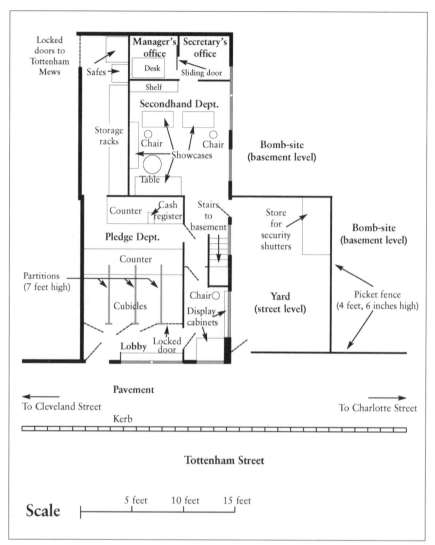

*Diagram of the interior of Jay's.*

search of the streets and alleyways around Jay's. As always, he was trying to see things from the criminals' point of view. It was a technique that had brought him plenty of success. If he had been part of the gang who had carried out the shooting, he would have been lying low in some alley or back-yard, waiting for the commotion to die down.

Higgins was instructed by Fabian to obtain written statements from everyone who had witnessed the robbery and shooting. Fabian had a knack of exercising authority with tact and breezy charm.

The task of putting together a detailed picture of the whole incident appeared fairly straightforward, all a matter of team-work and monotonous routine. As Fabian liked to tell people, ninety-nine percent of the CID's work was blood, sweat, toil and tears.

❖

A sign directing customers to the appropriate entrance had been fixed to the front wall of Jay's. For the pawnbroking side of the business, known as the Pledge Department, there was a door to the left of the front window. For the Sales Department, specialising in secondhand items, customers had to go through the rickety wooden gate on the other side of the front window. The gate led into a small, oblong yard.

While the witnesses were being rounded up, ready to be driven over to Scotland Yard, Fabian disappeared into Jay's where he commenced a meticulous examination of the scene of the crime. There was a saying in the CID which he sometimes quoted: 'Give your eyes a chance.' And that was precisely what he did.

Just inside the half-glazed door to the Sales Department were some stairs to the basement. A few feet ahead of these, there was another half-glazed door, this time fitted with frosted glass. The door had what appeared to be a bullethole in its upper panel. This jagged hole, not much wider than a golf ball, was near the righthand edge. But there was no broken glass on the floor. If the hole had been made by a bullet, the gun must have been fired from the side of the door closest to the yard. The irregular circumference of the break suggested either a low-velocity weapon or else one that had been discharged from close-range.

Through the hole, there was a view of the Pledge Department. A long, dark wooden counter, lined with cubicles for customers waiting to pawn or reclaim their possessions, ran down the lefthand side of the room. Opposite that, separated by a broad aisle, was a slightly shorter counter with assorted silverware and a big cash-register on it.

On the other side of the door into the Pledge Department, broken glass had been scattered across the worn linoleum, the shards sparkling in the light from the electric lamps suspended over the lefthand counter. From inside the Pledge Department, a tiny lobby was visible through the neighbouring cubicles. Among the silverware on the counter furthest from those cubicles, there was a rusty, snub-nosed .32 calibre revolver. Its grooved wooden grip was bloodstained, and all six of its chambers were loaded with cartridges. Unless the gunman had paused to reload, which seemed improbable, this couldn't have been the revolver used to shoot through the glass.

By following the imagined trajectory of the bullet, its eventual resting-

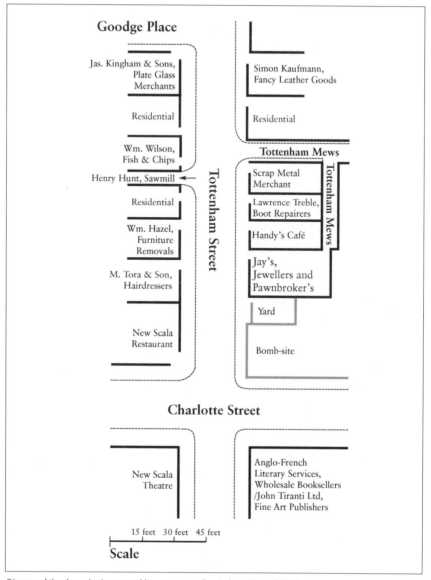

**Goodge Place**

Jas. Kingham & Sons, Plate Glass Merchants

Residential

Wm. Wilson, Fish & Chips

Henry Hunt, Sawmill ←

Residential

Wm. Hazel, Furniture Removals

M. Tora & Son, Hairdressers

New Scala Restaurant

**Tottenham Street**

Simon Kaufmann, Fancy Leather Goods

Residential

**Tottenham Mews**

Scrap Metal Merchant

Lawrence Treble, Boot Repairers

Handy's Café

Jay's, Jewellers and Pawnbroker's

Yard

Bomb-site

**Tottenham Mews**

**Charlotte Street**

New Scala Theatre

Anglo-French Literary Services, Wholesale Booksellers /John Tiranti Ltd, Fine Art Publishers

15 feet  30 feet  45 feet

**Scale**

*Diagram of the shops, businesses and houses surrounding Jay's on 29 April 1947.*

place could be found. It had travelled a mere twelve feet before piercing one of the white, wooden panels covering the wall on the far side of the shop. The point of entry, directly above a hospital-style radiator, was exactly three feet off the floor. Next to the radiator was a waste-basket around which scraps of torn paper had been scattered. As yet, Fabian couldn't tell whether these were related to the robbery.

The bullet's low trajectory showed that it must have been fired from the hip. Hardly the best angle from which to hit a target.

When Fabian examined the hole in the panelling, he could see the bullet, lodged in the wall behind. At that stage, though, he had no idea whether it would be any help to the investigation. The impact could easily have left the bullet so mangled that it would be useless as evidence. If he was in luck, it would be in good enough condition for a ballistics expert to match it to a specific weapon. Before that was possible, Fabian and his officers would have to track down the gun that had fired it. Easier said than done because, in spite of legislation that had been passed to restrict the sale of guns, London was awash with them, mostly souvenirs brought home by ex-servicemen.

Only the previous year when the Met had staged a firearms amnesty, 18,200 handguns, 352 machine-guns and 209,300 rounds of ammunition had been handed over. Even so, for a mere £5—equivalent to about £140 in 2007 currency—a high-calibre revolver could still be bought from the dealers who loitered in Ham Yard and on Great Windmill Street. For £10, an automatic pistol—a Luger or some other ex-German army weapon—could be purchased.

In addition to examining the bullethole, the room adjoining the Pledge Department had to be inspected. On a series of racks that extended from one end to the other, rows of pawned items were stored. Each of these had a ticket attached, recording the identity of the person who had pawned it. Beyond the racks was a double door that led into an alley at the back of the shop. The door turned out to be locked. At that end of the storage area, there were also two safes. One of these was large enough for a child to clamber into it. There were no tell-tale scratches round the doors or damage to the locks, nothing to suggest that the robbers had tried to force their way into either of the safes.

The Sales Department was the other part of the shop that needed to be looked over. It consisted of a spacious, square room with four free-standing display-cases, a circular table and a pair of easy-chairs. The room was lit by a combination of electric lamps and what little daylight seeped through the windows. Two of these had metal bars across them and most of the other window was blocked by rows of silverware.

Past the display-cases were a couple of small, interconnected offices, divided by a sliding door. The second of the offices was dominated by an enormous desk. It belonged to Bertram Keates, the manager, who was among the flock of witnesses being rounded up.

So far, twenty-seven of them had been assembled. Given that the incident had taken place in a busy street, it was likely that there were more witnesses than that, but those were the only people who had come forward. As Higgins knew to his cost, few people liked getting mixed up in crime enquiries.

Police procedure dictated that a group of plain clothes officers from the Flying Squad shepherded the witnesses into waiting cars—old but speedy black Railtons. The witnesses were told not to talk. Even with cooperative people like them, there was a danger that such conversations might distort their memory of events.

Known by crooks and police alike as the 'Heavy Mob', the Flying Squad's principal duty was to combat armed and professional criminals. It was, in consequence, staffed by some of the Met's toughest, most physically imposing men, many of whom relished the opportunity for violence. Until only a few weeks earlier, Fabian had been their boss but he had left the post on bad terms.

For the Squad's convoy of vehicles, the most direct route back to Scotland Yard was down Charing Cross Road. This went past the sheet music publishers' offices, outside of which buskers played the latest hit tunes; past the giant House of Foyle bookshop with its pavement stalls; past the Phoenix Theatre which was advertising a play starring the comedienne, Cicely Courtneidge; past the spot where a German bomb had left a crater so big that a temporary bridge had had to be rigged up; past the domed Astoria Cinema where *Gentleman Jim*, the Errol Flynn

*Fred Cherrill and Syd Birch studying fingerprints at New Scotland Yard.*
*(Copyright: Metropolitan Police Historical Collection)*

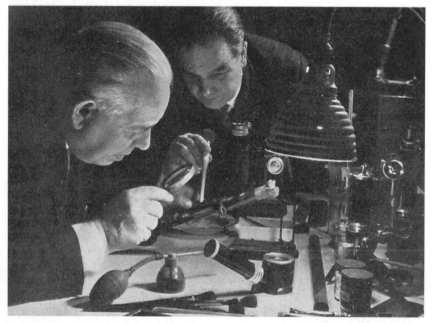

barenuckle boxing saga, was showing that evening; and past the junction with Shaftesbury Avenue where, even during the afternoon, heavily made-up prostitutes, their exposed calves muscular from hours of walking, patrolled its wide pavements on the lookout for likely customers.

❖

Aristocratic though his surname sounded, Alec de Antiquis was a working-class Londoner who ran L & A Motors, a garage that specialised in repairing motor-bikes. He'd set up the business in December 1945. Prior to that, he had worked at an air-craft factory and served as a cor-

*Fred Cherrill with a scene of crime box.*
*(Copyright: Metropolitan Police Historical Collection)*

poral in the Home Guard. To finance his business, he and his wife, Gladys, had pooled their savings and borrowed from friends. Their garage was based in bomb-damaged premises on the High Street in Colliers Wood, a south London suburb where he and his wife had family connections. He'd spent six months repairing the building and putting up a tiny workshop on adjoining land before he was ready to start trading. Besides housing his business, the main building provided rudimentary accommodation for him, his wife and their six children. Without a bathroom, they had to use a tin bath that was filled from the kitchen tap and carried into the living-room.

Despite the material sacrifices made in the hope of a more prosperous future, L & A Motors had struggled since its inception, handicapped by a spate of burglaries. Just two or three days previously, though, Alec and Gladys had congratulated themselves on what appeared to be an upturn in the business. The improved outlook had prompted them to hire a seventeen-year-old assistant and acquire a sought-after consignment of ex-army motorbikes.

On the morning of Tuesday 29 April—the day of the bungled robbery at Jay's—Alec, who had been working incessantly to support his family, had set off for London to buy hard-to-find spare motorcycle parts. He'd headed for Camden Town where he'd been led to believe he could obtain an exhaust-pipe and front wheel for the machine that his assistant was repairing. But he'd had no luck in tracking down either of these items. To ensure that his journey wasn't entirely wasted, he had ridden over to North Soho in search of other spare-parts. He'd bought enough of them to fill the rucksack now lying on the ground at the crossroads where Charlotte and Tottenham Streets intersected.

Ignorant of what had happened, his wife and children were waiting for him to arrive home for a hot lunch.

❖

Meanwhile the squad cars carrying the witnesses to the robbery and shooting drove down the broad expanse of Whitehall, ticking off a familiar sequence of landmarks. First, there was the War Office, then the Home Office, then the Colonial Office, then the Board of Trade, then Downing Street. When they reached the Cenotaph, its surface inscribed with the words, 'To The Glorious Dead', they turned left and threaded their way through the huge wrought-iron gates at the back of Scotland Yard.

Like taxis arriving at some popular destination, cars carrying witnesses were expected to form a queue to drop off their passengers. Escorted by officers from the Flying Squad, witnesses were taken past a large stone block, installed to help the Commissioner of Police mount his horse on ceremonial occasions. Not far down a bleak corridor, decorated in the

Officers at work in the Teleprinter Room at New Scotland Yard. (Copyright: Metropolitan Police)

building's standard colour scheme, the upper halves of the walls painted white, the lower halves mid-green, there were a couple of facing doors. Witnesses were guided through the door on the right. This opened into the Information Room where officers shuttled between the switchboard, map-tables and radio sets.

The Back Hall Inspector and his Constables were responsible for ushering witnesses into Room 114, the Waiting Room opposite. There the witnesses were guarded by the Constables who had to prevent them from speaking to one another.

Within a few yards of Room

114, there was a small office now used as the Teleprinter Room. It formed the centre of a network of teleprinters recently installed throughout the capital's 173 police stations. These devices, which transmitted typed messages, had evolved from the 'stock ticker machines' of the 1870s, used to relay stock exchange figures through telegraph wires.

One of the walls of the office was taken up by electrical circuitry. The teleprinter, comprising a bakelite box with a keyboard, stood on a nearby desk. A uniformed officer sat at

*A detective peers at a potentially useful fingerprint.*
*(Copyright: Metropolitan Police Historical Collection)*

this and typed a bulletin of the latest crimes. Every hour he circulated an updated list. The Charlotte Street shooting was certain to receive top billing on the next bulletin, due to be transmitted at 3:15pm.

❖

Fabian and Higgins were joined at the scene of the crime by Detective Superintendent Fred Cherrill from the Fingerprint Branch. This was the second time Cherrill had been over to Soho that day. On his last visit he and his deputy, Chief Inspector Syd Birch, who possessed the extraordinary ability to memorise fingerprints, had been called in to check the scene of the Eastcastle Street shooting.

A short, self-important man in a dark suit, Cherrill had a slow, confident voice, his manner calibrated to the status of the person he was addressing. To those below him in rank, he was curt and frequently acerbic. But those above him, Fabian among them, were treated with unctuous deference, accentuated by the way he had to peer up at colleagues. How he had circumvented the Met's height restrictions, which used to require that all recruits were over five feet nine inches tall, his colleagues couldn't understand. Those on the receiving-end of his sharp tongue joked about how he must have shrunk as he'd got older. He was now in his late fifties. His jowly face, hooded eyes and deep folds on either side of his mouth conferred on him the appearance of a truculent bulldog. His thick, silver hair was usually topped by a black bowler-hat, favoured head-gear for

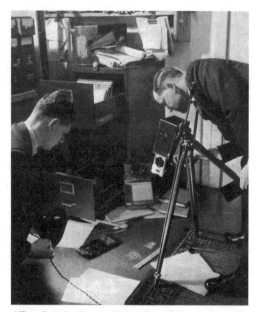

*Officers from the Photographic Branch working at the scene of a crime. (Copyright: Metropolitan Police Historical Collection)*

officers of his rank. He liked to wear it tipped back from his forehead in a raffish style at odds with his personality. Unprepossessing though his appearance was, he was vain enough to remove his glasses whenever he had to pose for a formal photograph.

To him, a fingerprint represented more than just a means of identification. He claimed it allowed him to classify its owner's intellectual status, an assertion eagerly endorsed by at least one gullible Fleet Street reporter.

The powders, brushes and other equipment vital to his job were carried in a flat-bottomed brown case called a 'scene of crime box'. Using a large magnifying glass and battery-powered torch, he peered at the surfaces where the gang might have left fingerprints. Witnesses had described how the Charlotte Street gunmen had vaulted the counter in the Pledge Department before making their escape, so Cherrill examined the woodwork. Through an atomiser that reminded Fabian of an old-fashioned car horn, grey powder was squirted over the counter and the partitions between the cubicles, exposing an array of fingerprints. These included two clear sets that had been left round the edge of the partition nearest the door into the Sales Department. For the time-being, though, it was impossible to know who had made them. They could have been left by customers or members of staff. Cherrill then transferred these onto a sheaf of five-by-eight inch cards which were divided into boxed sections, one for thumbprints and four others for the prints made by each finger.

Back at Scotland Yard Cherrill's assistants, to whom he seldom gave much credit for their work, would classify the prints according to the well-established system devised in 1901 by Sir Edward Henry, Inspector General of Police in Bengal. The system analysed what were termed the 'loops', 'whorls' and 'arches' on each fingerprint, reducing these to a numerical sequence. Equipped with this information, the staff at the Fingerprint Branch would be able to ascertain whether the prints obtained by Cherrill matched those of any convicted criminals whose particulars were already held in the Yard's enormous, meticulously indexed collection. A painstaking search of the files would also reveal whether the prints corresponded with any left behind at the scenes of other crimes, committed by criminals who had not yet been identified.

Once Cherrill had finished behind the counter in the Pledge Department, Fabian and his team were free to prize the panelling off the wall where the bullet had struck. Watched by Higgins, who was about to begin the protracted task of taking witness statements, they found a .45 calibre bullet embedded in the wall beneath the panelling. Luckily for him and unluckily for whoever had fired it, the bullet had missed the brickwork. Instead, it had struck the much softer cement pointing. A fraction of an inch either up or down, and it would have been crushed beyond recognition.

When it was removed from the grainy cement, it turned out to be in good condition, good enough for it to be matched to the gun that fired it. But Fabian's delight was offset by a report from one of the officers under his command, who informed him that they'd finished their search of the area around Jay's. The gang responsible for the robbery and shooting was nowhere to be found.

Still, it was reasonable for Fabian and his colleagues to assume that they wouldn't have too much trouble tracing the culprits. Promising leads weren't exactly in short supply. There were the witnesses, plus the getaway car, now on its way to the Forensic Science Lab. And there was the revolver left behind by the gang. There was also the bullet in the woodwork. As if that wasn't enough, there was the other bullet, buried in the unfortunate motorcyclist.

Fabian had cracked cases where there had been far less evidence. One of these, dating back fifteen years, had involved the hunt for the first armed robber to hold up a West End jeweller's shop in broad daylight. Despite the initial lack of clues, Fabian had succeeded in identifying and convicting the man responsible, a First World War veteran named Rudolph Franklyn. Ironically, Franklyn had just returned from a stint with the British-run Palestine Police.

News soon reached Fabian that Antiquis had died. His death had occurred only about ten minutes after his arrival at Middlesex Hospital's Casualty Department.

Like the rest of the population, Antiquis had been issued with an identity card that had to be carried at all times. The card listed his name, address and date of birth. Two officers were sent to the Collier's Wood address given on his card. They were entrusted with notifying his next-of-kin. It was a task most officers dreaded. Besides breaking the bad news, the officers in question needed to persuade the next-of-kin to agree to identify the body.

❖

Almost two hours had passed since Antiquis's death. In that time his corpse had been transferred from the Casualty Department to the mortuary at Middlesex Hospital. Higgins, who was en route there from the scene of the crime, wanted to take a quick look at the body before the following morning. That was when the next-of-kin had agreed to identify it and when the post mortem was due to be carried out.

At 4:30pm Higgins entered the mortuary. However clean these places were, they usually smelt the same, the heavy chemical tang of disinfectant mingling with the odour of blood, flesh, urine, the entire grisly cocktail.

The body of the murdered man was lying in the mortuary. His pallid corpse bore no resemblance to the serene corpses described in so many English detective novels of that period, novels in which murder victims look as if they've just gone to sleep. He could never have been mistaken for a living person. It was hard to believe that he had, only that morning, been walking round and talking and making plans for the future.

# II

# PERSONS
# UNKNOWN

After the police had left the scene of the crime and the crowd had dispersed, a cameraman from the Pathé company arrived at Jay's. Together with firms such as Gaumont and Movietone, Pathé was one of the foremost producers of newsreels. These were screened not only by specialist 'News Theatres' but also by conventional cinemas, which combined them with the shorts and cartoons that made up the often lengthy preamble to the main feature. In this era before most homes had been invaded by television, Pathé offered a popular source of news through its *Pathé Pictorial* and *Pathé News* programmes. Two years earlier it had provoked criticism by including footage depicting the horrors of the newly liberated Belsen concentration camp.

Standing on the side of Charlotte Street opposite where Antiquis had intercepted the gang, the cameraman set up his tripod. Right in front of him was a parked sportscar: a streamlined Jaguar with sinuous running-boards. On the pavement next to it, three men—who looked like reporters—were chatting, hands thrust into their pockets. With them in the foreground, occasionally sneaking self-conscious glances in his direction, the cameraman filmed a twenty second shot of Jay's, visible across the bomb-site on the corner. As he was doing this, a flat-capped old market trader wheeled a heavy wooden barrow down the middle of Charlotte Street. The cameraman then filmed the front of the Pledge Department, the entrance to the Sales Department, the 'Tottenham Street' and 'Charlotte Street' signs, plus the shop's side window, its shelves lined with silver cups, tankard and salvers. He also took a brief shot of the crossroads, seen from outside the New Scala Theatre. Before leaving, he filmed the south-eastward vista down Tottenham Street where the normal flow of cars and bicycles, not to mention pedestrians, had resumed. The street glistened in the drizzle that had started to fall. Beneath a black umbrella, a woman old enough to remember the era of horse-drawn carriages, top hats and crinolines walked past, clasping a chunky handbag. For the cameraman, it would have been difficult to imagine that this unremarkable spot had, only a matter of hours earlier, been the setting for a scene straight out of a Hollywood gangster movie.

❖

Chief Superintendent George Hatherill, Fabian's boss at CID Central Office, reckoned that, for every hour spent examining the evidence at the scene of a crime, it was necessary to spend a day interviewing witnesses. At irregular intervals the witnesses waiting in Room 114 at Scotland Yard were plucked from their seats and led up to one of the Interview Rooms on the third-floor. These small rooms were unfurnished, apart from a few chairs and a table.

Higgins, fresh from his visit to the mortuary at Middlesex Hospital, supervised the laborious process of taking witness statements. Irrespective of the pressure he was working under, he went about such routine tasks with quiet determination. He got on well with most of the detectives under his command, among them Detective Inspector Fred Hodge whom he had recruited as his assistant on the Antiquis case. A dapper man with a large nose, Hodge had sagging eyelids that conveyed an impression of sleepiness and inattention, yet he'd worked on an impressive number of successful murder investigations. He possessed a rare gift for interviewing witnesses, for exposing the side of his character best suited to that person. His attitude towards some witnesses was tough and unrelenting. Towards others, he was kind and sympathetic.

In theory, interviews had to be conducted in accordance with a checklist of procedures known as 'Judges' Rules'. Listed in the pocket-sized Police Code, issued to every officer, these procedures were partly designed to prevent the contents of statements being discredited and declared inadmissable in court. Judges' Rules specified, for example, that 'a prisoner making a voluntary statement must not be cross-examined and no questions should be put to him about [a crime] except for the purpose of removing ambiguities in what he has actually said.' But interviewing officers didn't always adhere to these strictures. Contrary to correct procedure, witnesses were often encouraged to delay writing anything down until they had talked about what they'd seen. That gave the interviewing officer the chance to point out everything worth including in the written statement.

To extract as much pertinent information as possible from a witness, the interviewer was supposed to maintain a relaxed and courteous tone. When dealing with a talkative person, he would have to listen to all sorts of irrelevant chatter before he was rewarded with something useful. Educated witnesses tended to be the worst in that regard. Interrupt the witness, though, and the interviewing officer would risk making him or her clam up. Likewise, a single brusque comment by the detective could result in the witness becoming indignant and unhelpful.

Over the ensuing hours, their passage marked by the sonorous chimes of nearby Big Ben, statement after statement was taken. These were written on Form 992s—Metropolitan Police 'Statement of Witness' forms. Once each statement had been completed, it was read to the interviewee who had the opportunity to make amendments or additions before signing the bottom lefthand corner of every page.

On major investigations, a few of the statements typically covered as

*A detective dusts for fingerprints.*
*(Copyright: Metropolitan Police Historical Collection)*

*An officer examines fingerprints at New Scotland Yard.*
*(Copyright: Metropolitan Police Historical Collection)*

many as thirty or forty pages of foolscap, but nobody had that much to contribute this time. Of the twenty-seven people interviewed, only six were particularly informative. Among them was Alfred Stock, whose gashed head had just been stitched up at Middlesex Hospital. There was also the firm's seventy-year-old Manager, Bertram Keates, a difficult interviewee because he was slightly deaf. There was William George Hazel, one of the shop's salesmen. And there was Abraham Buckner, the customer who had rushed over to help Antiquis after the shooting. The other useful witnesses were James Sadler, an advertising man who had been loitering outside the shop when the robbers had made their escape, and Charles Grimshaw, the bystander who had got into a fight with the smallest of the gunmen.

Through the witness testimony Higgins was able to build up a picture of how events had unfolded. Sometime between 2:15pm and 2:30pm, Alfred Stock got back from his lunch-break and popped into the Pledge Department. His return coincided with the arrival of Abraham Buckner, a salesman who had travelled into town from Westcliff-on-Sea. Faced by the row of four booths that bisected the Pledge Department, Buckner entered the lefthand booth. Stock had bought items from Buckner before. On this occasion Buckner wanted to sell him a couple of pieces of silverware. The two men soon agreed a price. As they did so, James Sadler was outside, peering through the window of the Pledge Department. He caught sight of the reflection of a car pulling up behind him. A man got out of the car but Sadler didn't notice where he went.

Back inside the building, Stock carried the newly purchased silverware into the Sales Department while Buckner pocketed the cash he'd just been paid. From the adjoining cubicle Buckner heard suspicious noises, made by someone clambering over the counter. Next thing he was confronted by a masked intruder with a revolver in each hand. Both weapons were pointed at him. The intruder said, 'Stand back and don't move.'

Buckner did as he was told. The same was true of Keates who was on the other side of the counter from Buckner. Keates obediently stepped backwards. Without the gunman realising, Keates pressed a button that set off an alarm-buzzer. Hearing this, Stock dashed through from the Sales Department. One of the shop assistants, a seventeen-year-old named Leslie Grout, threw a stool at the gunman. Moments after that, Stock ran straight into a second masked gunman, armed with a revolver. The collision provided the prelude to a brawl between Stock and the gunman. Stock remembered seeing the gunman raise his arm as if to take aim. Before he could fire his weapon, Stock tried to knock it out of his hand.

During the melee, the other gunman sneaked behind Stock and whacked him on the back of the skull with a hard object, most likely the butt of a revolver. Blood trickled down Stock's head but he continued trying to disarm his adversary. While both gunmen were distracted, Buckner charged through the doorway leading onto Tottenham Street.

In the meantime, a third gunman crossed the yard outside Jay's and went into the Sales Department. Anticipating a customer who might require assistance, William Hazel approached the incoming man. He found himself standing less than eighteen inches from a masked robber brandishing a revolver.

The gunman said, 'Stand still.'

With the barrel of the revolver angled up from his hip, the gunman fired what, Hazel suspected, was only intended as a warning shot. This was the shot that had pierced the glass-panelled door opposite and struck the wall. The man who fired it then went into the Pledge Department. Together with his accomplices, none of whom had taken anything, he jumped over the counter and headed for the getaway car which had been stolen from Whitfield Street just before the robbery.

Since there was nothing wrong with the engine, it appeared that that the gunmen had simply panicked, abandoning the car and bolting down Tottenham Street. Several people witnessed Antiquis swerve in front of the gang and fall to the ground after being shot.

Charles Grimshaw described his own subsequent attempt to make a citizen's arrest and how he'd earned himself a beating in the process. Grimshaw was lucky that he hadn't ended up in the mortuary next to Antiquis. Before the gunmen ran off, he got a clear look at the face of one of them. Grimshaw was confident that he'd be able to identify him. The trouble was, Grimshaw's description of the man differed from the description supplied by other interviewees, few of whom remembered much about the gang.

❖

A pair of police officers arrived at L & A Motors, where Mrs de Antiquis was still waiting for her husband. She was a matronly thirty-four-year-old with deepset eyes, plucked eyebrows and dark, shoulder-length hair pinned back from her high forehead. None of her children, aged between two and twelve, were present when the officers told her what had happened. The shock was so overwhelming she fainted.

She couldn't have been surprised to hear that her husband had tried to stop the gang of armed robbers from escaping. After all, he had a record of committing selfless acts of bravery. When he'd been working outside his garage only three weeks previously, he had dashed after a runaway horse, grabbed its bridle and brought it to a standstill. And he'd once risked his life by sprinting into a burning building to rescue a child, his courage earning him minor facial burns.

In a cruel coincidence he was the second member of his family to be killed by a gunman's bullet. More than half a century earlier, the same fate had befallen his great-grandfather, Alessandro Tempesta, a businessman living near the Italian town of Cassino. Tempesta had been kidnapped and held for ransom by a local mafioso named Domenico Fuoco who had been wanted by the police. The ransom had just been handed over when Fuoco and his gang had spotted a detachment of police officers. Fuoco had warned Tempesta that he'd kill him if he tried to attract the attention of the carabinieri. Despite the warning, Tempesta had yelled as loudly as he could, prompting Fuoco to shoot him. Several of the gang had died in the resultant gun battle with the police, yet Fuoco had escaped.

Tempesta's daughter, Rosa, had later married Alec de Antiquis's grandfather, Luigi. Together the couple had fled Mafia-ridden Italy and emigrated to the supposed safety of England.

❖

Even after the winter snows had thawed during the previous month, the fuel crisis had persisted. As a means of saving energy that would have been used for lighting, the government was experimenting with a novel measure. During the weeks leading up to the Charlotte Street shooting, the clocks had been put forward twice. Each time an hour had been added, initiating a period known as 'Double Summer Time', scheduled to continue until early November.

In London the light didn't start to fade until around 9:00pm, by which time Higgins and Hodge had completed the task of questioning the witnesses, none of whom had been allowed to leave. The interview process had yielded an impressive stack of signed statements. But Higgins was disappointed by the quality of the information contained in them. For even long-serving detectives like him, it was shocking to be reminded just how unobservant most people were. Under oath they would sometimes insist that they'd seen things they could not possibly have seen. A witness at a pre-war murder trial, for instance, had sworn under oath that she'd seen a plume of smoke emanating from the barrel of a gun which had turned out to have been firing smokeless ammunition.

The statements had given Higgins a clear idea of what had occurred in North Soho that afternoon, yet they didn't contain the type of leads that would help him and his colleagues apprehend whoever was responsible for Antiquis's murder. Any competent defence counsel would have had a field day pointing out the numerous inconsistencies.

One of the witnesses had referred to 'three enormous men' while someone else had stated that the gunmen were 'three dodgy little fellows'. Another witness had thought that one of the gang was lame, only to be contradicted by someone who had said, 'They all ran like blazes.' Someone had claimed that none of the gang had had their faces covered while someone else had sworn they'd had caps pulled down over their eyes. Someone had said that they'd been wearing battle-dress while other witnesses remembered them wearing raincoats, overalls or dungarees. There was even a witness who had expressed doubts about whether the gang had fired the fatal shot.

Higgins was beginning to run out of hope that he'd obtain a positive identification of any of the three gunmen.

❖

So lugubrious was Detective Superintendent Cherrill's demeanour that fellow officers could never tell whether he was about to dispense good or bad news. When Cherrill reported back to Fabian that evening, Fabian hoped that his colleague's search of the crime scene had yielded some incriminating fingerprints. But Cherrill disappointed him by saying, 'Nothing on the car to help you, Bob. Nothing in the shop either.'

Though Cherrill turned out to have found numerous fingerprints, most of these could be identified as belonging to the owner of the car or the shop assistants. None of the remaining prints matched any of those held in the archive over which Cherrill presided like some petulant monarch.

Fabian knew that if the gunmen had been linked to an unsolved crime or if they possessed a criminal record, no matter how insignificant, their prints would have been catalogued. All of which suggested that the gunmen were amateurs, a suspicion borne out by the botched robbery. If they'd been professionals, surely they would have been better organised. And surely they wouldn't have left the shop empty-handed. Then again, the fact that the prisons were full to bursting-point suggested that even hardened professionals were liable to make mistakes.

Perhaps the gunmen had left no prints because they had worn gloves. More and more criminals were getting wise to the power of fingerprinting. A few years earlier, an experienced burglar—whose prints had earned him several spells in gaol—had found an alternative to wearing gloves which detracted from his skills. Using acid, he'd started burning the skin off his fingertips. For a decade he'd evaded capture. Despite the acid damage, the original pattern of his skin had eventually reasserted itself, landing him behind bars again.

❖

Formerly dedicated to recording where German bombs had fallen, the Map Room took up the largest of three basement rooms at Scotland Yard. Most of one wall was devoted to a map of London. This was thirty feet long and extended from the skirting-board to the ceiling. To reach its upper edges, the staff needed a little wooden stepladder of the type used in libraries. The map's surface was studded with over twenty-thousand pins. Each of these represented a crime that had been committed. Unsurprisingly, the highest density of pins was in the section depicting the West End.

Once confirmation of Antiquis's death filtered through to the bowels of Scotland Yard, a smartly dressed civilian employee of S2—the statistical branch of the Criminal Record Office—headed for the relatively small 'Death by Violence' map, pasted across the wall in the far corner. Scrutinising the centre of the chart, he found the spot that marked the junction between Tottenham and Charlotte Streets. He held a pin with a tiny, triangular green flag attached to it. He thrust the pin into the spot where the shooting had taken place.

For him and his colleagues, the colour of the flag communicated the nature of the crime. Different colours were used to record manslaughters, abortions and infanticides. Miniature rings, like the hoops in some Lilliputian game of quoits, had been hung from the majority of the pins. Depending on the colour of these, it was possible to tell the outcome of each case. Black indicated 'death', yellow 'imprisonment', green 'guilty but insane', blue 'insane but not fit to plead', red 'suicide', and white 'crime unsolved'.

*The Map Room at New Scotland Yard. (Copyright: Metropolitan Police Historical Collection)*

During the previous year, there had been thirty-three murders in the capital. Of those, only eighteen had led to convictions, translating into an unimpressive 55% success rate for the police. From a purely statistical perspective, the portents were discouraging for Fabian and his team.

❖

When the News Editor of the *Daily Mail,* himself an ex-crime correspondent, had paired Syd Brock with Arthur Tietjen, he'd instructed them to find out the answers to three questions. One: was there any similarity between the bullets used in the Charlotte Street shooting and the earlier incident on Eastcastle Street when someone had opened fire on a police constable. Two: had the CID found any fingerprints and, if so, did these indicate that the raid on Jay's was a 'professional job'? Three: did the police know the identity of the culprits?

With forty-five minutes to spare before the first edition of his paper was due to go to press, the News Editor summoned Brock and Tietjen to a meeting. Over the intervening hours, the two reporters had, through their contacts with the police, unearthed the answers to their boss's questions.

Forensic evidence suggested that there was no link between the incidents on Charlotte and Eastcastle Streets. While the bullet extracted from the wall of Jay's was lead, the ammunition retrieved from the shop on Eastcastle Street was nickel-plated. Another tip-off from the police indicated that there were no obvious suspects in the Antiquis murder because the culprits were amateurs.

A cigarette drooping from his fleshy lips, Brock peered over the shoulder of Tietjen who was sitting at a manual typewriter. Their boss, clad in a hat and overcoat, also scrutinised the sheet of paper spooled onto the machine. In collaboration the three men composed a front-page story about Antiquis's death. Emphasising the significance of that afternoon's events, the reporters quoted an anonymous senior Scotland Yard officer's doom-laden pronouncement that 'This is a new era in crime.'

By 9:30pm the piece had been completed and hastily typeset, heralding the monstrous roar of the printing presses. The story, headlined 'THE AMATEUR KILLER', was juxtaposed with a selection of photos, one of them depicting the dead man's abandoned gloves, goggles and bloodstained rucksack.

After the paper had gone to press, Brock continued to harvest more information about the case, perhaps pausing to wolf down a sandwich, the crime reporter's usual dinner. Periodically, he phoned the *Daily Mail* News Room to pass on what he'd discovered.

❖

Tottenham Court Road Police Station was a gaunt-looking, late 1930s building near the noisy junction with Oxford Street. The building had six floors that extended down to a double basement. These backed on to North Soho. Since the scene of the crime was only a few hundred yards away, Fabian had decided to use the station's CID offices as the investigation headquarters. They consisted of four first-floor rooms on the Tottenham Court Road side of the building. Fabian had requisitioned one of them. It exuded an unmistakable aroma which, he'd noticed, was common to all police stations: a blend of soap, disinfectant and typewriter ribbons.

From his office he was able to see the massive Portland stone façade of the Dominion Theatre. Above the entrance, patrolled by commissionaires in pseudo-military uniforms, there was a canopy with 'CONTINUOUS PERFORMANCES DAILY' written round the rim. And above the canopy were three immensely tall windows bisected by a sign advertising the current films: Lon Chaney Jr. in *Son of Dracula* and Ginger Rogers in *Magnificent Doll*. Many of the people in the audience had probably read the first wave of press stories about the Antiquis murder. These had featured in two of London's evening papers: the *Star* and *Evening Standard*. Trumping their rival, the *Evening News*, which had missed the story altogether, both papers carried it as their front-page lead. In the *Star's* case, it appeared under the headline, 'GUN GANG KILL MAN IN LONDON: CHICAGO-STYLE JEWEL STICK-UP'

Not long after his discouraging conversation with Cherrill, Fabian was visited by Higgins who, prior to his promotion, had been based at Tottenham Court Road Police Station. During the Blitz, Higgins remembered sitting in his office with Detective Sergeant Saul, now an Inspector with the Colonial Force, vetting a report he'd submitted. Suddenly Saul had shouted, 'Never mind the commas, guvnor, duck!' Just as they'd both dived to the floor, a rocket had exploded behind the police station. The force of the blast had shaken the building, blown the windows off their hinges, scattered paperwork over the floor and coated everything in dust. Higgins and his colleague counted themselves fortunate to have survived the explosion which had, they later discovered, killed a policewoman who had been in the yard at the rear.

On being asked by Fabian how the interviews had gone, Higgins responded with a mournful expression and said, 'Well, Chief, I've got the descriptions. They're all different.'

Fabian flicked through the pile of statement forms that Higgins had brought with him.

Despite the discrepancies, Higgins said that all the witnesses had claimed they'd recognise the gunmen if they saw them again. Hearing that, Fabian

*Tottenham Court Road police station, c.1970s.*
*(Copyright: Metropolitan Police Historical Collection)*

made arrangements for the clerical staff at Department C4 of Scotland Yard—the Criminal Record Office—to search the files for case-histories and mug-shots of former convicts with a record of violence involving guns. Priority was given to those offenders who had just been released from prison or borstal. The witnesses could then inspect these mug-shots while their memories were still fresh. It was a tactic that had, eight years earlier, enabled Fabian to catch the killer of Mary Heath, the nightclub singer whose raven-haired good looks had led to her being billed as the 'Black Butterfly'. But mug-shots were seldom so effective, because most witnesses had trouble matching the culprits to their photos. The chances of success were further diminished by the fact that so many habitual criminals had evolved tricks intended to make themselves look unrecognisable in their mug-shots. Some prisoners distorted their faces by stuffing pieces of sponge or torn paper between their teeth and gums. Others sucked in their cheeks, clenched their nostrils and adopted uncharacteristic expressions. Higgins remembered Ruby Sparks, a self-confessed safe-cracker and gaol-breaker, being a master of that art. Sparks wasn't known as 'Rubberface' for nothing. When he'd broken out of HM Prison Dartmoor during the war,

*Staff look through index cards at the Criminal Record Office. (Copyright: Metropolitan Police Historical Collection)*

Higgins had been part of the team that had hunted him down. His mug-shots had, however, been useless for identification purposes.

Even if the CRO staff worked flat-out, it would take them at least half-an-hour to fish out the photos that Fabian had requested. Before heading over to Scotland Yard with Higgins, Fabian received a phone-call from the Forensic Science Lab in suburban Hendon. He knew the place well from his days at the Detective Training School which was located in the same, campus-like grounds. Often the white-coated boffins who staffed the lab were patronising in their dealings with mere detectives. This time, though, the man in question was perfectly polite.

'Mr Fabian?' he said. 'We've examined that stolen Vauxhall Fourteen Saloon, registration KPK 524, put a micro-camera over the upholstery and so on. There isn't a shred of a clue...'

❖

Stanley Firmin, an employee of the *Daily Telegraph and Morning Post*, had been reporting on crime for almost a quarter of a century. The Antiquis murder was the latest of many important cases he'd covered. As a junior reporter, he'd written about the death of the actress Billie Carleton from a cocaine overdose. He'd followed the hunt for the so-called Blackout

Ripper. And he'd also reported on the 'Brighton Trunk Murder', the 1934 case sparked by the discovery of a young woman's nude torso inside a trunk deposited in the cloakroom at the town's railway station.

Firmin had no great illusions about his chosen career. He saw himself as no more than a gleaner of facts. Like his fellow crime correspondents, he paid a heavy price to obtain those facts. Most weeks he worked punishing hours every day, hours that prevented him from enjoying a normal social life.

Late that evening he was still working on the Antiquis story. With little time to spare before he had to deliver his copy, he was snooping round Charlotte Street, alert for some telling detail that would give him an advantage over the other crime reporters. That detail took the form of an old woman in a funereal outfit. He watched her approach the spot where the shooting had occurred. She laid a small, homemade wooden crucifix on the ground. An arum lily was tied to it. To stop her tribute from being blown away, she weighted down the cross with a stone.

Kneeling for a moment, she bowed her head in silent contemplation. As she got up and walked away, Firmin intercepted her. Years of probing the aftermath of tragedy had, he knew, left him, if not downright cynical, at least unimpressed and untouched by whatever frailties and emotional dramas he witnessed. In reply to his questions about Antiquis, the old woman refused to give her name and said, 'I did not know him.'

After she had gone, a down-at-heel crowd of white, black and oriental passers-by converged on the crucifix she'd left. Relishing the added piquancy that they'd lend his story, Firmin noted that the crowd included 'Mr Tong, the barber', 'Jinghi, the fur dealer' and 'Mystic, the woman who reads your hands'.

❖

One by one the witnesses in the Antiquis case were escorted from the Waiting Room to the CRO, housed at Scotland Yard. The CRO was reached via either a cage-lift or the main staircase, the polished stone steps of which were so slippery that accidents were commonplace. Fabian had followed these routes countless times. In the summer of 1929 when he had been a detective constable, he had found himself re-assigned to the CRO. He could still recall his annoyance at being taken off active duties. He'd secured the conviction of numerous criminals, among them a big-time forger and two murderers, since joining the CID. With fifteen official commendations from the Commissioner behind him, he couldn't understand why he had ended up as a glorified clerk at the CRO. There his responsibilities had included copying information from police reports onto index cards and filing records of convicted criminals. He'd also been responsible for cross-indexing potentially useful information about their aliases, idiosyncracies, friends, favourite pubs, as well as their preferred methods of committing crimes, their so-called 'modus operandi' or 'MO'.

At first he'd been bored and frustrated by this posting, the deskbound routine making for a painful contrast with the previous five years of what he had regarded as proper detective work. Eventually, though, he'd got used to his new job and had even started to enjoy it. His renewed sense of job-satisfaction had been prompted by his contribution to the arrest of a thief, posing as a student at the Slade School of Art. The thief had specialised in robbing the tenants of boarding-houses. Whenever these robberies had been reported, Fabian had taken it upon himself to jot down details of the incident in his notebook, details contributing to the thief's arrest. This wasn't the type of story that made front-page news, yet Fabian looked back on it as an important case. It had taught him just how effective the pencil and paper detective could be. He'd been almost sorry to leave the place when, after eighteen months, he had received a transfer to the police station on Marylebone Lane.

Entry to the CRO was restricted to those on official business. Witnesses were ushered through the doors leading in to the Crime Index Room, a long, open-plan office that faced the Thames and the city beyond, where the lights tended to be blurred by a combination of mist and smog. Rows of dark wooden cabinets traversed the room. Each of these was equipped with a bank of slim, brass-handled drawers which made a low rumble when they were opened. Inside the drawers, the particulars of around a million criminals convicted in the United Kingdom were recorded on rows of stiff index cards. These were arranged in various sub-indices within the vast Crime Index. Under 'Breakings', for example, there were separate categories devoted to forced entry into churches, shops, cinemas, garages, offices, pavilions, schools, and warehouses. Those categories were, in turn, subdivided by the method of entry.

Many of the besuited officers usually to be seen marching from cabinet to cabinet had worked at the CRO for over twenty years. A few of them had been around in the days when Fabian had been posted here. So familiar were they with the Crime Index that they were capable of drawing up a list of likely culprits within about half-an-hour of being handed a Form 590—the standard form used to describe a suspect.

Beyond the labyrinth of filing cabinets, there was the Viewing Room, into which the witnesses were shown. Dubbed the 'Rogues' Gallery' by the CRO staff, it was as sparsely furnished as the Interview Rooms

*Officers in a Metropolitan Police wireless car. (Copyright: Metropolitan Police Historical Collection)*

downstairs. On the table in the centre, four-by-three inch mug-shots of possible culprits were laid out. Detectives were trained to arrange these face down like playing-cards in a multiple-deck game of patience. Before any of the photos were flipped over, the detectives had to tell the witnesses to point at pictures that showed anyone they recognised from the incident. With a sense of gravity, accentuated by the quietness of the room, the detectives then turned the photos face up.

The men portrayed in these black and white mug-shots were all convicted criminals. Had they been glimpsed in the street, passers-by wouldn't have automatically marked them down as people to be avoided, but Higgins knew just how deceptive appearances could be. Any doubts on that score were dispelled by the memory of Gordon Cummins, the Blackout Ripper. Higgins had been given the task of escorting Cummins on his trips to and from prison while he'd been on remand. Cummins had what Higgins regarded as the irritating habit of wanting to shake hands each time they met. Apart from that, however, he was not an obviously unpleasant person. Higgins remembered him being deceptively gentle in manner, someone who would not have attracted special notice if put among a group of ordinary people. Yet he was by far the most vicious killer Higgins had encountered in his police career. When Higgins had found Cummins's third victim in her flat near Broadcasting House, she'd been strangled and subjected to what the pathologist, Sir Bernard

Spilsbury, had described as a 'quite dreadful' ordeal.

Fabian and Higgins studied the witnesses' reactions as they examined the mug-shots displayed in the Rogues' Gallery. There were several exciting moments when witnesses, pausing to inspect particular photos, thought they'd recognised one of the gunmen involved in the Charlotte Street shooting. But those witnesses were, much to the frustration of the two detectives, uncertain about whether they had fingered the right man.

Whenever a witness left the Viewing Room, the layout of the photos on the table had to be rearranged in order to reduce the possibility of collusion. For the same reason officers had to avoid letting the outgoing witness see or speak to his or her successor.

At around 11:00pm, the last of the twenty-seven witnesses was led out of the Viewing Room and through the Card Index Room where the CRO staff were still busy searching the catalogues.

❖

In the average whodunnit Fabian had noticed that criminals were defeated by the efforts of a lone detective, grimly devising ingenious theories as he poured himself yet another double scotch. Steeped in fiction of this genre, Fabian had expected his preconceptions to be confirmed when he'd joined the CID. As he'd risen through the ranks, he had, however, come to recognise the importance of team-work in collaring criminals. The Antiquis investigation continued to endorse this ethos.

Officers were posted at each of the mainline London railway stations and bus termini where they checked passengers leaving the city. And pairs of squad cars were parked on outward-bound roads. Any vehicles with three or more occupants were stopped and the passengers' identity cards examined. In case the gunmen had already slipped through the cordon, a message was sent to the Chief Constables of all county police forces, asking them to keep watch over stations and roads leading into their counties.

Detectives, meanwhile, began to interview the residents of every London hostel for the homeless. Other detectives traced the whereabouts and checked the recent movements of former convicts whose records had been pulled out by the CRO. But these enquiries, many of them centred on the King's Cross area, hadn't produced anything significant by the time Fabian left Scotland Yard and was driven back to the investigation headquarters.

The streets en route were much less brightly lit than they'd once been. Due to the continued fuel crisis, electric advertising signs outside theatres, cinemas, shops and other businesses were prohibited, evoking memories of the wartime blackout.

Fabian was soon back at Tottenham Court Road Police Station, where he could deal with any important overnight developments in the case. Though officers were only supposed to work a maximum of eight hours a day, he had grown accustomed to putting in much longer hours without any prospect of overtime pay. Even when a CID officer signed off duty, the officer in question never really stopped working. That was something Fabian's wife, Winnie, could have confirmed. As a novice detective, he'd combined their courtship with unofficial, off-duty patrols of the West End. He had made his first arrest during one of their evenings out. While he and Winnie had been discussing whether they fancied going to the cinema, Fabian had spotted a couple of young men eyeing a parked car. He and Winnie had followed them well beyond the boundaries of C Division where he'd been posted. In Sloane Square, the two men had stopped next to an open-topped car, then reached across and helped themselves to a pair of expensive-looking rugs. Fabian had gone up to the thieves and arrested them, his heart thumping as Winnie went to look for help.

Pupils at the Detective Training School, where he had later received a grounding in CID work, were advised to have a few photos of themselves taken, photos which they could give to their families to remind them what they looked like. Each morning when Winnie said goodbye to Fabian, she could never be sure how long she'd have to wait before she saw him again. If he was involved in a big investigation like the Antiquis case, he might be gone for days at a stretch. Eventually he'd return exhausted, unshaven and fit company for no one, his mind already focused on the lengthy report he'd be expected to write. He sometimes joked about how an understanding wife was a most important part of a policeman's equipment.

Since receiving the initial call from Higgins, work had been so frantic that Fabian hadn't had time to phone Winnie and tell her that he wouldn't be coming home that night. Nor had he had a chance to send someone round to their house in Ashstead—well outside what was then London's south-western perimeter—to collect his shaving kit and other overnight things.

❖

As dawn broke on the morning after the shooting, bundles of newspapers were being delivered to shops and news-stands across the country. Following the precedent set by the *Star* and *Evening Standard*, events in North Soho received profuse coverage. From a journalistic point of view, they presented an irresistible story, combining the theme of the post-war crimewave with guns, gangsterism and the death of what, in present-day tabloid-speak, would be called a 'have-a-go hero'. Of the nine national daily newspapers, extending from serious titles such as the *News Chronicle* to populist ones such as the *Daily Graphic*, only the *Times* chose not to feature the story on its opening page. The headlines ranged from the *Daily Telegraph and Morning Post's* 'HOLD-UP MEN MURDER PURSUER IN LONDON' to the *Daily Express's* snappier 'MURDER, LONDON W1'. Several reporters gave the impression that the previous day's events, during which half-a-dozen gunshots had been fired in the West End, represented a pivotal moment in the war against the underworld.

Beneath the headlines, most papers carried what would become the defining image of the Antiquis murder: Geoffrey Harrison's photograph of the fatally wounded motorcyclist lying on the pavement. Thanks to recent technological advances that enabled the picture to be wired across huge distances, it made rapid appearances in foreign newspapers, bringing the Antiquis case worldwide notoriety.

❖

The morning rush-hour was underway when Fabian headed across the West End. At that time of day the pavements were always crowded, mainly with people who held down nine-to-five office jobs: dull jobs in the kind of dull offices Fabian knew from his days as a draughtsman. Many of the men would have been dressed in cheap, dark suits, as well as flat caps or trilbys, well-oiled hair glinting in the light if they were hatless. And many of the women, choices circumscribed by clothes rationing, would have been wearing the fashionable outfits of the era: autumnal-coloured, knee-length, belted coats with boxy shoulders, their hair swathed in headscarves or pinned back and teased into artful curls.

Fabian, who normally took such pride in his appearance, wasn't looking at his best because he hadn't had any sleep. Along with Higgins, he had been busy with the investigation all night. Earlier that morning he'd had to shave using ordinary soap instead of shaving-cream. This was guaranteed to leave his face looking raw and pink. All very unfortunate because he'd been summoned by the head of the Metropolitan Police, Commissioner Scott, to a press briefing at the Yard.

There was a time when the Met's top brass had treated reporters with regal disdain. Previous Commissioners had never even held press conferences. Instead, they'd relied on a tiny, basement Press Bureau for disseminating information. But that had changed since the appointment of Sir Harold Scott to the highest rank almost two years before. Scott considered publicity an indispensible part of his armoury. Whenever a major story such as the Antiquis murder broke, he liked to keep the Fleet

*Front page of the* Daily Telegraph and Morning Post, *Wednesday 30 April 1947. The story features an inaccurate diagram of the escape route of the two gunmen who got into the fight with Charles Grimshaw. (Copyright: the Daily Telegraph)*

Street reporters posted on the progress of the investigation. Not that Fabian was in a position to provide news of any dramatic breakthrough.

❖

Albert Pierrepoint was having breakfast in the large dining-room at the rear of the Rubens Hotel, just round the corner from Buckingham Palace. The Rubens had once served as the headquarters of General Sikorski, leader of the exiled Polish forces fighting Nazi Germany. Now it was being used as a so-called transit hotel. Its clientele comprised officers either on their way home or en route to postings abroad. The War Office had instructed the hangman to register at the Rubens under the honorary title of 'Lieutenant-Colonel Pierrepoint'.

From the tall rear windows of its dining-room, he and the uniformed guests had a dreary view of the buildings behind the hotel. Victoria Railway Station was near enough for the sound of trains coming and going to be heard above the usual hotel noises—the murmur of conversation, the rattle of tea-trolleys and the click of cutlery.

Over breakfast Pierrepoint perused the front-page of one of that morning's newspapers. His attention was caught by a report on Antiquis's murder. Shocked by the realisation that Antiquis must have been the man whom he had seen lying on the pavement near the Fitzroy Tavern, Pierrepoint could not bring himself to read the rest of the story. He had plenty of other things to worry about, though.

That morning he was due to check out of his hotel and fly to the Continent. As a child, brief train journeys had seemed to him like epic voyages of discovery, yet Pierrepoint now thought nothing of travelling to RAF Northolt where he'd board a plane and fly to Germany. Arriving at Northolt sixteen months earlier, a pack of newspapermen had chased him to the waiting plane. They'd wanted to question him about his assignment to execute Josef Kramer, former commandant of Belsen concentration camp. There was, of course, always the danger that news of his flight had been leaked to the press again and he'd have to go through the same ordeal.

As arranged, the War Office had provided him with the requisite travel documents. He had also been issued with a detailed itinerary for the three days he'd be spending in the Westphalian town of Hameln. There he was scheduled to execute thirteen more Nazis, guilty of war crimes committed at Ravensbrück concentration camp. He found multiple hangings hard work, not just physically but mentally as well. On top of his normal duties, he had to measure the height of the prisoners and weigh them, enabling him to calculate the drop required to break their necks. If he didn't make the drop long enough, he'd strangle them. And if he made it too long, he'd decapitate them. With multiple executions, he had to keep adjusting the drop and checking that the prisoners were being brought forward in the correct order. He knew that he could have got away with less exacting methods than he applied in Britain, where he worked under the watchful gaze of half a dozen officials, but he was too much of a perfectionist to succumb to that temptation. Added to which, he had a sense of obligation towards the condemned prisoners. Whatever unspeakable crimes they had committed, he felt compelled to treat them with humanity and allow them the final mercy of a quick death—a mercy seldom afforded the victims of Kramer, the so-called 'Beast of Belsen'. Yet Pierrepoint remembered feeling sorry for Kramer, Irma Grese and the eleven others as they had stared out at him from the darkened prison cells where they'd been kept before their execution. Pierrepoint had even gone so far as to lodge a complaint about the way that the prisoners were being treated. He realised they were guilty of all kinds of unspeakable acts, of whipping people to death and watching while inmates were torn to pieces by dogs, but he didn't think they should have had to listen to the interminable, tortuous noise of a group of workmen digging thirteen graves out of the frozen ground. When he'd told one of the young British soldiers stationed at the prison what he was thinking, the boy had replied, 'If you'd been in Belsen under this lot, you wouldn't be able to feel sorry for them.'

Each Christmas since the execution of Kramer and his subordinates, Pierrepoint had, along with the usual greetings cards, received a plain envelope with a £5 note inside. He presumed these were sent by a former concentration camp inmate. The first donation had been accompanied by a scrap of paper that had nothing but the word 'BELSEN' written on it.

❖

For important cases involving firearms, officers from the Met tended not to consult their own Forensic Science Laboratory. Instead, they preferred to seek assistance from Robert Churchill, the renowned gunsmith and pioneer in the emerging science of forensic ballistics. Such was his oracle-like reputation that a distressed Police Constable had once turned up at his shop with a brown paper parcel containing a human penis. With characteristically dry wit, Churchill had informed the officer that it wasn't his sort of shooting case.

The business, which Churchill had inherited from his feckless Uncle Ted, was based in a three-storey building on the corner where Orange Street met St Martin's Street, immediately behind the National Gallery. The building had a discoloured stone façade, leaded windows and a dark

Robert Churchill, c.1940.

shopfront with a sign reading, 'E.J. CHURCHILL, GUNMAKERS'.

Higgins went round there to deliver both the loaded revolver found at Jay's and the bullet extracted from the wall of the Pledge Department. Visitors to Churchill's combined shop, factory and ballistics laboratory were greeted by its long-serving manager, Jim Chewter, who had the shrewd, appraising instincts of a veteran butler. He used the shop's internal telephone to notify his employer of the arrival of friends or customers. Higgins fell into both categories.

A tiny lift connected the shop with the first-floor office, the walls and windows of which were covered by gun-racks. Churchill normally welcomed the occupants of the lift with a handshake and a warm smile. He was a squat, tubby sixty-year-old with broad shoulders, a neatly trimmed moustache and a bald crown unsuccessfully concealed beneath a few strands of hair, scraped back from what little remained of his widow's peak. A childhood bout of rheumatic fever had left him with a strange, tottering walk. His portfolio of physical defects was completed by a slight cast in one of his brown eyes, sometimes causing him to appear distracted. These impediments were counterbalanced by the vibrant personality and heavy-calibre charm that made him such a gifted salesman, his customers encompassing royalty, aristocrats and movie moguls to whom he sold made-to-measure guns in monogrammed cases.

Churchill regarded his police work as a hobby, for which he only invoiced Scotland Yard if a case went to court. He'd been introduced to forensic ballistics by his Uncle Ted who had hired him as an apprentice during the early 1900s. His uncle had been an occasional expert witness for the Met and, from the age of fifteen onwards, Churchill had helped him carry out rudimentary tests by shooting at carcasses purchased from the neighouring butcher's shop.

On examining the .32 revolver that Higgins had brought with him, Churchill noticed that there was blood on its handle, where it had been used to club the manager of Jay's. Churchill could see nothing to indicate that the revolver had been fired lately. Before testing it, he took it down to the shop's cellar where he had constructed a firing-range.

The cellar spanned two levels, the lower of these extending into a tunnel that ran beneath the road. Churchill had filled the far end of the tunnel with rubble. Behind that, there was a layer of iron-plating. These precautions allowed him to test anything from pistols to big-game hunting rifles in safety. Through testing, he could match a specific bullet to a specific gun, something that had been impossible in his uncle's day. Numerous murderers had been hanged on the strength of detective work conducted in Churchill's cellar. Late at night people sometimes walked past the shop and felt the faint thump of gunfire through the pavement.

When Churchill tested the revolver Higgins had given him, he found that the hammer didn't work properly. He thumbed it back, but it refused to stay at full cock. Only by pulling the trigger twice in rapid succession could he make it strike the cartridges. Even then, the revolver in his hand was no more dangerous than a toy pistol. Whoever had loaded it obviously knew nothing about guns because all six chambers had been filled with the wrong cartridges—what Churchill described as 'a very odd assortment of .320 rim-fire ammunition.'

❖

The briefing, to which Fabian had been summoned, was held in Scotland Yard's Press Room where the crime reporters were accustomed to working twelve-hour shifts, a dense cloud of cigarette smoke hanging over them. This pokey room, which had a small skylight that nobody bothered to open, was usually dotted with nondescript chairs arranged around a paper-strewn table. A worn and faded carpet, woven by the convicts at Wormwood Scrubs, represented the solitary attempt at homeliness. Down one side of the room, there were three wooden, soundproof telephone-booths. What appeared to be graffiti scrawled across the walls of these consisted, on closer inspection, of phone-numbers and shorthand notes relating to recent news stories.

Naturally, briefings on major cases like this attracted all the crime correspondents who had been granted accredited status by the Yard. Numbered among the senior reporters were Stanley Firmin, seventeen-stone Percy Hoskins of the *Daily Express*, and William Ashenden of the *Daily Graphic*. Ashenden's first

*Crime correspondents in the Press Room at New Scotland Yard.*

assignment had been back in 1911 when he'd covered the Sidney Street Siege. Alongside the newspapermen, there were journalists from two of the news agencies: W.G. Finch from the Press Association and the pint-sized, balding Charles 'Tich' Leach from the Exchange Telegraph Company.

Apart from the fact that they all chain-smoked, none of them, Firmin thought, bore any resemblance to the crime reporters portrayed so vividly in Hollywood films—the tough-looking gentlemen who were always in a tremendous hurry to get somewhere else. Firmin was impressed by how much better the relationship between the press and Scotland Yard had become. Until recently the higher-ups at the Yard had, he felt, regarded crime reporters as almost as big a nuisance as the criminals themselves. Courtesy of the new regime, Firmin had secured police cooperation for a book he was writing, entitled *Scotland Yard: The Inside Story*. For the purpose of research he'd been allowed to spend a night riding in a patrol car. Won over by this newfound spirit of cooperation, Firmin's book had acquired the breathless, uncritical flavour of a recruiting brochure.

Like Percy Hoskins and several other senior reporters, he had a symbiotic relationship with Fabian. Without their help, Fabian wouldn't have attained the celebrity status that he so enjoyed. Ever since the summer of 1939 when he had saved dozens of people from being killed by a New IRA bomb planted in Piccadilly Circus, he had been one of the CID's star turns. More by luck than skill, he had succeeded in defusing the homemade device, earning himself plenty of column-inches of gloating newspaper coverage as well as the King's Police Medal, presented at a Buckingham Palace ceremony.

During the briefing on the Antiquis case, P.H. Fearnley, head of the Yard's Press and Information Department, outlined the progress of the investigation. Appointed as part of the Commissioner's drive to improve the Yard's relations with the newspapers, Fearnley was a former journalist who had been a press officer for the BBC. He had a casual, confiding way of talking. Its down-to-earth quality was augmented by an appearance that spoke of solidity and trustworthiness, his craggy features topped by dark hair worn in a centre-parted style favoured by professional footballers of yesteryear. He'd already justified his appointment by establishing a valuable rapport with the press.

Reporters were told that the evidence pointed to one or more of the gang being inexperienced. And they were informed that fingerprints found in the shop and on the getaway car didn't belong to men who had been convicted of any offence. The gang were, in other words, not criminals 'known to the police'. Tracing them, Fearnley or one of his colleagues admitted, wouldn't be easy.

To supplement the briefing, a sheaf of flimsy, mimeographed news-sheets, containing descriptions of the three gunmen, was distributed among the audience. Derived from the most plausible of the twenty-seven witness statements, the following descriptions had been cobbled together by Fabian and his team:

*– Aged 25, height 5 feet 6 inches, slim build, pale complexion, broad forehead, thin jaw, clean shaven, long dark hair brushed back, wearing dark clothing and believed to have a light mackintosh.*
*– Aged about 25, 5 feet 10 inches, slim build, pale complexion, clean shaven, wearing a mackintosh.*
*– Aged between 30 and 40, 5 feet 8 or 9 inches, medium build, clean shaven, wearing a cap and dirty raincoat.*

Exposing a hint of the desperation Fabian felt about the case, an appeal was issued to law-abiding members of the public for any information that might help to track down the gunmen. 'Somebody somewhere knows who committed this murder,' the police spokesman declared. 'Somebody somewhere is giving shelter to these men. We ask them to come forward to the police at once. Their confidence will be respected. The perpetrators of this dastardly crime must not be allowed to remain at large.'

❖

Through his incisive contributions to the trials of such notorious murderers as Dr Crippen and George 'Brides in the Bath' Smith, Sir Bernard Spilsbury—Honorary Pathologist to the Home Office—had been a household name for more than three decades. Only a few weeks shy of his seventieth birthday, he betrayed no outward sign of the two strokes that had afflicted him in recent years. He was a tall, tired-looking man with a slight stoop which he'd deluded himself into regarding as a symptom of lumbago, not arthritis. Encroaching plumpness had blurred the placid, angular features that had once led a newspaper to proclaim him the 'Handsomest Man in London'. Since those far off days, Spilsbury's face had acquired the flushed complexion of a prosperous farmer. And his dense, light brown hair had turned white. His eyebrows had, however, retained their original colouring. These were visible above the rims of the round, tortoiseshell-framed glasses through which his sad, grey eyes peered round the cramped hotel room where he had been living for just over six years.

His room was on the second floor of a modest residential hotel on the edge of Hampstead. Not the type of establishment that befitted a man of his eminence. Spilsbury, whose marriage had long ago disintegrated under

Sir Bernard Spilsbury in his laboratory at University College, London. (Copyright: Metropolitan Police Historical Collection)

pressure of work, had moved there after his flat in Gray's Inn had suffered bomb damage. At that time the hotel had also been home to his late sister, Constance. He had envisaged it as no more than a temporary refuge while he searched for more convenient, centrally located accommodation. But he'd grown to appreciate the advantages of hotel life, chief among them being the relative anonymity and freedom from domestic responsibilities.

Spilsbury's room overlooked Frognal, the broad, sloping street that linked bustling Finchley Road with the bucolic expanses of Hampstead Heath. The room was furnished with only a bed, a wardrobe and a small writing-desk. When he had to contend with recurrent bouts of insomnia, Spilsbury would sit at his desk, making notes and filling in post mortem forms. Despite his age, he was working as hard as ever, partly because he needed the money. People tended to assume that he was well-off, but he had never been interested in exploiting his reputation for financial gain. His fees remained comparatively low. These were earned on a case by case basis, so he never refused any work offers. If he turned down a job, he was afraid that people would stop using his services. He had even continued working after the first of his strokes, a period during which he had been forced to hobble round with the aid of walking-sticks.

His days were filled by a hectic round of post mortems, visits to crime scenes, sessions in his laboratory at University College, as well as lectures at St Thomas's and the Royal Free Hospitals. In between all that, he lunched in the unlikely setting of the station restaurant at Euston where he often met his daughter Evelyn and her friends. Dinner was taken at one of his clubs, normally the United University Club, just off Pall Mall. On Sundays when he treated himself to a break, he listened to the evening concerts on BBC radio's recently launched Third Programme. In the music of Mozart and Beethoven, Spilsbury found solace from his sapping routine and, perhaps, from the depression that he had endured since tuberculosis and the Blitz had claimed the lives of his two grown-up sons.

Busy though he was, he always took the trouble to make sure he was dressed neatly before he went down to breakfast. The arthritis in his fingers rendered the task of buttoning his white shirt more time-consuming than it should have been. To avoid the risk of spattering his cuffs with blood while he was at work later on, he wore a custom-made shirt, fitted with detachable sleeves. Over his shirt he put on a three-piece suit, cut in an old-fashioned style. Together with his matching homburg, the suit heightened the aura of Edwardian decorum that he radiated.

Downstairs in the hotel's dining-room, he liked to breakfast alone, a newspaper or some notes spread out on his table. Here and in other communal areas of the building, he was sometimes waylaid by fellow residents who wanted him to diagnose their ailments. Thankfully, though, not many of them realised who he was. Talking about himself was not something he relished. In a typically polite, unemotional tone, his choice of words as fastidious as his dress sense, he replied to enquiries about peoples' ailments by saying that he wasn't a general practitioner. If he was feeling mischievous, he'd inform them that he wouldn't know what was wrong with them until he dissected them after they had died.

Each weekday morning he followed the same post-breakfast routine. Clutching the big black bag in which he kept his post mortem tools, he walked down the hill that led towards Finchley Road. The hill, steep enough for the return journey to leave him wheezing and exhausted, was lined with large, redbrick houses. Many of these had not even been built when, as a ten-year-old briefly at school in that area, he had first become acquainted with Frognal.

On reaching the main road, he turned left and walked towards Regency Parade, a row of small shops and other businesses just beyond Swiss Cottage Underground Station. From Blue Star Garages, the well-staffed parking facility next to Connolly & Eyles Tea Rooms, he retrieved his car. He drove a luxurious Armstrong-Siddeley which, in a rare display of self-indulgence, he had purchased before the last war. There was something vaguely American about its sleek profile and wide running-boards. It soon joined the rush-hour traffic flowing towards the centre of town.

The journey took Spilsbury past Regent's Park and into the less salubrious streets of Camden Town. Experience had not improved his skills behind the wheel. But he was such a respected figure among the Met's officers that they never fined or prosecuted him if they caught him skipping a red light or ignoring a give-way sign. By some miracle he'd only had one accident, a collision with a pony and trap. The accident, which had occurred well away from the forgiving gaze of the Met, had resulted in him being fined £10 and charged with dangerous driving.

His destination was St Pancras Coroner's Court, located in the grounds of the church on Camley Street, a side road that skirted the busy goods depot behind King's Cross Station. Both the court and adjoining mortuary were housed in a cluster of late nineteenth-century buildings. The single-storey mortuary had a large enclosed yard that was used as a car park. From there, the court building could be entered via double doors. Spilsbury parked his car, then went in search of W. Bentley Purchase, Coroner for the Northern District of London.

Purchase was a long-faced fifty-six-year-old with dark, thinning hair, owl-like eyebrows and a bulbous nose on which circular-framed glasses rested. He'd been a barrister before training to be a doctor. He was among Spilsbury's few close friends, their friendship spanning seventeen years. Since Purchase's appointment as Coroner during the early months of 1939, Spilsbury had become dependent on his friend—who ran the mortuaries at both St Pancras and Hackney—for the majority of his post mortem commissions. Aware that Spilsbury was not in good health, Purchase endeavoured to assign him as much work as possible. In doing so, Purchase hoped to spare him from the necessity of trekking across London to other more distant mortuaries.

Spilsbury had got into the habit of immediately handing over the previous day's completed post mortem forms, then asking Purchase whether there was any work for him. This time the pathologist was informed that an urgent post mortem needed to be carried out on the man who had been murdered on Charlotte Street. It was a street that already had grisly associations for Spilsbury. He'd once been called upon to examine a woman's dismembered body, part of which had been found in a cellar not far from the site of the Antiquis shooting. Wrapped in sacking and a bloodstained sheet, the trunk and arms had been dumped nearly a mile from there. The body turned out to be that of an emigrée Frenchwoman named Mme Émelienne Gérard, who had been murdered by her former lover and his new girlfriend. Spilsbury still possessed the notes that he'd made about the multiple wounds inflicted on Mme Gérard. He also had a souvenir from the case, kept at St Mary's Hospital where he used to work and where he'd built up a collection of hundreds of macabre relics from his career. Inside a tiny cardboard box of the type formerly used by chemists for dispensing pills and powders, there was a faded scrap of blood-soaked hearth-rug, taken from the kitchen where Mme Gérard had been murdered. Like all the other objects Spilsbury had accumulated over the years, it was capable of unleashing a sequence of gruesome memories.

❖

Habitually dressed in a plain blue-black suit and tie, Sir Harold Scott was due to celebrate his sixtieth birthday later that year. He had a long, thin face with a beaky nose, large, fleshy ears and a mouth bracketed by deep furrows. His hair was brushed away from his forehead. There was something faintly austere about him, about the way he appraised people through his round, horn-rimmed glasses while puffing on a large briar pipe.

Just under two years earlier, he had been summoned to a meeting with Herbert Morrison, Home Secretary in the wartime coalition government. Scott had at that time been employed as a senior civil servant at the Ministry of Aircraft Production. He'd assumed the meeting would be about some aspect of Civil Defence, so he was nonplussed when Morrison began by asking, 'Can you ride a horse?'

He had replied that he'd never been much of a horseman, but— stretching the truth—he could ride well enough not to disgrace himself.

Prompted by his reply, Morrison had invited him to take over from Air Vice Marshal Sir Philip Game as Commissioner of Police for the Metropolis, a job that involved ceremonial appearances on horseback. But Scott had had doubts about his qualifications for the role, traditionally filled by retired officers from the armed forces. For a start he had wondered whether the public would have faith in his ability to instil discipline. He had also wondered whether people under his command would respect someone from his humble, civilian background, grammar school having been his passport to the upper levels of the civil service. Conversely, he had welcomed the opportunity to escape from the burden of paperwork which bore down ever more heavily on senior civil servants. And he had relished the idea of contending with the predicted post-war crimewave. His initial doubts quashed by these powerful incentives, he had told Morrison that he'd be proud to undertake the work. Since embarking on the job, Scott had faced a crimewave far more severe than the comparable phenomenon that had occurred after the First World War.

Already under pressure to subdue the continued upsurge in violent crime, he had convened a meeting with the Met's top brass to discuss the Antiquis case. He was concerned that failure to find the killers might encourage other London criminals to resort to shooting when they believed they were in danger of being intercepted after a raid.

The meeting was held in Scott's office on the first-floor of Scotland Yard. Almost six years earlier, this had been wrecked by an unexploded bomb that had penetrated the roof and two floors directly beneath, scattering fragments of concrete, broken bricks, furniture, paperwork and a substantial portion of the Crime Index over the room. The office's consequent expensive refurbishment hadn't long been completed.

Unlike any of the Yard's other offices, Scott's was relatively plush and comfortable. In place of the brown lino seen throughout the rest of the

*Sir Harold Scott in his ceremonial uniform.*
*(Copyright: Metropolitan Police Historical Collection)*

building, there was an oriental carpet. And the walls weren't decorated with the institutional two-tone colour-scheme predominant elsewhere at the Yard. The office was equipped with padded leather chairs, a table, a glass-fronted bureau, a fireplace and a big, knee-hole desk. Scott liked to keep the dark, highly polished surface of his desk bare apart from a few neatly stacked papers, a calendar and a couple of ashtrays. Behind the desk was a large chart. This showed the number of arrests made in London over the past twenty-four hours, along with the location of crimes committed during that period. Antiquis's murder was destined to be incorporated into these alarming statistics.

Prior to meetings, Scott's predecessor used to have the chairs arranged in a semi-circle in front of his desk, from where he addressed his senior officers like a schoolmaster talking to his class. But Scott insisted on meetings being conducted around the table, a change of layout intended to create a friendly and informal atmosphere. Scott thought that he'd been successful in fostering an environment in which everyone felt free to speak his mind on any subject that came up. He was, however, yet to win over many of the officers under his command. To some of them, he had become a laughing-stock thanks to the incident when he'd fallen off his horse and broken several bones which had had to be encased in plaster beneath his uniform. Others saw him as a mere pen-pusher. Not that he fitted the profile of the average Whitehall bureaucrat because he had a refreshing hatred of waffle and unnecessary paperwork. Whenever Scott convened meetings, they tended not to drag on for hours, and this one was no different.

Fabian attended it together with four other chief inspectors from Central Office. Assistant Commissioner (Crime) Sir Ronald Howe and Commander Hugh Young, the two highest ranked officers in the CID, were also present. Aside from both being in their fifties, Howe and Young had little in common.

Grey-haired and softly spoken, Young was a working-class Scotsman, born on a highland croft. He'd taken decades to rise from the bottom of the police hierarchy to his present exalted position. He'd carved out a reputation as a crack detective with an unblemished record of leading murder enquiries. All those decades spent in London had left him with only a faint residue of his native brogue, yet it still offered a sharp contrast to Howe's well-enunciated, upper-class accent.

Howe was Young's antithesis in other respects, too. A public school and Oxford-educated barrister in his mid-forties, Howe had never had to suffer the boredom and danger of being a constable on the beat. Instead, he'd been appointed to the upper ranks by Scott's predecessor. Since being assigned the post of ACC the previous year, Howe had developed a fixation with criminal detection. He'd often drop in at crime scenes on his way to the Royal Automobile Club after work, his immaculate evening-dress rendering him conspicuous.

That morning's meeting was chaired by the Commissioner whose relaxed and undemonstrative manner was refreshingly different from that of his more formal predecessors. Far from impos-ing his opinions by virtue of his rank, Scott strove to do so through the force of his arguments. Even so, Fabian wasn't too impressed by some of the decisions Scott had taken. He felt that the policy of putting officers in wireless cars—officers who would otherwise have been on the beat—was misguided. Had Fabian been in Scott's shoes, he would have done things very differently. He would have made sure that the rates of pay for the police were increased and accom-modation provided for their families. By doing that, he concluded, the recruitment problem would have been solved, the Met would have attracted the best of Britain's youth and the crimewave would have been curtailed.

Though the multiple-carriage trams and other traffic moving along Victoria

The main entrance to New Scotland Yard.
*(Copyright: Metropolitan Police Historical Collection)*

Embankment were visible from the Commissioner's office, double-glazing ensured that the noise did not distract from what was being said. On being informed of the worrying shortage of promising leads, the decision was taken to put out another press release. The next comminiqué would consist of a second appeal for information, this time issued by the Commissioner and aimed at members of the underworld, at those who 'lived on their wits' but had no sympathy with criminals using guns.

The unprecedented decision was also taken to dedicate nearly all the Met's officers to the Antiquis case, making it the force's biggest murder-hunt so far that century. Besides contributing directly to the investigation, these extra officers would be used to clamp down on the London underworld. By flooding the streets with policemen and keeping watch over all the cafés and clubs where criminals met, it would be hard for them to go about their everyday business without being caught. Logic dictated that most criminals would be eager to help the police catch the killers, if only to ensure that life went back to normal.

Alongside the additional manpower provided by the CID, the Flying Squad was placed at Fabian's disposal, though his acriminious departure from the Squad meant he was none too happy about the prospect of working with its officers again. Such an arrangement raised what was, for him, the nightmarish possibility of them grabbing the glory by arresting the killers. But he had no choice. If he'd tried to talk the Commissioner out of involving them, he would have laid himself open to accusations that he was giving his own feelings priority over the investigation.

❖

Shortly before 10:30am that morning, Higgins and Donovan de Antiquis, the victim's brother, made their way across the courtyard around which the St Pancras Mortuary buildings were arranged. Sparing his widowed sister-in-law further pain, Donovan—who, like her, lived in Colliers Wood—had agreed to carry out the formal identification of the body. Until this had been completed, the post mortem could not proceed, yet there was little or no chance that the murdered man would turn out to be anyone other than Alec de Antiquis. For Higgins, this was one of those stressful formalities that he had to endure.

To the left of Higgins and the dead man's brother were the Mortuary for Infectious Cases, the Store Room and the Microscope Room. Ahead there was the larger Mortuary for Non-Infectious Cases. The Viewing Lobby, from where the body could be inspected, ran parallel to the righthand side. Despite being roofed over, it had no door. It consisted of a long dead-end passageway with a picture-window that afforded a clear view of the slate slabs where the bodies were laid out.

London's mortuaries were kept scrupulously clean and tidy, but that hadn't always been true. At the height of the wartime bombing they had sometimes been used to store the dusty corpses of air-raid victims for whom there hadn't been space in the Civil Defence Mortuaries. These bodies, many of them crushed and mangled by the impact of bombs and falling masonry, had been left on the floor, tiny children side by side with the elderly. Serenaded by the nervous chatter of relatives waiting in the yard outside, the mortuary staff had gone round tying little cardboard identity discs to the bodies. Higgins could count himself lucky that his wife Jean and their three children—Ronald, Anthea and Peter—hadn't ended up somewhere like that, their names part of a long casualty list.

Donovan de Antiquis looked through the window into the mortuary. The body of the murdered man was arranged face up on one of the slabs. Identifying the victim of a gunshot wound to the head could be difficult, but that wasn't the case this time. Other than the fatal wound, marked by a patch of dark, clotted blood, Alec de Antiquis's face was clean and unblemished.

❖

Detective Sergeant Bill Cramb was a good-looking young man who worked for the Yard's Photographic Section. He had dark, crinkly hair and a facetious, bantering manner that made him popular with other members of the CID. His affable presence helped to create a relaxed atmosphere at the regular dinner dances staged by the Met.

Cramb had been sent to St Pancras Mortuary that morning to take pictures of Antiquis. He was also scheduled to photograph the gang's getaway car and the scene of the robbery. Kitted out with a wooden, telescopic tripod and a box-camera that had a flashlight-reflector the size of a large saucepan-lid, he was now in the Post Mortem Room, through which a cold draught invariably blew.

The impressive trio of Fabian, Higgins and Spilsbury were there with him. While the two detectives had to wear white surgical gowns over their ordinary clothes, Spilsbury liked to don rubber overalls which, coincidentally, matched his hair colour. When he was out of earshot, the mortuary staff affectionately referred to him as the 'Great White Chief'.

At his insistence, nobody present smoked at post mortems: a considerable imposition in those days of ubiquitous tobacco smoke. Once a fifty cigarettes-a-day man, Spilsbury had kicked the habit because he felt that it had exacerbated his bronchial problems. But his health concerns were not the sole motive for the ban. He objected to smoking in the Post

*Bill Cramb (directly behind the man with the moustache) at a Metropolitan Police dinner.*

Mortem Room because the heavy odour of tobacco could mask other potentially revealing smells given off by a corpse.

Antiquis's naked body lay on the ceramic table in the centre of the room. To stop blood and other fluids from trickling onto the floor, the table had a slight rim. When the body had been transferred from the adjoining mortuary, a chunky wooden block had been placed under Antiquis's head. Someone had also wiped the blood from his face and the area around the fatal wound. The dead man's eyes were closed, his hair neatly combed back, and his mouth open just wide enough to reveal his front teeth.

Next to the table, Cramb set up a tripod. He then fixed his box-camera onto this and lined up what would be the first of however many eight-by-ten-inch black and white shots Fabian required.

There were a surprising number of police photographers whose pictures were no better than the smudgy, sometimes blurred pictures of nude women sold under-the-counter in Soho. But Cramb had a reputation that placed him several notches above the average police photographer. With him assigned to a case, Fabian could bank on receiving a series of nice, crisp shots which would be invaluable if the case ever went to court.

Cramb was standing on the lefthand side of the mortuary-slab, from where he could get the best view of the bullet-wound. Over the next few minutes he composed a couple of flashlit, landscape-format photos of the murdered man, the light from the flashbulb accentuating his pallor and making the wound appear even darker than it was. Each time Cramb released the shutter, the bulb made a loud pop not unlike the noise of a gas-stove being lit.

One of the photos, taken from such a low angle that Cramb could see the cotton-wool plugging Antiquis's nostrils, depicted his head and torso. The other photo was a tightly framed close-up of his profile. Thrusting the lens so near to him that the individual bristles on his cheeks and the faint wrinkles under his eyes were visible, Cramb made sure that the bullethole was in the centre of the picture.

❖

Whenever Spilsbury carried out a post mortem, he gave the Mortuary Keeper a generous tip of at least ten shillings. In exchange duckboards were laid round the slab. These formed an improvised walkway which spared Spilsbury the discomfort of standing for hours at a stretch on the cold cement floor. No longer as resilient as he had once been, he found it hard to cope with the nagging chill, aggravated by the damp from the frequently washed cement.

Higgins always felt happy when he heard Spilsbury was scheduled to undertake the post mortem on a murder victim. With Spilsbury's assistance, he was confident that they'd finish with an accurate picture of what had happened. Through regular encounters here and at numerous West End crime scenes, Higgins had got to know Spilsbury quite well. The famous pathologist's unobtrusive charm had become more apparent with each encounter.

For all Spilsbury's fame and professiol success, Higgins had never seen him exhibit any of the bombastic traits which so many men seemed to acquire when they achieved a little authority. Whether Spilsbury was talking to a senior investigating officer or some fresh-faced Constable, he was, Higgins thought, extremely modest, courteous and helpful. People who met him off-duty were unlikely to guess that he was a man of such eminence, someone whose opinions were regarded as gospel-truth by juries. Even so, Higgins could not help feeling in awe of him.

Most pathologists merely got in the way when they attempted to play detective, but Higgins rated Spilsbury's deductive powers more highly

*One of Bill Cramb's photographs of Alec de Antiquis lying on the slab in St Pancras Mortuary.*
*(Copyright: Crown Copyright)*

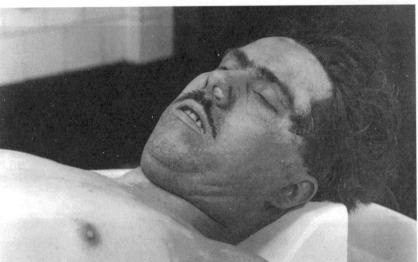

than those of himself or Fabian. In Higgins's opinion, Spilsbury was the greatest detective. Higgins had once told him about a case he was working on, a case involving a woman who had ostensibly died from a self-administered abortion. Hearing the evidence, Spilsbury had explained that the dead woman couldn't possibly have inflicted the wounds. His deduction had led to the arrest of a professional abortionist whose trade was, at that stage, illegal.

As a preamble to each post mortem, Spilsbury stooped over the body and subjected it to a thorough and systematic external examination, beginning with the head. He appeared more comfortable touching corpses than living people, contact with whom tended to make him recoil.

Unlike other pathologists who provided a commentary, Spilsbury preferred to work in silence, broken only when someone asked a question. On the lookout for clues, he subjected the body to careful scrutiny. In archaic mortuaries like this, though, it wasn't easy for him to see what he was doing because he was reliant on the skylight overhead.

Annoyed by what he regarded as the backward state of forensic science in England, Spilsbury had campaigned for improved mortuary facilities. He was angered by the lack of any mortuaries comparable to the Paris Morgue where bodies could be preserved for long periods. But there was little incentive for politicians to sanction the required investment. A campaign to refurbish mortuaries could never have been construed as a vote-winner. Besides, the beleaguered Labour government, elected in a wave of post-war euphoria, had more urgent problems to contend with, not least how to feed the population.

The bullet wound in Antiquis's head was about half-an-inch in diameter. Spilsbury noticed the absence of any gunpowder burns on the surrounding skin. This indicated that the murder weapon was likely to have been fired from a distance of a few feet or more. Until the mid-1930s, such telling observations would have been recorded by Spilsbury's secretary, the unshockable Mrs Bainbridge, who had accompanied him to many a murder scene. Since her death, though, he had managed without a secretary. If he spotted anything pertinent, he had to stop what he was doing and make a note of it himself. Idiosyncratic as ever, he didn't use a notebook like other pathologists. Instead, he recorded his observations on index-cards, decks of which he carried round with him. He had several thousand such annotated cards filed away in his office at University College. One day he hoped to use them as reference material for a textbook on medical jurisprudence.

Higgins got the impression that Spilsbury would have been lost without his index-cards. Sometimes Higgins, who found Spilsbury's looping, unexpectedly flamboyant handwriting difficult to read, had deciphered the brief, telegraphic notes written on them. The detective had been impressed by the way that they recorded apparently superfluous details which often turned out to be invaluable.

Pathologists were taught to move down the front of the body once the external examination of the head had been completed. When they reached the arms, they had to test for rigor mortis by manipulating them. In Antiquis's case, the tell-tale stiffness had set in overnight.

As soon as the pathologist was satisfied that he had noted everything worth recording about the front of the body, he had to examine the back of it. Before that could be done, though, the cumbersome, stiff-limbed corpse had to be picked up and turned over—never an easy process.

On completion of the exterior stage of the Antiquis autopsy, Spilsbury positioned himself, ready to make the preliminary incision with his short, broad-bladed post mortem knife. The majority of his colleagues started under the chin, but he preferred to begin on the lower slopes of the neck, moving the blade towards the genitals.

At first he had to apply only enough pressure to slice through the skin and moist layer of subcutaneous tissue below. Varying the pressure, he had to draw the knife down the body. With the ease of a jacket being unbuttoned, flesh and skin were opened to reveal glimpses of bone, cartilage, and glistening innards.

For the first few occasions on which Higgins had been present at autopsies, he had found it a disturbing and unpleasant experience. But he had soon become inured to the unique horrors of the process. Nowadays he was fascinated by it, by the way that a pathologist of Spilsbury's calibre could arrive at all kinds of ingenious deductions on the basis of apparently minor details. Higgins had even been fortunate enough to have been invited by Spilsbury to hear him lecture on the subject at University College.

In the years that Higgins had been working at West End Central, initially as a plain Detective Inspector, he had witnessed Spilsbury perform autopsies both at St Pancras and Paddington Mortuaries. Regardless of whether the cause of death was obvious or uncertain, Higgins knew that there were never any half measures at Spilsbury post mortems. Every aspect of the body would be examined with characteristic diligence.

Spilsbury tended to go about his unvarying routine with the matter of fact demeanour of a mechanic stripping down a car engine. Whenever the situation demanded, he would shift his instruments from hand to hand, having trained himself to be ambidexterous.

Every so often, he paused to sniff the body, just in case it was emitting some tell-tale odour. To refresh his deteriorating sense of smell, he liked periodically to down tools and hurry out of the Post Mortem Room and into the yard where he would gulp down a few lungfuls of fresh air before going back to work.

Higgins could see that Spilsbury was not quite his usual confident self. Mentally, he seemed just as sharp as always, but the old magic didn't seem to be there. The incisions were no longer as neat as they had once been. And he no longer proceeded with the same serene confidence, exactitude and speed. There had been a time when he would race through an entire post mortem in two hours or less. It now took him the best part of a week to accomplish what had once been a day's work.

Reticent though Spilsbury was, Higgins knew that the celebrated pathologist was worried by the prospect of age eroding his skills. But Higgins hadn't, until that moment, witnessed the decline in those much-admired powers. Higgins was saddened by the realisation of how far Spilsbury's work had fallen below the standards which he had set himself, yet he showed no inclination to reduce his workload. Asked what he would do when he retired, he'd said to someone else, 'I shall go on to the end, and die in harness.'

Among Higgins's colleagues there had been talk of how, under the strain of work, Spilsbury was cracking up. Higgins felt that Spilsbury drove himself too hard for a man of his age. The way things were going, he'd end up having another stroke, only next time he might not achieve such a remarkable recovery.

The crucial stage of the Antiquis post mortem was imminent. To dissect the head, Spilsbury had to make a shallow incision along the centre of the scalp, allowing the skin to be peeled away from the skull in two sections. The front half could then be folded over the face while the rear half could hang over the nape.

Spilsbury's attention was caught by a sizeable, recent-looking bruise on the crown. He concluded that Antiquis must have either banged his head on the pavement or, more likely, been struck by a hard object.

In preparation for opening the skull, an adjustable metal ring had to be placed over the bloodied scalp. At equidistant intervals round the ring, known in the trade as a 'coronet', there were four screws. These had to be tightened until the coronet was clamped to the skull. Holding the skull steady with a strip of metal that arced over the coronet, Spilsbury was then free to saw through the bone—always a messy business. As he moved the saw back and forth, each stroke accompanied by a dull grinding that sent vibrations through the floor, the pathologist had to be careful not to allow the saw's teeth to become clogged. When he'd finished cutting round the

*View of Jay's, taken from the intersection between Charlotte and Tottenham Streets on the afternoon of the police reconstruction. (Copyright: Crown Copyright)*

dome of the skull, a chisel had to be used to lever it away, exposing the brain's familiar topography, undulating greyish-pink hills flanked by a network of sinuous valleys.

His every move studied by Higgins and Fabian, Spilsbury employed his custom-made forceps to trace the bullet's trajectory after it had pierced Antiquis's skull. From its entry point just beyond the tip of the left eyebrow, it had drilled a two-inch hole through the left hemisphere of the brain.

As well as noting the cause of death—'meningeal haemorrhage'—Spilsbury observed that Antiquis was an otherwise healthy man, no other factors contributing to his untimely demise. Since there was no exit wound, the bullet must have been somewhere inside the dead man's skull, but Spilsbury couldn't find it. Desperate to get their hands on this valuable evidence, Fabian and Higgins were becoming ever more agitated.

Spilsbury said there was a million-to-one chance that the bullet had somehow been deflected, making its exit through the entrance wound. If he'd believed in his far-fetched theory, though, he wouldn't have resumed his search for the elusive bullet.

Lost in thought, Spilsbury didn't notice the bullet drop out of the entry wound. Nor did he notice the click of it landing on the floor.

Fabian tried to spare Spilsbury any embarrassment by promptly picking it up. It was a mangled .320 calibre bullet, large enough to explain why it had caused so much damage. With a few diplomatic words of congratulation, Fabian handed it to Spilsbury.

❖

Once the post mortem was finished, Fabian and Higgins went over to the scene of the crime. In an attempt to jog memories and bring forward additional witnesses, a reconstruction of the robbery and shooting was being staged that afternoon. The stretch of Tottenham Street between Jay's and the Charlotte Street crossroads resembled a film location, only the role of the director and technicians had been usurped by CID officers. At their behest the cast was being manouevred into position, ready for the action to begin.

Intrigued by what was going on, a dense crowd of passers-by had assembled. The crowd, which included at least one press photographer, was being held back by a cordon of Police Constables who had sealed off the area around Jay's.

For the second time in the space of twenty-four hours, a gang of three masked men fled the shop and sprinted towards the crossroads. Second time round, however, there was a feeling of inevitability about the outcome. The fugitives were predestined to confront the approaching motorcyclist, unlike the previous afternoon when things could have turned out differently. Had one of the links in the chain of cause and effect been broken, had the gang headed the other way down Tottenham Street, had they left the shop a few seconds later, had the traffic in the West End been heavier, had the missing motorcycle parts been available in Camden Town, Alec de Antiquis would still have been alive.

# III

# MURDER GUN

J ust over twenty-four hours had elapsed since the Charlotte Street shooting, yet Fabian and his team had found no promising leads. As if that wasn't frustrating enough, the police suspected members of the public were withholding vital information. There was no shortage of credible explanations for why those people hadn't come forward. Maybe they were friends or relatives of the gang. Maybe they were afraid of the culprits. Maybe they'd supplied the guns used in the robbery or been implicated in some other way. Maybe they were criminals who didn't want to acquire a dangerous reputation as informers. Then again, maybe they belonged to the transient kerbside population of 'grafters': street musicians, beggars, barrow boys, match-sellers and sandwich-board men, all inclined to be wary of the police, nicknamed the 'bogies'. For the sandwich-board men who tended to work for agencies under assumed names, calculated to conceal their criminal records, such wariness was understandable.

Detectives were sent round to question the innumerable grafters plying their trade in the West End. On previous investigations Fabian had sometimes received assistance from this section of society. He knew they were alert as monkeys and wouldn't shield a gunman from justice.

Another source of fresh information was the so-called 'bookies' runners' who stood on street-corners taking bets. Strictly speaking, they were liable to arrest because they were breaking the law against off-course gambling, but the police regarded this statute as unenforceable. It was also unfair because wealthy gamblers could bend the law by maintaining accounts with trackside bookies whom they phoned when they wanted to place a bet. Consequently, the Met did little to disrupt street bookmaking. In return, a significant slice of the business was distributed among the police. Payments would go to the Constable patrolling an area where bookies' runners were posted. More generous bribes would make their way to the officers above him in the hierarchy. Some of the Chief Inspectors in charge of the smaller police stations, scattered round each division, had accumulated tidy pension funds, courtesy of these backhanders.

To create the illusion that they were enforcing the law against street bookmaking, senior officers would collaborate with big-time operators such as Harry White, boss of the 'Kings Cross Boys'. The bookies would pay men with no criminal record to stand at a pre-arranged spot, pretending to take bets. These men would then be arrested and brought before a magistrate, their lack of previous convictions ensuring that they were given no more than a fine and a stern reprimand. While this charade was being enacted, the genuine bookmaking operation would carry on unhindered.

The secret, undercover branch of the CID, dubbed the 'Ghost Squad', was an additional source of possible new leads. Set up at the beginning of

1946, the unit was run by Detective Inspector John Capstick, who regularly rubbed shoulders with Fabian in the Fitzroy Tavern. Known among criminals as the 'Grey Fox' or 'Charlie Artful', Capstick was a red-faced, grey-haired pipe-smoker with a relaxed manner and soft voice. He had three experienced officers under his command, dedicated to infiltrating the underworld where they groomed potential informers and picked up rumours.

Fresh leads on the Antiquis case were also sought through the criminal contacts established by CID officers across London. Fabian and Higgins had built up an extensive network of these. Ever since their early days in the CID they had been encouraged to fraternise with the local criminals who, like members of any other profession, were liable to gossip about their colleagues. No matter how trivial it sounded, gossip could provide the key to a police investigation. For the likes of Fabian and Higgins, a casual, apparently innocuous reference to a criminal who had just bought his wife a fur coat or taken her to an expensive restaurant might connect that person to some recent, lucrative crime.

Fabian was on surprisingly good terms with many underworld figures, from whom he'd earned grudging respect. After he had foiled the New IRA attack in Piccadilly, during which several gangsters had narrowly avoided being blown up, a group of them had lured him to a surprise party, thrown in his honour. At the party, a leading gangster had made a speech expressing their thanks. The speaker had gone on to present him with a mysterious package. Fabian had been deeply touched by what he'd found inside. Attached to a blue ribbon was a bronze medal no bigger than an old penny. The medal bore embossed laurel wreaths on one side. On the other side was an inscription that read:

*To Detective Inspector Bob Fabian*
*For Bravery, 24.6.39*
*From The Boys*

Fabian kept it in the same drawer as the medal he had been awarded at Buckingham Palace.

From the ranks of the local criminals, both Fabian and Higgins had recruited a string of informers. Higgins bragged about having more informants and contacts than any of his colleagues, many of whom disapproved of the practice and considered it far too risky. By grooming informers, detectives laid themselves open to baseless accusations of corruption. Accusations of this nature could precipitate a disciplinary enquiry, generally conducted by a senior officer from a provincial police force. If evidence was found to corroborate the allegations, the detective could be dismissed from the Met and stripped of pension rights. But officers as experienced as Fabian and Higgins were well aware of the risks.

Nicknamed 'squealers', 'narks', or 'snouts', informers were normally recruited by turning a blind-eye to some offence they had committed, then blackmailing them with the threat of arrest. Prominent among Fabian's long-term informants was the professional gambler, Harry 'Big Hubby' Distleman. Nearly six years earlier

*Detectives question a barman.*
*(Copyright: Metropolitan Police Historical Collection)*

Distleman's brother, 'Little Hubby', had been fatally stabbed in a brawl at a Soho nightclub. Out of gratitude for Big Hubby's services, Fabian had lobbied successfully for the culprit, an Italian gangster named Antonio 'Babe' Mancini, to be hanged.

Meetings with informers like Distleman had to be arranged at discreet rendezvouses. One of the cardinal rules of these 'meets' was that the detective never made the first move when he arrived at the chosen venue, often an obscure pub or café. Billiard halls were also favoured for these clandestine encounters, the detective positioning himself at the adjoining table to the informant, with whom a furtive conversation could be held or a surreptitious note exchanged.

Care had to be taken not to use the same meet too many times and to avoid being seen alone with the informer. On entering the venue, the detective had to avoid approaching or acknowledging whoever he was meeting. First, the detective had to wait for the 'show out'. This consisted of a brief nod, signalling that there was nobody around who might blow the informer's cover.

Detectives frequently handed over cash for tip-offs or 'whispers', as these were termed. The money paid out was regarded as a sound investment, good inside information leading to arrests and the increased likelihood of promotion. If the tip-off resulted in a conviction, the informers also stood to earn a tax-free payment from Scotland Yard's Information Fund. Payments went up to £15—around £425 in 2007 currency. Informers had the extra incentive of reward-money if an insurance company got involved in the case. Substantial rewards were offered after major robberies, but these earnings carried with them considerable risks. Whenever informers were exposed, the victims of their tip-offs were prone to exact violent retribution, sometimes culminating in the informer's lacerated corpse being found floating in the Thames. More commonly, though, the punishment entailed being slashed across the face with a cut-throat razor, leaving the victim with a lifelong scar—the 'mark of the nark'.

❖

Through the remainder of Wednesday 30 April, information poured into the CID offices at Tottenham Court Road Police Station. Some of these tip-offs were obviously worthless, others had a whiff of authenticity. Yet Fabian and his team couldn't afford to make assumptions. All of these potential leads had to be followed up. As a result, numerous houses and business premises were raided by the Met, these raids bringing the police no closer to solving the case.

Higgins was conscious that he and Fabian were in need of a lucky break—what his friends at the golf club termed the 'rub of the green.' If only, he thought, real life was like a crime novel, where the novelist could fit all his imagined facts and events into a logical pattern and the solution was always just round the corner. But, as Higgins lamented, there was no such pattern for the real-life detective. Sometimes the harder he strove and the more ingenious his theories and ideas, the more he faced a blank wall and the public began to mumble about the police not knowing what to do.

❖

Each evening the crime correspondents from the London-based newspapers made a habit of gathering in the St Stephens Tavern. This quaint Victorian pub, nicknamed the 'Dive', was on the corner of Bridge Street and Cannon Row, close to Scotland Yard. Here, the reporters—who tended to be generous in praising a rival's scoop—liked to discuss the latest stories. And the Antiquis murder was the dominant story in that evening's newspapers. Their front-pages emblazoned with the headlines, '4 GUN GANGS ROAM LONDON' and 'SIX GUNMEN ON THE RUN', both the *Evening Standard* and *Evening News* placed it in the context of other recent gun-crimes perpetrated in the city. Robert Hoare, the *Evening Standard's* crime correspondent, even went so far as to make the claim that Antiquis's murderers belonged 'to a "guns for hire" gang of about twenty desperate characters who are always ready to be hired by a leader for an armed raid.'

Taking a different approach to its rivals, the *Star* focused on the plight of Antiquis's widow. Headlined 'GANG VICTIM'S WIDOW FACES POVERTY', the story pointed out that her husband's contributions to the government's National Health Insurance scheme entitled her to a weekly income of only ten shillings, plus five shillings for each of her children. The item was lent emotional resonance by a brief interview with Mrs de Antiquis, who talked about her late husband's struggle to build up their business. 'It is all I have now,' she told the *Star's* reporter, 'and I hope it can be kept going with the help of my brothers.'

Since the police had broken the bad news to her the previous day, she and her two eldest children, twelve-year-old Pearl and eleven-year-old Shirley, had been staying with her mother-in-law who lived in a bungalow close to L & A Motors. The couple's four other children were being looked after by relatives.

That evening Syd Brock, the *Daily Mail's* crime correspondent, visited the bungalow on Cavendish Road where Mrs de Antiquis had sought sanctuary from the tragedy that had suddenly engulfed her. Brock was accompanied by a press photographer. Her expression conveying her despair, Mrs de Antiquis allowed herself, Shirley and Pearl to be photographed. Shirley wore the new Girl Guide uniform her father had bought her shortly before his death. She was a pretty, dark-haired girl who had put on lipstick which made her look older than her sister. When the photographer had finished what he was doing, Shirley kissed her mother and went off to a Guides meeting.

Interviewed for at least the third time that day, Mrs de Antiquis explained that she had debts of £650—£18,500 in 2007 terms. Without

*Mrs de Antiquis with her daughters, Pearl (left) and Shirley (right). (Copyright: Solo Syndication)*

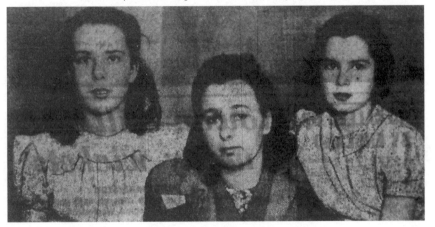

her husband, she was worried about keeping the business going and the family together. She added, 'Alec would never forgive me if I failed in that.'

❖

Most of the Met's police stations had a supply of camp-beds, ready for an emergency. One of these was set up in Fabian's office that night, but the inevitable background noise—the frequent voices, the phone-calls, the traffic—must have made sleep difficult.

Far from ideal though the arrangement was, it could hardly have been more uncomfortable than the Section House on Beak Street where Fabian had had to live when he had first joined the force. There he'd been allocated a cubicle with just enough room for a bed, a steel locker, a chair, a cardboard hat-box and a desk-top that folded out from the low partition separating his cubicle from its neighbour. Behind the door, there was a coat-hook which he and the other residents were permitted to use only when they were at home. Not that there was anything homely about the place. Residents weren't even allowed to display more than a single photograph of either their parents or a girlfriend. And the bolt on the door, which could be opened from both sides, meant that Fabian and his colleagues were never guaranteed privacy. All for a meagre pay-packet of £3 a week. Yet Fabian had no misgivings about joining the police. He did, however, feel mildly envious of the current crop of recruits, who were given proper rooms, fitted with an armchair and a radio, not to mention hot and cold water.

❖

Several other big news stories had broken since the Antiquis murder. Even so, the following morning's newspapers still carried prominent coverage of it, coverage that incorporated the Met's appeal for information.

The lack of major developments in the murder-hunt encouraging Stanley Firmin to weave a story from the sparsest of material, the *Daily Telegraph and Morning Post* ran a front-page article based on a leak from the police. Firmin's unnamed source said that a tip-off had been received just before midnight. The tip-off had indicated that the raid had been planned more than two months ago. The raid had, Firmin speculated, been organised by some master criminal—a concept that was among the biggest clichés of mid-twentieth-century Fleet Street reporting.

In parallel with the news stories, the Antiquis case provoked outraged editorials about the gun-crime epidemic. 'A dead man lies on a London pavement,' the *Daily Mail's* 'Comment' column began. 'He has been shot through the head by armed villains in broad daylight. It is a sight we associate with Chicago, but not with the capital of Britain. Yet it has

happened here. The picture of this victim at the scene of his murder has
been published in the papers. That grim photograph has shown millions of
horrified people, as little else could have done, the reality of the armed
menace to law and order existing in our midst today.'

According to Stanley Bishop of the *Daily Herald*, that menace had arisen
through the absence of a suitable legal deterrent. Anyone caught carrying
an unlicensed gun was subject to a maximum of three months' in prison or
a £50 fine. But Bishop revealed that most offenders were given paltry fines
of between £1 and thirty shillings.

All this continued press attention had so far produced no firm leads. The
police had come to the conclusion that the Charlotte Street gunmen were
being shielded by friends who may have been unaware of the gravity of
what they were doing. In the eyes of the law, those friends were accessories
to murder, an offence that carried a stiff gaol sentence. Unless one of those
friends could be frightened into breaking the silence, there was every
chance that Antiquis's killers would never be caught.

Such inconclusive cases could, as Fabian knew to his cost, be the source
of lingering frustration. During the closing months of the Second World
War, he had led the unsuccessful investigation into the macabre murder of
an old man near Stratford-upon-Avon. In what had appeared to be an
occult ritual, the victim's throat had been slashed with a sickle and his body
pinned to the ground with a pitchfork. The press had referred to it as the
'Warwickshire Witchcraft Murder'. Though Fabian's team had devoted
countless hours to the case, amassing some four-thousand statements in the
process, there had been insufficient evidence to arrest the prime suspect.
Despite that, Fabian still nurtured tenuous hopes of some hitherto
unknown information coming to light, information that would enable the
suspect to be prosecuted.

❖

Mrs de Antiquis was on her way to St Pancras Coroner's Court to attend
the inquest into her husband's death. As she travelled from Colliers Wood
to Camden Town, she was bound to have been recognised by a few
strangers who had seen her photograph in that morning's edition of the
*Daily Mail*.

The Court's main entrance consisted of a grand doorway topped by
scrolled stonework. Visitors stepped into a small lobby with a door on the
righthand side, leading into the spacious courtroom. Mrs de Antiquis had
to sit on one of the three benches opposite the large desk occupied by W.
Bentley Purchase, coroner in charge of the obligatory inquest. These seats,
reserved for family members, reporters and anyone else who wanted to

attend, were immediately behind the bench set aside for witnesses, Sir Bernard Spilsbury among them. Called to give evidence soon after the jury had been sworn in, he surprised no one by testifying that Antiquis had died from a gunshot wound.

❖

None of the CID's underworld contacts had thrown up any plausible suspects. This suggested that the gang behind Antiquis's murder might not be from the capital. On that assumption Fabian sent out instructions to every CID office in London to check up on everyone who had registered at hotels and boarding-houses in the city over the past three weeks. At the same time detectives from C Division were posted in every West End pub and drinking club, where they examined peoples' identity cards, allowing the police to compile an inventory of visitors to the capital.

A much more solid lead, meanwhile, came Fabian's way. Like most leads in major murder investigations, it was the product of patient, unspectacular detective work. By sifting through list after list of property stolen from addresses in London, the source of the .32 revolver, left in the Pledge Department at Jay's, had been pinpointed. The serial number on the revolver matched that of a weapon taken during the weekend of 26-27 April. The theft had been from Frank Dyke & Co, a gunsmith's on Union Street which ran through the south London district of Southwark. During the robbery, several other revolvers and three shotguns had been stolen. So had a cache of ammunition and, as Fabian jokingly commented, enough cleaning stuff, oil, brushes and flannel to supply a platoon of soldiers.

Orders had already been issued to the CID in M Division, which covered Southwark, to investigate anyone who might have participated in the Union Street robbery. While that lead was being pursued, Fabian and his team were examining the possibility that the gang behind the Antiquis killing might have carried out other recent armed raids. If so, Fabian knew that each robbery was likely to share the same MO. He had been taught that no two criminals approached the same crime in precisely the same way. They were bound to adopt different habits and develop idiosyncracies, akin to leaving a business card. These habits and quirks were recorded in Supplement A of the CRO's Modus Operandi Index which had helped Fabian solve many cases in the past.

On Wednesday 30 April—the day after Antiquis's death—a group of armed men had had the audacity to hold up a Military Police truck near a camp for exiled Polish soldiers at Malmesbury in Wiltshire. The gang, which had wrongly assumed that the Military Police were delivering the unit's monthly pay, had escaped in the hijacked truck. But a combination of geography and the gang's MO suggested that they weren't responsible for the more amateurish Tottenham Street robbery.

The masked raiders who had killed Antiquis were more likely to have been behind the bungled raid that had taken place in London later that Wednesday. Mrs Eveline Arthur, owner of a dress-hire agency near Victoria Railway Station, had been poised to enter her shop when she had been set upon by two or three men. Before they could force their way into the building, a brave passer-by had come to her rescue. Like Antiquis, the passer-by—an engineer named George Mitchell—had been shot and fatally wounded by the gang.

Fabian and his team were struck by the similarities between this and the Antiquis shooting. In both incidents, the culprits had tried to rob somewhere but panicked when a passer-by had intervened. The men behind both robberies had also displayed an alarming readiness to shoot anyone who got in their way.

❖

It was almost 9:30pm on Thursday 1 May. During the fifty-five hours since the Charlotte Street shooting, the police files on the case had grown fat. The stack of witness statements had been supplemented by the half-dozen glossy black and white photos that Bill Cramb had taken. Two of these showed Antiquis on the mortuary slab. The others depicted the gang's getaway car, the exterior of Jay's, the side entrance to the shop, as well as the interior of the Pledge Department, its counters and partitions still dusty with fingerprint powder. Included in the file, there was also a large, detailed plan of Jay's and two carefully scaled maps of the surrounding area. These had been produced by a Constable from C Division whose technical drawing skills can't fail to have reminded Fabian of his days as a draughtsman.

Despite the volume of paperwork generated by the Antiquis case, Fabian's initial optimism about catching the gang responsible had evaporated. He was aware that the file was in danger of joining the Yard's collection of 'open—unsolved' case records. Row upon row of these mouldering files were stored at the CRO, each of them offering a silent rebuke. Some of the cases dated back more than a decade, during which many of the investigating officers had fretted over their inability to bring the culprits to justice.

Failure to catch the gang behind the Antiquis killing would have represented a rare blemish on Fabian's record—a record which he viewed with justifiable pride. He was certain that some of his former colleagues from the Flying Squad were hoping to see him fall flat on his face. If he did, it wouldn't be for lack of effort. Right then, he could have been at home with his wife or downing another pint in the Fitzroy, instead of which he was at Tottenham Court Road Police Station, anxiously awaiting developments in the case.

Just over two days of intense work without a good night's sleep had left Fabian looking far from his normal immaculate self. Colleagues sometimes referred to him as 'Beau Brummel', but they would never have made the comparison if they'd seen him that evening. Besides being unshaven, he had bloodshot eyes and rumpled clothes. To stave off tiredness, he was sipping yet another cup of strong canteen coffee. Though the coffee had gone cold, he drank it all the same.

Downstairs a man in the type of dark leather coat favoured by taxi drivers had already strode up the steps and into the police station's lino-floored entrance hall. As the double doors closed behind him, the low swish and hum of passing traffic was muffled. The door opposite connected the hall to what was known as the 'Front Office', which consisted of a large, oblong room with a wooden counter facing the door. In a few hours from then, the room would be echoing to the drunken shouts of the troublemakers routinely arrested after closing-time in the local pubs.

Under the supervision of the Station Sergeant, dubbed the 'Skipper', the counter was staffed by uniformed officers. The taxi driver announced that he had some information about the Antiquis murder. He appeared very apologetic and didn't think there was anything in his story, but felt duty-bound to tell it. Hundreds of such stories had been reported, so there was nothing to suggest that this would be any more helpful than the others. Yet the taxi driver was taken to see Fabian. Purely by looking at his coat, the surface of which glistened with raindrops, Fabian could tell how he earned his living.

'D'you want to know anything about two young fellows I saw disappear into a building off Tottenham Court Road just after the murder?' the taxi driver asked. Before Fabian could reply, he added, 'They had handkerchiefs knotted round their chins.'

The taxi driver proceeded to identify himself as Albert Grubb. He explained that, around 2:30pm on the day of the murder, he'd been driving a fare towards the Warren Street end of Tottenham Court Road. Past Heal's department store, he had taken a righthand turning down Torrington Place, a relatively narrow side-street. As his taxi swung round, a man had leapt onto the running-board next to the passenger-seat, causing him to brake sharply. Even though the man had a white handkerchief tied across the lower half of his face, Grubb claimed to have seen enough of his features to know that he was young.

Grubb said he'd told the man that the taxi was already taken. The man had reacted by jumping off the running-board, then dashing round the back of the vehicle and over to Brook House, an office block on the other side of Torrington Place. According to Grubb, another young man—also wearing a mask—had been holding the door open for him. Both men had disappeared into the building. And that was the last Grubb had seen of them.

❖

Ever since he'd been a lowly Constable on patrol duty, Fabian had been aware of the crucial role that luck played in police work. For ambitious young patrolmen like him, impatient to secure promotion by chalking up regular arrests, much depended on going down the right street at the right moment. Fabian was energised by the possibility that the information volunteered by Albert Grubb was the equivalent of one of those lucky streets.

Everybody who worked at Brook House had gone home, so Fabian was unable to search the building until the following day. Before that could happen, he had a tip-off that one of the Charlotte Street gunmen was a deserter from the American military. Officers under Fabian's command found that the description of the deserter matched a description provided by witnesses to the Antiquis murder. In the wake of this discovery, over 300 addresses across London were raided by the CID. One such raid was led by Higgins who, together with eight detectives, targeted a house in Camden Town which, according to his informant, was being used as a 'drum'—an underworld hideout. When Higgins and the other detectives arrived there, the suspect was nowhere to be seen. They were told that he'd left a few minutes previously.

An hour and a half later, the police received a tip-off announcing that the suspect was being sheltered by a woman who lived just off Kennington Road in Lambeth. Higgins and his men would have taken too long to get to south London, so another group of detectives was sent there. They surrounded the house and entered it through the front and back doors. Written statements were obtained from everyone in the building, but this line of enquiry proved a dead end.

❖

The majority of the following morning's newspapers carried updates on the Antiquis investigation. Beneath the headline, 'MURDERERS SHIELDED', *The Times* cited yet another disturbing example of the wave of gun-crime sweeping England. George Tyler, a taxi-driver who had picked up an airman from New Street Railway Station in Birmingham, had been found shot dead on the road between Burton-on-Trent and Derby.

Well ahead of daybreak, Fabian, Higgins and a colleague drove round to Brook House, an old office block just a few hundred yards from the investigation headquarters. Though the block's address was 191 Tottenham Court Road, its entrance—protected by a steel security-door—was on Torrington Place.

In their eagerness to look round Brook House, Fabian and his colleagues got there before anyone who worked in the building. The three unshaven, red-eyed detectives sat and waited in their squad car, the collars of their coats turned up against the cold. Fabian and Higgins used the opportunity to catch up on some sleep. Like Fabian, Higgins was accustomed to sleeping in uncomfortable places. During the war, he'd often had to bail out rainwater from the air-raid shelter in his garden where he had spent many nights with his wife and children.

The sky was just starting to brighten when Fabian and Higgins woke up. Soon afterwards, the first of the people who worked at Brook House arrived. Fabian got out of the car and spoke to him. He was a porter named Leonard Joel. On being told the reasons why the police were there, Joel said, 'Ah, that might account for the little key I found when I swept the stairs yesterday. It didn't belong to any of the people in these offices, for I asked 'em all.'

Joel showed him the key. Fabian took this and handed it to the officer who had accompanied him and Higgins to Brook House.

'Try it in the stolen Vauxhall,' Fabian told the officer, who climbed back into the squad car. It roared off in the direction of Scotland Yard, where the Vauxhall had been taken after the shooting.

While the officer was gone, Fabian and Higgins embarked on a thorough search of the offices. These were occupied by six separate companies, specialising in areas ranging from glassmaking to optometry. But the two detectives had not made much progress by the time Fabian received a phone-call from their colleague.

'It fits, Chief!' the officer said with palpable excitement.

The key turned out to be the Vauxhall's ignition key.

As Fabian and Higgins continued their search of the building, more porters and other staff rolled up for work. All of them were surprised to find CID officers there. For Brian Cox, a freckly, mischievous-looking fourteen-year-old office boy and kitchen assistant, the presence of the police must have provided a welcome dash of drama to enliven his day.

The officers questioned him about Tuesday afternoon. He said he'd popped downstairs at about 2:45pm to fetch the latest delivery of post from

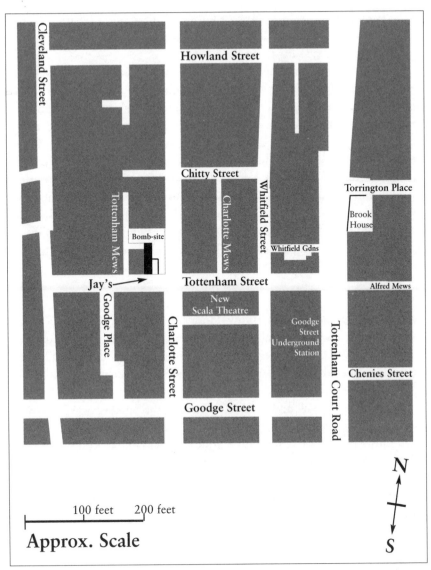

*Diagram showing the locations of Jay's and Brook House.*

the letterbox just inside the front door. There he'd chatted with an East End lorry driver who had been making a delivery. Cox had been locking the lid of the letterbox when two men had barged past him and the lorry driver. The men had then taken the lift upstairs.

Cox revealed that he'd seen the men again about five minutes later. En route back from his next errand, he had spotted them loitering on the staircase, halfway between the ground floor and first floor. One of them had been sitting on the window-sill while the other had been standing next to the bannisters. They'd wanted to know whether 'Mr Williams was in', but Cox had told them he didn't know of anyone by that name. The two men had swiftly made for the exit.

Quizzed about whether they had been wearing overcoats or mackintoshes, Cox said he couldn't remember. He did, however, recall noticing that one of the men had been wearing a white scarf when he'd first set eyes on him. But the scarf had gone by the time Cox had next seen him. Cox's memories of that afternoon were endorsed by the lorry driver, Percy Skinner, whom the police succeeded in tracing. Skinner described how the two men had nearly knocked him and Cox over as they'd pushed past. He said that the shorter of them was clad in a 'fawnish' raincoat while his accomplice wore a 'bluish' mackintosh. Both men looked as if they had been running because their faces were slick with sweat. The taller of them, Skinner told the police, appeared to have discarded his coat before leaving the building.

❖

The detectives had been at Brook House for over four hours, yet they hadn't completed their search of the building. So far, they'd encountered nobody else who had seen the two gunmen. To compound their frustration, they'd found neither the discarded raincoat nor any other relevant evidence.

With the search still underway elsewhere in the building, Reg Hyam— foreman at Rogerson & Co. a firm of builders and decorators based there— went into a store-room on the first floor. Stuffed behind a dusty old shop counter, close to an open lift-shaft, he found a mackintosh, made from RAF blue material criss-crossed by a fine red check pattern. When he picked up the grubby coat, a white scarf dropped out. This had been folded into a triangular mask and knotted at both ends.

Just after 10:45am, Higgins and Fabian heard about Hyams's discovery. They headed straight to the store-room where they examined the coat and scarf. These were ordinary, mass-produced items, so Fabian knew it would be hard to trace who had bought them.

In the pockets of the raincoat were a pair of gloves and a dirty grey cap. The material under the brim of the cap was so ragged that the cardboard beneath was exposed. Fabian and Higgins were disappointed to discover that the manufacturer's labels had been carefully removed from the cap, gloves and coat. Referring to the coat, Fabian said, 'I think we should tear it open and see if we can find any other labels.'

He and Higgins spread the coat out on a table and ripped away the lining. There was a linen tab protruding from the seam that ran between the righthand pocket and the armpit above. The tab had a number and several symbols written on it in scarlet ink. Arrangements were immediately made to show this to experts in the clothing business, commonly referred to as the 'rag trade'.

By lunchtime those experts had informed Fabian that the tab was a 'stock ticket', the number on which indicated that the coat had been manufactured by Montagu Burton Ltd. Besides owning a factory in Leeds, the company had an extensive chain of gentlemen's outfitters. The experts said that the number should correspond to a specific consignment. If that could be identified, Fabian and his team would be able to locate the shop from which the coat had been purchased.

A police driver was ordered to take the stock ticket up to the factory in Leeds while the coat was dispatched to the Forensic Science Lab, just in case the scientists were able to find other potentially helpful clues. Even a single item of clothing could reveal a lot about whoever had been wearing it. Higgins had once secured a conviction thanks to the dust that had accumulated in the turn-ups of a suspect's trousers. Scientific analysis had demonstrated that this was identical to the wadding used in the body of the safe which the suspect had been accused of blowing open.

On the afternoon of his visit to Brook House, Fabian returned to Tottenham Court Road Police Station. While he waited for news from both Leeds and Hendon, he took another well-earned nap. When he woke, he was informed by an undercover detective that a member of the Charlotte Street gang—possibly the American deserter about whom they'd been tipped off—was rumoured to be hiding at 15 Hillgrove Road in the north London suburb of Swiss Cottage.

Fabian and Higgins assembled a raiding party of thirty detectives, drawn from several police divisions. They boarded a couple of police vans waiting at Tottenham Court Road Police Station. With Fabian in one van and Higgins in the other, they drove to Swiss Cottage and parked in a side-street near Hillgrove Road, a short street adjacent to South Hampstead Station. Officers then surrounded the house and banged on the front door, their arrival startling the couple who lived in the downstairs flat. Fabian and his men spent more than two hours searching every room, but their efforts yielded nothing pertinent to the case.

❖

'The essence of good crime reporting is,' Stanley Firmin wrote, 'the possession of really first-class contacts. They will consist of individuals on both sides of the fence—detectives on the one hand, crooks or near-crooks on the other. Obviously neither type will pass on the tiniest shred of

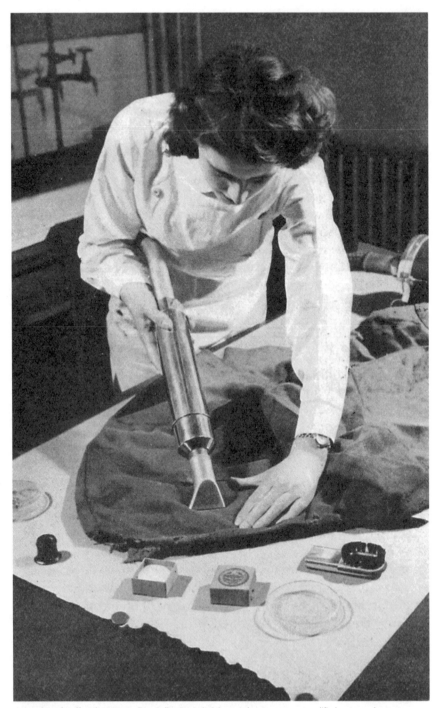

*A member of staff at the Metropolitan Police Forensic Science Laboratory uses a modified vacuum-cleaner to collect dust and fibres from a jacket. (Copyright: Metropolitan Police Historical Collection)*

information unless he has complete confidence in the integrity and discretion of the recipient. And it is the creation of that confidence that takes time. Neither the detective nor the crook will ever take a man on face value alone.'

Robert Hoare of the *Evening Standard* had acquired the trust of just such a contact among the officers leading the Antiquis investigation. Secure in the knowledge that Hoare would preserve his anonymity, the officer granted an interview which took place while the latest wave of police raids was in progress.

'There is no doubt that a number of armed men have got together into gangs,' the officer declared. 'They are dangerous men. They are young and reckless—possibly men from borstal backgrounds and with one or two other men connected. They have formed themselves into bands of villains—stop-at-nothing boys. It is possible that they are led by several old lags who are dealing with the receivers... They are the type of men who will fight it out, even with the police if they are cornered.'

❖

Fabian was back at Tottenham Court Road Police Station by the time the detective sent to Leeds phoned him. 'Sorry, sir,' the detective said. 'All they can tell us is that the raincoat was delivered to one of three branch shops in London.'

Two of these were situated in what Fabian regarded as fairly high-class suburban districts. The third shop was 'over the water' in Deptford, a rough dockside area south of the river. There wasn't much likelihood that Fabian and his officers would be able to find out which of these branches had sold the coat, let alone who had bought it. Each shop probably sold dozens of such coats every year. On top of that, there was no reason why any of the sales assistants would remember who had bought them or know where the customers lived.

Before Fabian could set off on a tour of all three shops, he was given more disappointing news. This took the form of a teleprinter message from the Forensic Science Lab. The message—printed on thin, crackly paper which, only a few moments ago, had spooled out of the machine downstairs—read, 'REGRET NO IDENTIFICATION IN RAINCOAT, CAP, SCARF OR GLOVES.'

❖

Higgins and his immediate superior had just entered the second of the two suburban branches of Montagu Burton's. Luckily for the investigation, they discovered that the branch in question—like many other clothing retailers at that time—recorded the names and addresses of its customers. It did this as a precaution against people purchasing clothes using forged ration coupons.

The shop's manager wasted no time in finding the sales ledger which he then flicked through. 'Ah, yes, here we are…,' he said as he located the appropriate entry. He gave Fabian and Higgins the name and address of the man who had purchased a mackintosh of the same style, colour and size as the coat left at Brook House.

Fabian dispatched a team of detectives to question that customer. Detectives were also sent round to interview the man whose address had been provided by the previous suburban branch that Fabian and Higgins had visited.

With closing-time imminent, Fabian and his second-in-command went back to their car, a powerful black Railton. Accompanied by at least one other detective, they sped round to the Deptford branch of Burton's. It was a triple-fronted shop, sandwiched between the Expert Denture Repair Service and Sandford Brothers' Greengrocers on the High Street, where several buildings had either been destroyed or damaged by German bombs aimed at the docks.

Marching into the shop, Fabian asked Arthur Amos, the manager, whether he had the name and address of someone who had purchased an RAF blue raincoat with the serial number '7800'.

'Why, of course we have a record of sale,' Amos replied. He thumbed through his ledgers with breezy confidence. When he found what he was looking for, he said, 'Here we are—sold on December 30th 1946.' He went on to reveal the details of the purchaser, who had an odd-sounding name: Mr Kemp Thomas of 160 Park Buildings, Paradise Street, London SE16. Not far from the gunsmith's that had been robbed the previous weekend.

Amos turned out to have dealt with Thomas himself, so the entry was in his handwriting. Since the sale had required ration coupons, he'd copied the details from the customer's ration-book. Mention of this prompted Fabian to glance at his own book of clothes coupons. Noticing that 'Fabian Robert' was written on the cover, he enquired whether Amos had inadvertently copied the purchaser's names in reverse order. Amos remembered selling the coat on the final Saturday before Christmas when the shop had been besieged by customers. In his haste to serve everyone, Amos had done exactly what Fabian had suspected. The purchaser's name was Thomas Kemp, not Kemp Thomas.

❖

Equipped with the coat, which had by then been sent back from the Forensic Science Lab, Fabian and his team were poised to visit Kemp who was now the main suspect. When Kemp realised that he was cornered, there was every likelihood that he might try to shoot his way out. Before confronting him, Fabian secured the support of a squad of armed officers. Though Fabian disapproved of the concept of routinely arming policemen because he felt it might lead to an arms race, he was prepared to make an exception in situations such as this.

Kemp's address was just over two miles away in Rotherhithe. Fabian and his colleagues were soon driving through this dockside area. Here, truant children, their shouts juxtaposed by the melancholy hooting of ships, were often to be seen scrambling across makeshift playgrounds provided by the bulldozed ruins of bombed buildings. And long, sagging clothes-lines laden with washing usually extended between tenement blocks. Fabian was convinced that the material hardship experienced in these slum districts was among the main factors behind people turning to crime.

Park Buildings were made up of several large, seedy blocks of flats. These were next to the Queen's Head pub on the inappropriately named Paradise Street, midway between Southwark Park and the Upper Pool of the Thames. Elsewhere on this short side-road were a greengrocer's, a shoe-repairer's, an ironmonger's, a laundry and a small police station.

Armed officers encircled the block before Fabian paid Kemp a visit. Vera Kemp, the young wife of the man they wanted to interview, opened the door. She appeared predictably nervous when Fabian showed her the raincoat.

'Does this belong to your husband?' Fabian asked.

'Yes. He lost it in a public house about, er, five weeks ago.'

Fabian pressed her to name the pub.

She replied that it was the Green Man, a pub on the fringe of Soho.

❖

Once Fabian and the others had driven away from Park Buildings, Mrs Kemp left as well. She was followed by a plain clothes officer who had been posted outside. The officer was adept at shadowing people. Fabian regarded this as an underrated skill. If the officer got too close to Mrs Kemp, he would be spotted. But if he didn't get close enough, he risked losing her in a crowded street or if she boarded a bus or tram. As a rule, it was easiest to tail someone from the opposite side of the road, often by watching his or her reflection in shop windows. To his embarrassment, Fabian had messed up a surveillance operation when he was younger. The man whom he had been following had abruptly swivelled round, gone up to him and presented him with a visiting-card which, the man had announced, would save Fabian a lot of trouble.

The officer shadowing Mrs Kemp tailed her for about half-a-mile through the battered streets that connected Rotherhithe with neighbouring Bermondsey. She walked into Weller House, an inter-war block of council flats on George Row, close to the warehouse-fringed waterfront.

Under the watchful gaze of the surveillance officer, she subsequently reappeared and made her way home. In the meantime Fabian had redeployed detectives around Park Buildings. The detectives had been ordered to pick up Mrs Kemp's husband. Fabian wanted to interview Kemp before he talked to his wife and devised an alibi that fitted in with what she'd already said.

❖

On returning to his office Fabian was informed that a loaded revolver, possibly the missing murder weapon, had been discovered. It had been handed to the nearest Constable by a ten-year-old named George Mizon. Someone had left it on the steps at Shadwell docks, just across the river from where the Kemps lived. Fortunately the gun hadn't gone off when Mizon and one of his friends had pulled the trigger.

Fabian arranged for Robert Churchill to examine the weapon and ascertain whether it had fired the .45 bullet retrieved from the wall of the Pledge Department at Jay's. Despite where the revolver had been found, there was no guarantee that it had any connection with the Charlotte Street shooting. The police often presented Churchill with guns plucked from the riverside, guns that turned out not to have been used in whatever crime the CID were investigating.

This particular weapon was identified by Churchill as a .455 English Bulldog revolver, manufactured by the London firm of E.M. Reilly & Co. Its five chambers were all loaded with what Churchill described as 'very ancient' .45 calibre cartridges. Even though these were slightly too small, one of them had been fired. He could see no marks on the other cartridges to suggest that an attempt had been made to fire those as well.

Churchill went down to his firing-range to test the revolver. Before that could be done, he had to replace the spent cartridge with a live round. He also had to arrange a line of old twelve-bore cartridge boxes, packed with cottonwool. He liked to ensure that the line was fifteen boxes deep because he'd discovered that no handgun bullet could penetrate all of them.

Within the confined space of his cellar, guns made a deafening noise. Churchill knew where to look for the bullets he test-fired. The bullet from a Webley revolver would go through six boxes while the ammunition from a Mauser would reach the eleventh or twelfth box. Irrespective of which box it ended up in, the slug was always encased inside a tight ball of cottonwool only a bit smaller than an orange. After the ball had been peeled open, Churchill marked the base of the bullet and dropped it into a buff envelope. On this, he wrote the date of the test, the details of the weapon and something to indicate its role in the case.

He then took the envelope up to his attic. Though he liked to claim that he was more

*The .455 calibre English Bulldog revolver found by George Mizon and friends.*

orderly and well-organised than his late uncle who had founded the business, the attic floor was littered with walnut gun-stocks as well as cobwebbed ammunition boxes, filled with anything from yellowing press cuttings to flashlit photos of murder victims. There were also filing-cabinets stuffed with a seemingly random assortment of paperwork: old music hall programmes, bills and cheque-stubs, notes on his cases, letters from the Director of Public Prosecutions, pathologists' rep-orts, and records of long-gone shooting parties.

Amid this chaos, Churchill kept his comparison microscope, a double microscope with a single eyepiece that allowed him to compare the test bullet with the one provided by Fabian. Connected to the microscope was a camera with which he could take 'photo-micrographs' of whatever he was examining.

Peering through the microscope's eyepiece, he examined the two bullets. Inside the barrel of every rifle or pistol there is a set of spiral grooves called the 'rifling', the purpose of which is to make the bullet spin, ensuring that it travels in a straight line. These rifling grooves leave their imprint on the bullet. Such marks vary in frequency, width, depth and direction. No two weapons will leave identical markings.

Hunched over his microscope, Churchill slowly rotated the bullets as he studied the scratches on them. He spotted similarities between those on both bullets, yet he wasn't certain that the revolver found at Shadwell docks had been used during the raid on Jay's. Always wary of making assumptions that weren't justified by the evidence, he was only prepared to admit that the Shadwell gun could have been the one fired in the shop.

❖

When Fabian and Higgins heard about Mrs Kemp's visit to Weller House, they made a stab at finding out who she might have been visiting. They did

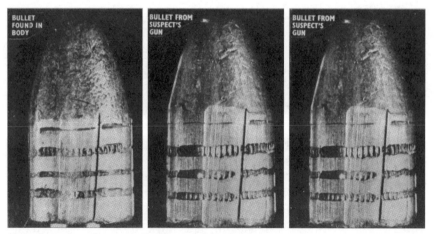

Photo-micrographs used to compare the rifling marks left on bullets.
(Copyright: Metropolitan Police Historical Collection)

this by checking the list of residents. One of the names on that list prompted the two detectives to exchange knowing glances. The name in question was 'Jenkins'. Both Fabian and his second-in-command knew all about Thomas J. Jenkins and his wife Mary, residents of Flat 21. Their eldest son, Tommy, had been involved in one of the most well-publicised criminal cases of the past few years. A member of the 'Elephant Boys', the notorious south London gang which had originated in the Elephant and Castle district, Tommy Jenkins had, in December 1944, helped to carry out a smash and grab raid on a jeweller's shop near Cannon Street Station. As Jenkins and the others had driven off, a passer-by had tried to stop them. The would-be hero—a retired naval officer named Captain Ralph Binney—had been left clinging to the getaway car. Dragged along the road for half a mile, he had sustained fatal injuries. While Ronald Hedley, the driver of the car, had been sentenced to death, later commuted to penal servitude for life, Tommy Jenkins had received an eight-year sentence for manslaughter.

An urgent request submitted to the CRO for further information on the family revealed that Tommy's younger brother, twenty-three-year-old Charles Henry Jenkins, known as Harry or 'Harryboy', also had a record of violence. He'd first appeared in court at the age of twelve, after which he'd been convicted seven times, twice for assaulting a police officer. During one of those assaults, he'd broken the victim's jaw. For that he was sentenced to three years in borstal. Undiscouraged, he'd gone on to be convicted of theft and receiving stolen property, his conviction earning him another spell in borstal. On 23 April 1947, a mere six days before the Antiquis murder, he had been released on parole from the borstal in Nottingham where he'd served twenty-one months of his sentence.

Whether this date was a mere coincidence, Fabian and Higgins were not yet in a position to say. But experience had taught Higgins that ex-prisoners seldom learned their lesson. He'd arrived at the gloomy conclusion that most criminals lacked the willpower and determination required to get back on the paths of righteousness once they had allowed themselves to go downhill and live a dishonest life.

❖

Soon after Fabian had learnt about the link with the Jenkins clan, Tom Kemp was escorted into the investigation headquarters. Kemp was an unlikely suspect in a murder investigation. Enquiries into his background had unearthed nothing suspicious. Unlike his brothers-in-law, Harry and Tommy Jenkins, there was no file on him at the CRO. And he had a reputation as a hard-working, law-abiding person.

Fabian showed him the raincoat found at Brook House and asked if it belonged to him. This was a question to which Fabian knew the answer. The coat must have belonged to Kemp because the two other suspects who had purchased matching garments from branches of Burton's still possessed theirs.

Without hesitation, Kemp replied, 'Yes, that's mine. I lost it at the pictures a few weeks ago.'

'Your wife said you lost it in a public-house. Who's making the mistake?' Fabian asked.

After a brief hiatus, Kemp said, 'We both are. She lent it to her brother, Harry Jenkins.'

❖

Fabian decided to bring Harry Jenkins in for questioning. Since being released from borstal, Jenkins had been living partly with his parents at Weller House and partly with his wife Louisa and their baby at 235 Riverside Mansions, an even larger block of council flats on Garnet Street in Wapping. The odds on him being at either address on a Friday evening, though, were slim. If Fabian did catch him at home, there was a distinct possibility that Jenkins would put up a fight. Still, Fabian had had plenty of practice at defending himself. In addition to all the experience he'd accumulated in the boxing-ring, he had taken lessons in judo. On three occasions he had been assaulted by members of the public. Not that there was anything unusual about a policeman being attacked. He could remember years when, in London alone, well over a thousand people had been charged with assaulting, obstructing or resisting the police. Almost two decades earlier, a conman whom he'd arrested had pulled a gun on him while they had been standing in the Front Office at Vine Street Police Station. But Fabian had flung himself at the man and succeeded in wrenching the revolver out of his grasp.

Just to be on the safe side, Fabian was joined on the trip to south London by the strapping duo of Higgins and Hodge. Police officers were meant to use the minimum force necessary to restrain a suspect, but Fabian always bore in mind the advice he'd been given when he was younger. It's better, the advice went, to end up hurting a crook than getting injured yourself—or, worse still, letting him get away.

The three detectives were chauffeured through the West End which tended to be busy on Friday nights. Red London buses, emblazoned with adverts for products such as Fry's chocolate, Brooke Bond tea and Craven 'A' cigarettes, disgorged dozens of passengers. Groups of men, keen to celebrate the end of another working week, hurried towards their favourite pubs. Courting couples headed, arm in arm, for a night on the town. And buskers entertained queues of cinema and theatregoers. A matter of months earlier Higgins had briefly appeared on screen in many of those cinemas when they'd shown *Post-War Crime*, a short documentary made by Rank Film Studios. To dampen down the fear aroused by the press, it strove to reassure the public with a voice-over saying, 'The present crimewave is universal throughout the world and a legacy of war...' Higgins was described as being part of 'an army of experts at Scotland Yard' arrayed against 'the individual criminal—a man against a machine.'

Before long, the car carrying him and Fabian crossed the Thames, the banks of which bristled with dockside cranes. In the soft glow of the streetlights, the jagged silhouettes of gutted buildings could have been mistaken for ruined castles rather than merely the remains of warehouses or humble terraced homes. During the height of the Blitz, London's riverside districts had been devoured by a nocturnal conflagration from which even the shipping wasn't immune. Blazing barges often broke loose from their moorings and went spinning lazily down the river, only for the tide to wash them back next day, cargo still smouldering.

❖

Earlier on Friday 2 May—well over twelve hours before the police went in search of Jenkins—the *Daily Mail* had featured an article about the financial plight of Antiquis's dependents. Its message was reinforced by the accompanying photograph of his wife and two eldest daughters. Their obvious grief unleashed a surge of donations, offers of support and letters of sympathy which flowed into Northcliffe House where the paper was based. Consisting of anything from small gifts to large cheques from businesses such as the motorbike manufacturer, BSA, the donations amounted to £1,521, comparable to £43,000 in 2007. Other *Daily Mail* readers offered to help by taking the murdered man's children on holiday and even adopting them. Also there were offers of benefit performances of the opera, *Cavalleria Rusticana* and the West End play, *Power Without Glory*.

Scenting a popular cause behind which its readership could rally, the *Daily Mail* prepared to launch a fund-raising campaign on behalf of Mrs de Antiquis. That evening she read the letters forwarded by the paper. They included a letter from a former squadron leader who declared that 'The peerless courage of Mr de Antiquis in tackling armed bandits stirs the courage of a true Englishman.'

After the murdered man's widow had ploughed through the letters, her response was canvassed by a *Daily Mail* reporter. 'So many kind people,' she replied, 'so much sympathy. I can never thank them enough for this help and understanding. Some kind and well-meaning people have sent offers to adopt some of my children, but please do tell them I want to keep my family together and keep Alec's business going.'

❖

When Fabian and the other officers turned up at Jenkins's current address, they found him at home. A tall, tough character who exuded a potent mixture of confidence and intelligence, he spoke in quickfire flurries. His heavy south London accent made it hard for anyone not from that part of the city to understand him.

Both Fabian and Higgins were struck by what they regarded as his good looks. He had long, gently arching eyebrows, high cheekbones, a square jaw and a pallid complexion which contrasted with his black hair. This was normally combed back, exposing a widow's peak.

Higgins discerned a sardonic glint in his grey eyes. The sight of three detectives standing outside the flat left him unruffled. So nonchalant was he that he treated Fabian and Higgins to a wry grin. Higgins was annoyed by Jenkins's arrogance and refusal to be overawed.

As soon as the detectives got him back to Tottenham Court Road Police Station, they took him up to Fabian's office.

Jenkins said that he'd heard that they had talked to his sister, so he'd been expecting them to pay him a visit.

Asked what he had been doing on 29 April 1947, he replied that he knew exactly what he'd been doing all that day. 'But I'm not going to tell you now. I don't want to be funny, but that's how I feel about it.'

Fabian showed him the raincoat found at Brook House and said, 'I understand that you borrowed this from your sister, Mrs Kemp.'

Betraying no sign of panic or obvious guilt, Jenkins gave them another of his mirthless smiles. For several defiant seconds he maintained this expression. At last he said, 'It looks like Tom's coat, but I'm not saying anything more now, as it all looks serious to me.'

True to his word, Jenkins remained silent. Nevertheless Fabian didn't release him. Instead, he was led out of the CID offices, past the toilets and the Sergeants' Writing-up Room, then down to the ground-floor where officers issued him with a blanket, plus food from the canteen. He was taken to the men's cell-block which overlooked Kirkham Place, a narrow alley separating the police station from the adjacent Parthenon Restaurant.

At 5:00pm Fabian paid him a visit and told him that he was going to be placed in an identification parade the following day. Suspects were entitled to refuse to take part in such parades, but they had little to gain by doing that. Failure to cooperate would only heighten the suspicion surrounding them.

Jenkins was informed that the parade was being staged in connection with an attempted robbery and murder which had taken place in Soho on 29 April. Fabian then gave him a formal caution, the words of which were usually spoken with the uninflected tone of a schoolboy reciting the Lord's Prayer. 'Do you wish to say anything in answer to the charge? You are not obliged to say anything unless you wish to do so, but whatever you say will be taken down in writing and may be given in evidence.'

Yet Jenkins seemed to be treating the whole thing as an elaborate game. No sooner had he been cautioned than he said, 'I suppose it's because I had the coat. If I get picked out, I'll tell you about the coat, but I shan't tell you where I was until it comes to the last. I'm not a grass but I'm not having this on my own. You surely don't think I'd do any shooting?'

❖

During what was left of that evening, Fabian arranged for the CRO to send over Jenkins's file. On receiving it, Fabian looked through the contents. These provided details of the suspect's previous convictions, behaviour while he was at borstal, favourite haunts and known associates. All of this served to endorse the negative impression made by Jenkins, a former merchant seaman whose knack of attracting followers had earned him the sobriquets of the 'guvnor' and the 'King of Borstal'. Outside prison he was the leader of a gang of local youths. The most prominent of these were twenty-year-old Christopher James Geraghty, known as 'Chris', and seventeen-year-old Terence John Peter Rolt, known as 'Terry'.

It transpired that the CRO also had a file on Geraghty. Like Jenkins, he had a record of violent crime. Foremost among his previous offences was the armed robbery of a Grafton Street jewellers, from where he'd stolen

*Staff at the Criminal Record Office search for files. (Copyright: Metropolitan Police Historical Collection)*

goods worth £6,000, approximately £170,000 in 2007 money. He and Jenkins had been imprisoned at Sherwood Borstal, located in a suburb of Nottingham. Geraghty, for whom this was his second spell of imprisonment, had twice escaped from Sherwood. He'd been released on parole the previous November.

Fabian had strong opinions about the insanitary, overcrowded conditions prevalent in most borstals and prisons, all but one of which had been built in the nineteenth-century. Such conditions were, he believed, designed to confirm the prisoners' grudge against society. He agreed with the Commissioner who had said that the best thing to do with these insanitary, depressing places would be to blow them up.

Reading the files persuaded Fabian that it was worth interviewing Geraghty and Rolt straightaway. If he was right about Jenkins being one of the gang that had raided Jay's, then they could well have been his accomplices. Through the CRO, Fabian obtained their home addresses. Both of these were in rundown, working-class districts with a reputation for spawning young criminals. While Rolt lived in Bermondsey, not far from the Jenkins family, Geraghty's home was at the Angel end of Finsbury, around which the so-called 'Angel gangs' flourished.

With midnight approaching, Fabian and his officers called on Geraghty and Rolt. Geraghty lived at 23 Liverpool Road, a building that backed onto Chapel Street Market. He and his parents had rooms above Chas Smith Gents' Hairdressers. When the police arrived there, they discovered that 'Jim'—as his parents called him—wasn't at home. The detectives left a message asking him to report to Tottenham Court Road Police Station.

Fabian and co. had more luck with their search for Terry Rolt, who shared a flat with his widowed mother and older brother Ted in the St John's Estate, a series of inter-war council blocks between Tower Bridge and Bermondsey Leather Market. He was a small, muscular boy whose attempts at making himself appear grown-up only served to emphasise his youth and vulnerability. Along with so many London boys of his age who imitated American styles, he wore his longish, mousy hair slicked back.

The detectives escorted him from his flat to the waiting squad car, in which he was driven over to the investigation headquarters. Just before the clocks struck midnight, he entered the police station.

Urged to give an account of his movements on 29 April, Rolt said that he'd stayed in bed all day because he had felt ill. Even though there was no clear evidence against Rolt, Fabian didn't believe him. But Rolt stuck to his story.

Unlike Jenkins, still languishing in a downstairs cell, he was released once the questioning had been completed. From Fabian's point of view, there was more to be gained by keeping him under twenty-four hour surveillance than by putting him in an identification parade.

A single plain clothes officer followed Rolt as he left the police station.

❖

For the fourth consecutive night, Fabian failed to return home, though he still hadn't got round to sending someone over to his house in Surrey to collect his shaving kit or a change of clothes. When he began work on

Saturday 3 May, his eyes were encrusted with grit and his unevenly shaven face looked sore. A few minutes before 10:00am that morning—three and a half days after the Charlotte Street shooting—Geraghty presented himself at Tottenham Court Road Police Station. He was a tall, well-built young man with high cheekbones, a broken nose and light brown hair which he usually teased into a generous quiff.

From the lobby, he was taken for questioning by Fabian and Higgins. Knowing Geraghty's background, Higgins wasn't surprised to discover that he was a hard, shrewd youngster, unabashed by the precarious position in which he found himself.

'I am enquiring about an attempted robbery and murder at Charlotte Street on 29 April,' Fabian said. 'Can you tell me where you were that day?'

But Geraghty didn't respond until he had studied the calendar on the wall. After a protracted, suspicious pause, he said, 'As a matter of fact, I was in bed, queer. I had some boils and was away from work all that week.'

Fabian asked whether he'd seen a doctor.

He replied that a doctor wouldn't have been able to help. 'I just felt run down.'

Question after question was fired at him. Neither Fabian nor Higgins were, however, able to coax anything incriminating out of Geraghty who insisted that he had been nowhere near Charlotte Street at the time of the shooting.

It was approaching 11:00am when Fabian released him. As he made his way out of the building and onto Tottenham Court Road, he too was tailed by a CID officer.

❖

Just over an hour later Jenkins was led out of the cell-block and down to the first of the two basements. He was wearing a fresh suit with sharply creased trousers and a crisp silk shirt acquired from friends who had visited him earlier. They'd also brought him the late morning edition of one of that day's newspapers. He carried this with him.

Next to Jenkins, Fabian felt scruffy and resentful. For someone who took such pride in his appearance, he was vaguely embarrassed to be seen wearing clothes that were creased from days of camping out at the police station.

Fabian told Jenkins that the identification parade was about to take place and that Mr O'Connor, his solicitor, would be allowed to attend, just to make sure everything was above board.

Exuding his usual self-assurance, Jenkins needled Fabian by saying, 'I shouldn't be picked out. And if you play fair, I'll tell you something interesting after I've been stuck up.'

Clearly, Jenkins was still treating his detention as if it was part of a meaningless game.

He was escorted into the sizeable, T-shaped Parade Room, the ceiling of which had been fitted with two large skylights. A row of other young men had already formed across the parquet floor by the time Jenkins got there. The dozen or so other men who had been recruited from the nearby streets would all have shared his hair colour, build and approximate height.

In accordance with Judges' Rules, Jenkins was allowed to choose his position in the line-up. He did so with an air of calmness and composure. Innocent or not, he was evidently well versed in the tricks used on such occasions by professional criminals. To convey the impression that he was someone who had been plucked from the street purely to make up the numbers, he slipped his rolled newspaper into his jacket pocket. The newspaper was arranged so that anyone standing in front of him could see that it was a late morning edition.

Of the twenty-seven people who had witnessed the raid on Jay's and the consequent shooting, all but five of them attended the identification parade. They included everyone working in the shop, plus Albert Grubb, Brian Cox, and Albert Buckner. One by one, without the benefit of the protective glass used nowadays, they each spent a few minutes strolling pensively up and down the line of young men. But none of the witnesses identified Jenkins as a member of the gang that had raided Jay's.

When the last of the witnesses was shown out of the Parade Room at 1:10pm, Fabian caught sight of Jenkins whose smirking expression conveyed defiance and disdain. The cool, insolent challenge of his stare left Fabian more convinced than ever of his involvement in Antiquis's death. Perhaps sensing the high stakes for which they were playing, Jenkins had second thoughts about telling Fabian 'something interesting'.

Reluctantly, Fabian said to him, 'All right, Jenkins. You can go.'

Along with Geraghty and Rolt, Jenkins was placed under discreet round-the-clock surveillance.

❖

Even though the inquest into Antiquis's death had been adjourned, the coroner had already released the body of the murdered man, enabling his grieving family to hold a funeral that day. The cortège set off from his mother's bungalow in Colliers Wood. Hundreds of people watched from either side of the street as it gradually made its way up Cavendish Road. Reporters from newspapers as diverse as the local *Mitcham News & Mercury* and the national *Sunday Dispatch*, were among the watching crowd. At the junction with the High Street, the cortège turned left and, in a moment of slow-motion poignancy, passed the workshop where Antiquis had struggled to support his family.

❖

Word reached Fabian that the gang behind Tuesday afternoon's murder had used a building on nearby Percy Street as their headquarters. Immediately this tip-off came through, a large, unmarked police van was sent there. The van contained uniformed officers and detectives, some of the latter armed with automatic pistols. Policemen were stationed at either end of Percy Street while detectives not only searched the cafés, houses and other businesses but also ordered everyone to show the identity cards which they were required to carry.

After about an hour of this, it became apparent the tip-off had been no more reliable than the one that had propelled Fabian and Higgins over to Swiss Cottage. Yet Cecil Catling, the *Star's* crime reporter, misread the situation and filed what became a front-page story headlined 'STREET SEALED IN SOHO AS KILLER HUNT NARROWS'.

❖

When Fabian was a young Detective Constable he'd avoided alcohol. In those days the French prostitutes who frequented Soho's seedier cafés called him the 'Little Water-Drinker', yet it was a nickname that had long since ceased to be appropriate.

Taking a break from the investigation's excessive demands, Fabian decamped to the Fitzroy Tavern which he regarded as an amazing place. Over the years he'd become great friends with Charlie and Annie Allchild, whom he considered two of the largest-hearted people he knew. Conveniently for him, their celebrated pub happened to be within easy walking distance of Tottenham Court Road Police Station. He was such a well-known character in North Soho that barrow-boys and shopkeepers would shout greetings to him whenever he walked past.

In the Saloon Bar of the Fitzroy where he liked to sit, smoking his pipe, there was usually an array of famous, flamboyant and eccentric customers, guaranteed to distract him from the rigours of his work. The regulars included the ageing, bearded painter Augustus John; the tubby Welsh poet Dylan Thomas; the emerging Labour MP Hugh Gaitskell; the radio broadcaster Wynford Vaughan-Thomas; and the bestselling writer Gerald Kersh who had bestowed Fabian's surname on the protagonist of his twice-filmed 1938 novel, *Night and the City*. Another of the Fitzroy's devotees was Tom Driberg, the louche politician who penned the *Daily Express's* widely read 'William Hickey' gossip column. Driberg and many of the other regulars were homosexuals who made no secret of their erotic interests, which were illegal at that time, placing Fabian in an awkward spot. Though he viewed homosexuals as perverts liable to destroy the moral stability of the nation, he tolerated their uninhibited antics in the Fitzroy out of loyalty to the Allchilds.

Lately the Allchilds' inner circle of favoured customers, Fabian among them, had expanded to accommodate Robert Capa, the handsome and urbane Hungarian war photographer. Capa, who spoke in spurts of broken English that his friends called 'Capanese', was often accompanied by his adulterous girlfriend, the exquisitely beautiful Hollywood film star Ingrid Bergman. She had caused quite a stir when she'd taken a blue handkerchief from her bag, wrapped thirty shillings in it and pinned the money to the ceiling with a well-aimed dart. A flurry of customers had then tried to get their darts as close to her's as possible, bringing in a tidy sum for the Pennies From Heaven charity.

What would become the familiar sight of Fabian conferring with Higgins, Hodge and other detectives over a pint of beer led to the Fitzroy acquiring the reputation as the unofficial investigation headquarters. So inseparable were Fabian, Higgins and Hodge that reporters started referring to them as 'we three', a phrase lifted from a speech by the three witches in Macbeth.

While Fabian was out of the office, a phone-call came through for him at Tottenham Court Road Police Station. It was from Albert Pierrepoint, who had just got back from Germany. Pierrepoint was keen to meet Fabian for a drink. The officer who took the call informed Pierrepoint that Fabian had gone to the Fitzroy.

Pierrepoint was soon making his way through North Soho. Fabian had sometimes taken the genial hangman on informal tours of the area, reminiscing about all the tough times he'd had there as a young policeman. The two friends were reunited in the Saloon Bar of the Allchilds' famous pub, where they'd often chatted about their shared passion for professional boxing.

Unlike so many other people, Fabian never asked Pierrepoint prying questions about his work. Grateful for this rare discretion, Pierrepoint refrained from quizzing Fabian about the Antiquis murder hunt, though he was curious to know how it was progressing. Unprompted, Fabian started talking about the case.

Before exiting the pub, Pierrepoint had a drink with Charlie and Annie Allchild. Not that Annie touched alcohol, something she had in common with Pierrepoint's wife.

*Bob Higgins (left), Fred Hodge (centre) and Bob Fabian. (Copyright: Metropolitan Police Historical Collection)*

Fortified by drink, Pierrepoint headed back to Manchester. Euston Station, from where his train departed, was only a brisk walk from the Fitzroy. The station was a colossal Victorian building, guarded by a stocky-legged triumphal arch which, Pierrepoint felt, lent some dignity to the occasion of the northern traveller entering or leaving London.

❖

Several hours after Jenkins and his two friends had been placed under surveillance, the tactic paid dividends. Fabian and Higgins were notified that the suspects, all of whom had seemed anxious, had met in a Clerkenwell pub. There the three of them had held a whispered conversation, the contents of which could not be overheard by the detectives spying on them.

Though Fabian's suspicions were bolstered by what he had been told, he resisted the temptation to bring Jenkins, Geraghty and Rolt in for further questioning. Instead, he kept up the surveillance.

❖

At 11:15pm that night William Setter, a thirty-five-year-old former member of the RAF, returned to his flat in Wilton Place, Belgravia. As he was unlocking the door, Setter felt a gun barrel being jabbed into his back.

From behind him, the gunman said, 'Get in and don't start anything.'

Forced through the door into his flat, Setter turned to face a powerfully built man of about thirty. The man, who was wearing a shabby raincoat, pointed a small revolver at Setter and ordered him to take off his clothes. While Setter was removing his brown herring-bone patterned suit, green shirt and suede shoes, he heard a neighbour arriving home.

Fearing that Setter might try to raise the alarm, the gunman cuffed him across the mouth and said that if he made a sound he'd regret it. Still at gunpoint, Setter was told to pack his clothes into a suitcase. Recurrent shortages meant that secondhand clothes like these commanded a healthy price on market stalls. Not content with stealing Setter's clothes, the gunman also compelled him to hand over his wristwatch, £2 in cash, and his allocation of clothing coupons.

The gunman threatened him again, then picked up the suitcase, backed out of the flat and left the building. Setter phoned Scotland Yard's Information Room rightaway. Despite sending a couple of squad cars round to Belgravia, cars that spent the night patrolling the surrounding streets, the police failed to arrest the gunman.

Continued surveillance of Jenkins, Geraghty and Rolt showed that none of them could have been the man responsible for this bizarre robbery. A senior CID officer nevertheless admitted to Bill Jones of the *Daily Herald* that he and his colleagues were 'considering whether the man might be one of the murderers of Alec de Antiquis'. Jones used this and an interview with Setter to construct a story destined to appear in the Monday morning edition of the *Daily Herald*, complete with the risible headline, 'ARMED "STRIPPER" HUNTED BY YARD'.

❖

No more useful information had been channelled back to Fabian by the detectives who were shadowing the three suspects. Meanwhile, the mooted link between the murder of George Mitchell and the Antiquis shooting had been discounted. Mrs Eveline Arthur—whom Mitchell had been trying to help when he'd been shot—must have been certain that Jenkins, Rolt and Geraghty were not the men responsible.

Early on the afternoon of Sunday 4 May, Fabian sent an officer down to Bermondsey. The officer was instructed to ask Jenkins and his sister to go over to Tottenham Court Road Police Station and answer some questions about the raincoat that Mr Kemp had lost at the Green Man Tavern. Not that Fabian believed Mrs Kemp's story about her husband mislaying the coat.

Neither Jenkins nor Mrs Kemp could afford to risk stirring up more trouble for themselves by refusing this request. They were soon sitting in Fabian's office. Under renewed questioning, cracks were likely to appear in Mrs Kemp's story. Even if that didn't happen, the encounter offered other rewards. Fabian hoped to learn something from the way Jenkins and his sister behaved when they were interviewed together.

Facing them across his desk, Fabian asked Jenkins and Mrs Kemp to make full statements about the missing coat. Jenkins must have realised that he was in a dangerous position because he was much more cooperative than he had been during his previous interview.

'Let us tell Mr Fabian who I lent the coat to,' he said to his sister. He hesitated while he lit a cigarette. Fabian watched his hands for any sign of a nervous tremor, but he struck the match without the flame flickering. He went on to admit that he had borrowed the raincoat, later found in the store-room at Brook House, from his brother-in-law. 'I'm not a grass,' he added prior to revealing that he had subsequently lent the coat to a man called Walsh. Bill Walsh. 'We saw him about a week ago in Southend. He's knocking around with a blonde girl named Doris Hart, who works in a café in Southend on the front.'

Both Fabian and Higgins had already encountered Walsh in the course of their CID work. He was a professional criminal with a record as an armed robber. There was something about his rather menacing appearance that always reminded Higgins of Humphrey Bogart, star of recent hit films such as *The Maltese Falcon* and *The Big Sleep*. Walsh had a similarly lean physique, long, careworn face and dark, receding hair.

Fabian was taken aback by Jenkins's willingness to inform on Walsh. Habitual criminals like Jenkins didn't normally turn on their colleagues, especially when the case against them seemed to have collapsed. Fabian didn't comment on this, preferring instead to make a mental note to find out why Jenkins had betrayed Walsh.

❖

A request was submitted to the CRO for Bill Walsh's file, which was soon delivered to the investigation headquarters. The file provided a resumé of Walsh's extensive criminal career. Aged thirty-seven, William Henry Walsh had a wife and family who lived in Plumstead, a south-eastern London suburb. He had not, however, spent much time there lately because he'd been in prison, from where he had recently been freed on parole. The arrangement, known as 'ticket of leave', required him to report to the police on a regular basis, but he'd missed his appointment on Saturday 4 April, leading to a warrant being issued for his arrest.

Since Jenkins had mentioned seeing Walsh in Southend, a well-known hiding-place for London criminals, that appeared to be the obvious place to begin the search for him. Before setting off on the 38 mile drive there, Fabian, Higgins and Hodge obtained guns from the station's well-stocked armoury.

From central London, Southend was best reached via the East End which had suffered badly from the wartime bombing. Entire streets had been levelled and the fronts of other buildings had been peeled away, exposing tattered wallpaper, fireplaces stranded in mid-air and staircases leading nowhere. Beyond the East End were the sprawling, grey suburbs, row upon row of shabby houses giving way to the Essex countryside. Navigating roads outside London had become a lot easier now that the signage, previously removed to confuse potential German invaders, had been reinstated.

When Fabian and the others reached Southend, they made for the Central Police Station. It was a homely-looking two-storey, Dutch gabled Victorian building on Alexandra Street, flanked by a wool shop and some council offices. Above the porch was the usual dark blue lamp with the word 'Police' written on the glass in white lettering.

The visiting detectives were plied with cups of tea while they leafed through the bulky Occurrence Books, maintained by the local uniformed branch. In these hard-cover tomes, each Constable made a daily entry, recording every noteworthy or suspicious event that had taken place on his beat. These tended to be trivial: sightings of stray dogs, lost property, drivers warned for parking in the wrong places.

If Walsh *had* been in Southend, he might have made a guest appearance in one of the Occurrence Books, perhaps giving a clue to his whereabouts, though the chances of this were remote.

Fabian and his colleagues were, however, rewarded by the discovery of a particularly eye-catching entry. At 9:40pm on Friday 25 April 1947, PC Frederick Jauncey had reported the suspicious behaviour of two young men who had been standing in a telephone box near the main post office. Jauncey had questioned the men and asked to see their identity cards. These had given their names as 'Christopher James Geraghty' and 'Michael Joseph Gillam'. Satisfied that their identity cards were legitimate, Jauncey had detained neither of the men.

There was another, potentially even more important entry in the same Occurrence Book. At 7:15am on the day after Jauncey's encounter, PC James Bunn had found a .455 revolver concealed in a shrubbery next to the footpath on Royal Hill, close to the immensely long pier that was the town's main landmark. All six chambers of the revolver had been loaded.

By contacting the CRO, Fabian discovered that Michael Joseph

Gillam, the man seen with Geraghty, also had a criminal record. More to the point, he had been at borstal with Geraghty and Jenkins.

❖

The next step in the Antiquis investigation entailed tracking down Walsh's waitress friend, Doris Hart, whose distinguishing feature was her peroxide blonde hair. To find her, Fabian and his team embarked on a laborious trek round all of the town's sea-front cafés, ranging from cheap refreshment rooms to the comparatively expensive Peveril Restaurant on Marine Parade. Higgins got the impression that there were more cafés and restaurants in Southend than anywhere in England.

At last the CID men discovered where Doris Hart worked. It was among the boarding houses, shops, cafés and amusement arcades on the Eastern Esplanade. But the detectives were informed that she no longer worked there. They were, however, able to find out that she lived with her parents at 124 Southchurch Avenue.

Fabian and his team then visited this address. It was part of the way down the sharply sloping road that led to the Kursaal rollercoaster and adjoining ballroom, already advertising a forthcoming appearance by Geraldo and His Orchestra, one of Britain's top dance bands.

The Harts lived in a bay-windowed Edwardian villa with a black and white tiled porch inset into the front. When the detectives rolled up there, Mr and Mrs Hart were at home. Fabian and his colleagues quizzed them about their daughter who turned out to be twenty-four-years-old. In 1944 she had married an American paratrooper named 'Marshall', but she and her husband had since separated and divorce procedings had been initiated. Until recently, the former Mrs Doris Marshall had been living with her parents. Where she was now, her parents couldn't, or possibly *wouldn't*, say.

Under questioning, Mr Hart admitted to having seen Walsh and someone called Jenkins in Southend the Friday before last—four days prior to the Charlotte Street shooting. Walsh had stayed with Mr and Mrs Hart for a few nights, during which he'd taken their daughter to the cinema once or twice. 'Suddenly Bill Walsh seemed to disappear,' Mr Hart added. 'Nobody knew where he'd gone. Then Jenkins said Walsh had double-crossed him, and something about getting his revenge.'

Meaningful expressions flashed between Higgins and Fabian, both of whom had reached the same conclusion. Here was an explanation for why Jenkins had been willing to inform on Walsh. The two of them must have staged a robbery together, only for Walsh to abscond with the proceeds.

❖

Assisted by the Essex police, Fabian and his men drew up a list of everyone in Southend who had connections with Walsh. The remainder of Sunday 4 May was devoted to visiting people on that list and searching their houses. The list featured a cabinet-maker who lived on the eastern side of town. When Fabian and co. turned up there, making enquiries about Walsh, the man admitted to knowing him. He told Fabian that he'd met Walsh in a Southend café. There Walsh had sold him a gents' wristwatch for £7. The man handed over the watch to the police. It was a very expensive-looking gold timepiece with a black dial. Clearly, it was worth a lot more than he had paid for it.

As soon as Fabian and his team had worked their way through the available leads in Southend, they drove back to London. They then went round to talk to Walsh's wife. Like many other families who had lost their homes in the wartime bombing, she and their two children were living in temporary accommodation. This consisted of a so-called 'prefab': one of numerous prefabricated bungalows with white metal walls and shallow-pitched roofs, sealed not with tiles or slates but with tar. Their compact, modern design, electrical fittings and bathrooms made a pleasant contrast to the housing they had replaced. Set in a small garden intended for growing vegetables, the Walshes' home was located at 27 Voce Road, only a few streets from Plumstead Common.

The knowledge that Walsh had left his wife for another woman offered Fabian convenient emotional leverage. But Mrs Walsh didn't provide clues as to her husband's whereabouts. The possibility that she was sheltering her errant husband seemed so remote that Fabian didn't bother searching the house.

During the interview, she mentioned that Walsh had given her a present when she'd last seen him. It consisted of a jewel-encrusted bracelet. Common sense decreed that Walsh must have stolen it. After all, it wasn't the sort of thing that a man like him would have been able to afford, especially when he had just been released from prison. Before Fabian and his team left Voce Road, Mrs Walsh surrendered the bracelet.

By going through the daily lists of stolen property compiled by the Met, Fabian and his officers discovered the source of both the bracelet and wristwatch that Walsh had sold in Southend. These matched the description of items reported missing after a raid on a jeweller's shop in west London. While the wristwatch, which had an eighteen-carat gold case, retailed at £22 10s, the bracelet was even more pricey. Altogether the stolen goods, comprising several dozen watches and assorted items of jewellery, were valued at £4,517 12s 3d, equivalent to about £128,000 in 2007 terms. That said, the recorded value of stolen goods was often unreliable due to businesses exaggerating their losses in order to increase their insurance pay-outs.

From the CRO, Fabian obtained a file on the robbery. Inside there were witness statements which, when pieced together, gave him a precise picture of what had taken place. At about 3:25pm on Friday 25 April 1947, three men entered the showroom of A.B. Davis Ltd at 89-91 Queensway, right next to Bayswater Underground Station. Stanley Coleman, the owner of the shop, was dealing with a couple of customers when he heard the front door

*A suspect is brought in for questioning.*
*(Copyright: Metropolitan Police Historical Collection)*

open, followed by the shuffling of the intruders' shoes on the floor. By then, a masked man with a pistol had shoved Coleman's young assistant against a glass cabinet. The assistant was forced to stand face to the wall. As Coleman glanced up from the counter, he saw a second armed man approaching. He also spotted a third intruder, scooping up the contents of the window-display. Determined to stop him, Coleman advanced towards the window and said, 'What's the game?'

Before Coleman was able to do anything else, though, he was intercepted by another of the thieves. The man pushed Coleman in the direction of the safe, which had been left open. Reaching into it, the man helped himself to the contents of one of the drawers.

All this must have taken a minute at most. The gang hurried towards the exit. The first of them had already left by the time Jenkyn Leonard, who worked at Bayswater Underground Station, suspecting that a robbery might be in progress, came through the door. He was confronted by a man with a gun who told him to 'Get out of it.'

With the pistol still pointed at his chest, Leonard backed across the pavement. Meanwhile, the third member of the gang dashed over to a black saloon car parked outside. The gunman who had left the shop first was sitting in the car, waiting for his accomplices. When they joined him, the car sped off. It was later found abandoned on Bishop's Bridge Road, about a quarter of a mile from D.B. Davis's.

Edward Ludlam, an accountant who worked at the Ministry of Supply, had provided a statement declaring that he had seen three men get out of the car. He'd said that one of them hailed a taxi, but the taxi drove past without stopping. The men ended up boarding a Number 36 bus which was, luckily for them, coming round the corner from Eastbourne Terrace.

❖

Everything pointed towards Walsh being part of the gang behind both the Queensway robbery and the raid on Jay's, staged only four days afterwards. For a start, there was the shared MO: three masked men barging into a jeweller's shop early in the afternoon, threatening the staff with guns, then sprinting over to a stolen getaway car. There was also the link with Harry Jenkins and his friends, a link that was unlikely to be coincidental.

Certain that Walsh and Doris Hart had to be found before Walsh robbed more jeweller's shops and, in the process, endangered any more lives, Fabian ordered Hodge to pass on their details to the *Police Gazette*. To oblige, Hodge filled out two Form 590s, one for William Henry Walsh, the other for Doris Brenda Hart. The forms had spaces set aside for the person's full description, associates, known addresses, aliases, habits and any criminal record. On Walsh's form, Hodge made a note of the fact that he was likely to be armed, that he was a teetotaller who frequented pubs, and that he was probably accompanied by Hart.

Both of the completed forms were submitted to the CRO, which was responsible for producing the *Police Gazette*, a confidential newspaper containing descriptions as well as grainy black and white photos of people wanted for questioning. Published every day except for Sundays and Bank Holidays, it had an enormous print-run and was distributed to every police station in the country. But there was no guarantee that overworked officers wouldn't flick past the pages devoted to Walsh and Hart. As a precaution against that, Fabian issued instructions via the recently established national police radio system that every policeman should be briefed on the case. From the south coast of England to the north of Scotland, nearly 60,000 uniformed officers and detectives were told that Walsh and Hart were being sought in connection with the Antiquis investigation.

Making the most of the considerable manpower at his disposal, Fabian ordered CID men in the West End to interview every informer and known criminal about Walsh. On top of that, Fabian summoned all the detectives who had previously arrested Walsh. They were questioned about him, about his associates and the places he frequented. The names of various clubs and gambling dens in Southend and Brighton were mentioned. Primed with this information, detectives—chosen by Fabian

*Staff at the Criminal Record Office print the* Police Gazette.
*(Copyright: Metropolitan Police Historical Collection)*

because they had good memories for faces—were sent in search of Walsh.

If Walsh hadn't already discovered that he was the focal point of a nationwide manhunt, he would now, perhaps leading him and his girlfriend to attempt to leave the country. Fabian arranged for the staff at ports and airports throughout Britain to be on their guard and report any sightings of the fugitive couple.

❖

Over the next few days, the CID's underworld contacts provided a succession of tip-offs about various houses, hotels, and boarding houses where Walsh and his girlfriend might have been hiding. Backed up by one of several squads of armed officers that had been placed on standby across the country, Fabian and his team swooped on addresses in areas extending from wealthy Mayfair to poor parts of the city such as Elephant and Castle, Soho, Camberwell, Wapping, Bermondsey and Notting Hill. But Walsh

*The .320 calibre revolver used to kill Alec de Antiquis.*

had disappeared from his usual haunts.

Oddly enough, the comings and goings of Fabian and his officers were watched by Geraghty who had a labouring job with Burgess & Son, the company hired to repair some bomb-damaged offices almost opposite the investigation head-quarters. In between the many police raids, coordinated from Tottenham Court Road Police Station, Fabian was informed that a revolver had been found lying on the muddy foreshore at Wapping where it had been exposed by the low tide. As with the weapon discovered only about a mile away, it had been spotted by a schoolboy, this time a seven-year-old named Edward King who lived at Riverside Mansions. The boy had repeatedly tried to pull back the hammer, but lacked the necessary strength.

Still coated in Thames mud, the weapon was taken to Robert Churchill for examination. Unlike the revolver left near Southend Pier, he was able to glean crucial evidence from it. He identified it as a centre-firing .320 calibre revolver. All six of its chambers contained cartridges, one of which had already been fired. He could tell by the slight indentations on the base of three of the other cartridges that an unsuccessful attempt had been made to fire those, too. But he was unable to say how recently the gun had been used.

Just as he'd done with the weapon found at Shadwell docks, Churchill test-fired it. In Fabian's presence, he used his comparison microscope to study the test bullet and the murder bullet. After what must, for Fabian, have been an anxious wait, the gunsmith looked up from the eyepiece and gave an emphatic nod.

'That's the one!' he said. 'It fired the shot that killed Antiquis.'

# IV

# ARMED AND DANGEROUS

Events on Charlotte Street and the subsequent press coverage had given the impression that the Met was powerless to protect Londoners from a new breed of vicious, gun-toting gangster. Plentiful newspaper reports on the capital's latest spate of gun-crimes only reinforced that impression.

On Monday 5 May two young men had burgled a flat in St John's Wood and fired at a constable who had tried to arrest them. And in the early hours of Tuesday 6 May, a gang of six masked men had robbed a factory on the outskirts of London, having threatened to shoot a seventy-six-year-old nightwatchman and one of his colleagues.

Reports on these incidents, spiced up by headlines such as 'BANDIT SHOOTS IT OUT WITH POLICE', were interspersed with continued stories about the Antiquis case. Between Monday and Thursday of that week, the police succeeded in keeping any mention of the hunt for Walsh and Hart out of the papers. Instead, journalists from the *Evening Standard* and other newspapers wrote about earlier developments which had just been made public by Scotland Yard, developments that included the discovery of the raincoat at Brook House.

Pursuing a different angle on the story, the *Daily Mail* concentrated its fund-raising campaign. By that Wednesday, it had received in excess of 4,000 letters, along with cheques and postal orders amounting to a massive £4,250. Alfred Stock was among the readers who had contributed to the fund. 'I am sending my cheque as a small token of my appreciation for Alec de Antiquis,' he declared in the accompanying letter. 'It was a miracle that I and several members of my staff were not also killed by the same assassins.'

❖

The outcry on behalf of Antiquis's widow and orphaned children presented Conservative MPs with an opportunity to gain political advantage over the embattled Labour government. On the afternoon of Thursday 8 May, the matter was raised in the House of Commons where James Chuter Ede, the Home Secretary, was present to answer questions about his area of responsibility. Within about twenty minutes of the prayer session which, at that time, prefaced the parliamentary day, E.P. Smith—a Conservative MP for a Kent constituency—launched his opening sallie. He asked Ede 'what official means exist of providing for the dependants in necessitous circumstances of citizens who may have been gravely injured or lost their lives in going to the assistance of the law by endeavouring to detain criminals in the act of committing or immediately after the commission of a crime.'

Smith's concern was reiterated by his fellow Conservative MP, Sir Jocelyn Lucas, who asked what compensation would be paid to the widow of Mr de Antiquis and out of what government fund.

Three more MPs spoke in the same vein, the final question carrying a plea 'to award a special grant to the widow and six children of this gallant citizen.'

Chuter Ede, a balding, beaky-nosed, former schoolmaster, now in his mid-sixties, rose from his seat. Through a spell as a magistrate and nearly a quarter of a century as an MP, during which he had served in the wartime coalition government, he'd accrued a detailed knowledge of crime and its causes, knowledge that he was capable of deploying in a plain-spoken, unsentimental style. He was nonetheless renowned for the sly asides and flashes of irony that enlivened his parliamentary performances. Responding to the previous flurry of questions, none of which gave any scope for humour, he said, 'I am sure the House would desire me to express their sympathy with the wife and orphans of this man who lost his life voluntarily discharging the duties of a good citizen.' He paused while his remarks were greeted by a chorus of cheers from both sides of the House. Once the noise had subsided, he added, 'The question of making an appropriate grant from the Metropolitan Police Fund is receiving my sympathetic consideration.'

These words provoked more cheering which echoed round the ornate neo-Gothic chamber.

For a few minutes longer, the ritual of question and response continued. Changing the opposition's angle of attack, Smith enquired whether Ede was aware of public concern about the alarming increase in cases of robbery with violence by armed men in London. 'How many such cases have been reported since 1 January 1947, and in how many instances have the culprits been convicted?'

In reply the Home Secretary said, 'During the first four months of this year, twenty-five robberies occurred in the Metropolitan Police district where a firearm was known to have been used. Eight of these cases have been cleared up, involving the arrest of fourteen persons, thirteen of whom have been convicted and one of whom is awaiting trial. The Commissioner of Police is giving every attention to dealing with this series of crimes.'

Ede must have hoped his reply would be sufficient to repel the opposition attack. Smith was, however, unwilling to let him steer the debate onto less fertile ground.

'Is it not really astonishing that so many crimes of this nature should escape solution?' Smith enquired. 'And can nothing be done to tighten up public security in this regard?'

'I imagine that criminals of this type are pretty astute, and that they take steps to assure themselves that the coast is reasonably clear before they commit their crimes. I think the number of detections that I have been able to announce is not unsatisfactory, having regard to the number of desperate men there are about at this time, but the Commissioner of Police and myself are fully seized of the importance of putting down this form of lawlessness. And I am quite sure that we shall have the support of all law-abiding citizens in the efforts we make to achieve our object.'

Another hostile MP joined the fray by saying, 'Is my Right Honourable Friend aware that, in the main, the illegal possession of firearms is punished in the lightest possible way by the magistrates who are not using the maximum powers they possess? Would my Right Honourable Friend consider issuing a recommendation to the magistrates for the imposition of maximum sentences for the illegal possession of firearms...?'

'It is my endeavour to issue as few recommendations as possible to magistrates because, having been a magistrate myself, I know the resentment with which the Home Secretary's circulars are sometimes received. But I have no doubt that the question put by my Honourable Friend will draw the attention of magistrates to this matter, and I hope they can feel that the House is behind them in seeing that the law is enforced.'

No sooner had the Home Secretary seen off his latest adversary than another sprang up in the form of a naval officer turned politician. Lieutenant-Commander Gurney-Braithwaite said, 'May I ask whether the Right Honourable Gentleman is in consultation with his Right Honourable Friend, the Minister of Fuel and Power, with a view to the immediate termination of the blackout conditions in the streets which give these thugs an excellent opportunity of making their escape?'

Before the Home Secretary could reply, a supplementary question was lobbed in his direction by one of Gurney-Braithwaite's colleagues. 'Is it the case, as I have been told, that the police are sometimes very badly handicapped in that they have not sufficient power... If this *is* the case, will my Honourable Friend ask the House for further powers?'

'No, sir,' the Home Secretary responded. 'One has to be very careful how one arms the police with additional powers. I am quite sure of this. The police themselves are very keen to bring this form of crime to an end. After all, they quite frequently are the persons most in danger from these illegal weapons.'

❖

The closure of the *Daily Mail's* campaign to raise money for Mrs de Antiquis and her children was announced in the Saturday 10 May edition.

Though the fund had only been open for eight days, a little over £5,300 had been raised, comparable to around £150,000 in 2007.

That afternoon a meeting was held at Scotland Yard to discuss the progress of the Antiquis murder-hunt. During the meeting, senior CID officers were told that a young man detained in a south-west London police station had just confessed to the crime. Within minutes of receiving the message, two car-loads of detectives were speeding over Westminster Bridge.

When they arrived at the police station, they interviewed the man who had claimed responsibility for the Charlotte Street shooting. Already facing a minor charge, the supposed culprit said he wanted to make a clean breast of his past. He added that he'd got himself arrested on the minor charge because he was scared of his former associates. But there were discrepancies between his account of the shooting in North Soho and the evidence so far amassed, these discrepancies compelling the police to rule out his confession.

Higgins had experienced a similar scenario when he'd been investigating the previous year's shooting outside the Blue Lagoon night club on Carnaby Street. Like the man who had falsely confessed to that crime, the prisoner in the south-west London police station suffered from what Higgins termed a peculiarity in a certain type of deranged person. Higgins sensed that this could be motivated by a general disinterest in life, a desire for notoriety, or genuine delusions. Whatever the reasons behind a false confession, he took pride in the Met's perceived reluctance to grab the first person who confessed and pin the affair on him.

❖

On Monday 12 May Fabian and Higgins made up their minds to bring Jenkins and Rolt back to Tottenham Court Road Police Station for another round of questioning. By going over and over a suspect's alibi, there was always a possibility that inconsistencies would appear. With patience, the faintest of cracks could be chiselled open.

As ever, each of the suspects was interviewed separately. Jenkins's account of what he had been doing on the day of the Antiquis killing remained unaltered, so he was released.

The two senior detectives didn't get round to questioning Rolt until 11:30pm. Rolt was still wearing his blue raincoat, presumably because the building was cold due to the lingering fuel crisis. Fabian began by telling Rolt that they were making enquiries respecting the murder of a motorcyclist on Charlotte Street on 29 April. The young suspect was then asked if he could remember where he had been that day.

'No, I can't, but I expect I stayed in bed in the morning.' He added that he didn't usually get up until midday. He also said he'd heard about Jenkins—whom he called 'Harryboy'—being brought in for questioning, so he had been expecting to be picked up as well.

His response differed from the reply he had given at his first interview when he had claimed that he'd stayed in bed all day. This discrepancy encouraged the detectives to persist with their questioning. The interview continued for about fifteen minutes.

Rolt concluded by saying, 'I know nothing about the job and I can't help you anymore.'

Once Fabian and Higgins had checked Rolt's alibi with his mother, who unsurprisingly corroborated what her son had told them, they informed him that he was free to go. He was instructed—with an undertone of sarcasm—to come back to the police station if he remembered anything that might help the investigation further. At 1:00am he was given a lift home in a squad car.

❖

Through the CID's underworld contacts, Fabian learned that Walsh had sold the bulk of the stolen items from the Queensway robbery to someone in Southend. Suspicion fell on Arthur Birchall, a known fence who lived in the suburb of Westcliff-on-Sea. A message was sent to the local CID to place Birchall under observation and to stop him if he showed any sign of fleeing.

Both Fabian and Hodge returned to Southend. During the early hours of Tuesday 13 May, the same night that he'd interviewed Rolt, Fabian initiated a major police operation. In search of Walsh and Hart, local detectives and uniformed officers combed the town. To prevent news of the operation filtering through to the missing couple, Scotland Yard instructed the press that no reference should be made to it.

Fabian was still in Southend when the investigation took an unexpected detour. At 8:00am a railway worker found the body of an unidentified man lying in the train tunnel connecting Chalk Farm with Hampstead. The tunnel was promptly closed and the police notified. With the Divisional Detective Inspector of D Division in charge, officers formed a cordon at both ends. Railway workers who attempted to enter were stopped and questioned by detectives.

Inside the tunnel, a huddle of photographers and fingerprint experts from the Yard converged round the body. It was that of a middle-aged man in a brown jacket and light grey cap. Under his arm, he appeared to have been carrying a raincoat. Though he had most likely been struck by an express train, there remained a suspicion that he'd been murdered. If he had been murdered, there was an outside chance that he might have been a victim of Antiquis's killer, regarded by the police as someone who would not hesitate to kill again. That prospect injecting additional urgency into the case, a squad car rushed the dead man's fingerprints over to the CRO. But these revealed no link with Walsh or the other suspects in the Antiquis case.

❖

Sightings of Walsh and Hart in Southend were reported to the police. These suggested that Hart didn't know that Walsh was wanted in connection with a murder.

Officers involved in the hunt for them worked without sleep for forty-eight hours following Fabian's arrival in Southend. The radius of their search soon expanded to cover the whole of south-east Essex.

As part of the police operation, Birchall—the local fence who had been under surveillance—was taken to Southend Central Police Station. In an Interview Room there, Hodge questioned him about Walsh. Birchall admitted that Walsh had sold him a consignment of stolen watches and jewellery. This turned out to include a gold wristwatch that Birchall had with him. Hodge confiscated the watch.

Asked which day Walsh had sold him the goods, Birchall said he couldn't be sure.

Hodge wanted to know whether Birchall was certain that he'd bought the watches and jewellery from Walsh. There was no doubt, Birchall said, that Walsh was the bloke who sold them to him.

The detective quizzed Birchall about Walsh's current whereabouts. Birchall gave Hodge an address where, he said, Walsh and Hart were staying. The address was in the area around Richmond Avenue, near the centre of town.

Before paying Walsh and his girlfriend a visit, Hodge arranged for Fabian and several carloads of armed officers from Southend CID to accompany him. The alleged hideout was an unprepossessing two-storey boarding-house at the end of a Victorian terrace. Jutting from the side of the building, a sign advertised 'APARTMENTS'.

Hodge and his fellow officers surrounded the building before Fabian approached the front door. When he was let in, he discovered that the fugitive couple had paid their bill and departed with their luggage about half-an-hour earlier. Though they couldn't have gone far, the police were unable to find them.

Still, there was always the possibility that they might have left clues as to where they had gone. Walsh might even have hidden items stolen from the shop on Queensway. Driven by these suspicions, Hodge ordered a thorough search of the building. Detectives went to the lengths of lifting the floorboards and slicing open mattresses, yet they found nothing significant.

❖

For the past week Jenkins had been working as a labourer on a building site. On Thursday 15 May his routine was disrupted when he was brought over to Tottenham Court Road Police Station where he faced another interview with Fabian, who had just got back from Southend.

In the presence of Higgins, Fabian questioned Jenkins about his brother-in-law Tom Kemp's raincoat and how it had come into his possession. Jenkins was shown the coat found at Brook House and asked whether he recognised it.

'I am quite willing to tell you the truth about the coat,' Jenkins replied, implying that he might not have been truthful before. 'On 24 April 1947 in the morning, a man I know as Bill Walsh called at my house and asked me if I could lend him an overcoat. I had only one decent one of my own, so—to oblige him—I took him over to my sister's at 160 Park Buildings to see if my brother-in-law had one he could borrow. I asked my sister if Tom, her husband, had a coat the fellow could borrow, and she brought a raincoat from the bedroom and lent it to the man.

'The man was already wearing a black herringbone-pattern overcoat and my sister said something about it, but the man I was with—Bill Walsh—said he wanted to borrow the mac. My sister gave the man the mac and we left her flat, Bill Walsh promising to return the mac as soon as he could. So far as I can say, the mac shown to me is the one my sister lent to Bill Walsh.'

Few people, least of all a pair of experienced detectives, were likely to fall for such an implausible yarn. If Walsh already had a coat, why did he need to borrow a raincoat? And why would Mrs Kemp have lent her husband's coat to a stranger?

❖

It was almost two weeks since Walsh and Hart's details had appeared in the *Police Gazette*. Despite having thousands of uniformed officers and plain clothes CID men on their trail, neither of the fugitives had been located, though there had been reports of them being seen in towns and cities as far afield as Sheffield. One of the more credible sightings was from someone in Southend who remembered Hart having a frightened look about her eyes.

Picture of Doris Hart circulated by New Scotland Yard.
(Copyright: Metropolitan Police Historical Collection)

Believing that she might be in grave danger from Walsh who would do his utmost to prevent her from talking to them, Fabian and the Yard's other senior officers took the decision to involve both the press and public in the hunt for the couple.

40,000 copies of Hart's photo were printed and distributed. Her picture was also circulated around all the Fleet Street news rooms. In the accompanying press release, the Met made an appeal to the public. 'It is vitally important that anyone who has seen Doris Hart within the last few weeks should contact the police immediately.' Another appeal was directed at the fugitive herself. 'Come and tell us what you know,' it urged. 'We will protect you.'

The press release described the missing woman as twenty-four-year-old Doris Brenda Hart, who sometimes used the names 'Doris Graham', 'Norma Marshall', 'Mrs Doris Stephens', and 'Mrs Brenda Harcourt'. She was also described as being five feet, five inches tall, and having an olive complexion, brown eyes and dark hair that had been dyed 'very blonde'.

For fear of prejudicing any future identification parade involving Walsh, the press release omitted either a description or photo of him. Instead, it noted that Hart was likely to be travelling with the man that the police wanted to interview in connection with the Antiquis murder. And it warned that Hart's companion was probably armed and might be dangerous.

❖

Duncan Webb was a beefy man in early middle-age whose tiny, watchful eyes were set in a pock-marked face that had already acquired a hint of the puffiness characteristic of heavy drinkers. He had sandy hair which he doused with Brylcreem, enabling him to part his hair as sharply as the gap between two columns of newspaper text. For most of that Thursday afternoon, he had been walking round the West End. There was a stiffness to his stride which served as a constant reminder of the wounds he had suffered while working as a war correspondent. During an assignment to cover the Battle of the Bulge, his plane had been shot down, forcing him to parachute into the snowy Ardennes. A bad landing had left him with a fractured right arm, two crushed vertebrae, several broken ribs and a punctured lung. He'd also sustained frostbitten feet before he'd been rescued.

Back home in London, he had written a memoir of his wartime experiences and resumed his embryonic career in the newspaper business. He'd made considerable progress since the pre-war period when he had been a cub reporter on the *South London Press*. It was there that he had developed an obsession with crime stories, along with an aptitude for covering them. In between hazardous stints as a war correspondent, flying bombing missions with the RAF and taking part in the Normandy landings, he'd demonstrated his facility as a crime reporter by delivering well-researched investigative pieces about what had come to be known as the 'Cleft Chin Murder'. This had been committed by Karl Hulten, an American army deserter who had fantasised about being a Chicago gangster. Together with a former stripper named Betty Jones, Hulten had carried out a string of hold-ups during the autumn of 1944. One of these had involved the fatal shooting of a London cabbie, owner of the eponymous dimpled chin.

More recently, Webb had covered two other prominent murder-hunts: for the sadist, Neville Heath, and for the men behind the shooting of Reuben Martirossof, the blackmarket kingpin nicknamed 'Russian Robert'. Only eighteen months earlier, Martirossof's body had been found in an abandoned car in Notting Hill. He'd been shot in the back of the neck by Henryk Malinowski and Marion Grondkowski, two Polish army deserters turned spivs. By a peculiar coincidence, Webb—who seemed to generate coincidences—had crossed paths with both Malinowski and Heath before they'd committed the murders for which they had been executed. Webb had first encountered Heath in a Knightsbridge pub. On the evening of the murder Webb had bumped into him again, this time in a Fleet Street drinking club where Heath had bought Webb a glass of light ale. In a similarly strange coincidence, Webb remembered sitting opposite Malinowski on a District Line Underground train. Malinowski had been wearing the uniform of a Chief Officer in the British merchant navy, but his battered, unpolished shoes and dirty shirt had persuaded Webb that he was an imposter.

Webb's diligent coverage of the garish crimes committed by Heath, Malinowski and their ilk had helped to secure his promotion to the post of

Marion Grondkowski (left) and Henryk Malinowski (right), the killers of Reuben Martirosoff.

Deputy News Editor at the *Evening Standard*. Though the job had brought with it a welcome pay-rise, it did have one major disadvantage. Nowadays he seldom got the chance to report on crime stories. Crime was, in any event, an area that appealed to neither his editor nor the senior management. Under the influence of the newspaper's meddlesome Canadian owner, Lord Beaverbrook, they felt that murderers were vulgar and had no place in a respectable newspaper.

Vulgar or not, Webb's fixation with crime had intensified over the years. Despite his recent marriage, he devoted most of his spare-time to befriending members of both the CID and the underworld. His diverse contacts ranged from Bob Fabian to the gangster Billy Hill, freshly released from a four-year spell at HM Prison Dartmoor.

Using these connections, he had got into the habit of producing dossiers on the latest criminal cases, even though his job didn't require him to cover most of them. Officially, he wasn't reporting on the Antiquis case, yet that hadn't stopped him from spending time on it. He had heard rumours from his contacts that Bill Walsh was the main suspect. Confident in his ability to succeed where the police had—so far, at least—failed, Webb set aside all his other work and decided to look for Walsh. If he could find Walsh and interview him, it would be a career-transforming scoop.

From a criminal whom Webb had known since his days as a cub reporter, he learned that Walsh's home was in Plumstead. For that reason Webb, who used to live near there, had revisited the area the previous day and sought out several criminals whose trust he had first gained when he'd worked for the *South London Press*. He'd asked them if they had any idea where Walsh might be. They had been unable to help, but they'd suggested he should have a word with a man named George—someone Webb had befriended during the 1930s. Webb's contacts had said that George was 'grafting' in the West End.

Keen to find him, Webb had spent several hours the previous day, plus several more that day wandering round central London. Every so often he darted into pubs and basement drinking clubs where he bought drinks for people and held hushed conversations with them about George.

Eventually Webb's persistence paid off. He saw the elusive George selling fruit from a barrow outside the broad-fronted Dolcis shoe shop. This was on the corner where Leicester Street met prostitute-filled Leicester Square.

Twelve years had passed since Webb had last set eyes on George, yet he had such a good memory that he still recognised him. He and George were soon ensconced in the White Horse pub on Rupert Street. Adept at gently probing people for information, Webb resisted the urge to ask George about Walsh straightaway. Instead, he bided his time. Without arousing George's suspicions, he manouevred the conversation onto the subject of various long-lost friends and acquaintances. Webb mentioned Bill Walsh in this context. When George admitted knowing Walsh, Webb said that he'd like to see him. From George's reaction, Webb sensed George didn't realise that Walsh was Britain's most wanted man.

*The psychopath, Neville Heath, pictured in the back of a squad car.*

George was curious as to why Webb had this sudden urge to see Walsh after so many years.

Webb said he just wanted to ask Walsh something.

You should go round to Walsh's home near Plumstead Common, George advised.

As a subtle means of confirming what George had just told him, Webb said he was under the impression that Walsh had gone away.

'Gone away? Well, he might have done, but I thought he was with his missus. Fact, I'm sure that's where you'll get him.'

❖

In the streets around the pub where Webb and George had been drinking, hoarse-voiced news vendors were a familiar sight. Encamped at strategic positions, they advertised their wares with barked shouts of 'Paper! Paper! *Star, News 'n' Standard!*' Under the headline 'ANTIQUIS: HUNT FOR WOMAN', that day's *Evening Standard* featured a front-page story about the hunt for Doris Hart and her unnamed companion.

The search for them had become an even bigger news story by the following morning when Webb arrived at work. Most of the national newspapers featured a large picture of her on their front-pages. It was the heavily retouched black and white studio portrait supplied by Scotland Yard. Taken before she had dyed her dark hair blonde, it showed her smiling broadly, an unforced expression borne out of happier times.

Webb was based in a scruffy, architecturally undistinguished office block on Shoe Lane, close to where the road met Fleet Street. The building's inadequacies were thrown into sharp relief by the flamboyant, shiny black Art Deco edifice several doors away. This housed the *Daily Express*, another of Lord Beaverbrook's stable of newspapers.

Overnight Webb had been weighing up the available options. If he went round to Walsh's house, there was every chance that Walsh would open fire in a bid to prevent Webb from passing on details of his whereabouts. On the other hand, if the tip-off proved inaccurate and Walsh wasn't there, Webb hoped to redeem the situation by interviewing the wanted man's wife, which would still provide the basis for a worthwhile story. Nevertheless Webb recognised that it was his duty as a citizen to ring Fabian and reveal where Walsh was hiding.

Ultimately arriving at a compromise, Webb decided to go down to Plumstead, land his scoop, then get in touch with Fabian. As a prelude to all that, just before lunchtime he headed for the Cashier's Office. When he got there, he attempted to draw £5 to cover his travel expenses for the journey to south London.

Instead of meekly complying with his request, the cashier refused to advance any money without a signed chit from the editor. Webb knew that there wasn't, for the time-being, any chance of obtaining such a chit because the editor had left the building. Worse still, Webb didn't have sufficient cash in his wallet to circumvent this exasperating process by paying for the trip himself. Infuriated by the bureaucracy that was preventing him from obtaining the biggest story of his career, Webb buttonholed his boss, the News Editor. Webb explained the situation before pleading with his immediate superior to lend him the money to get to Plumstead by taxi or whatever means necessary. But the News Editor wouldn't stump up the required cash. When Webb asked round the office, he received a similar response, so he announced that he would just have to write himself a cheque and go round to his bank and cash it. Even that didn't work because the News Editor insisted that he wanted Webb to stay in the office.

Webb's frustration manifested itself in a queasy sensation that persisted through lunchtime, during which he brooded over George's tip-off. The more he thought about it, the more plausible it seemed. Unable to devise any pretext that would permit him to leave the building and get down to Plumstead, he arrived at the reluctant conclusion that he might as well call the police. That way, the information wouldn't be entirely wasted. At least it would place Fabian in his debt.

Picking up the phone, Webb dialled Museum 113, the number for Tottenham Court Road Police Station. When someone answered, Webb asked to speak to Fabian.

The officer on the other end of the line went off to fetch Webb's friend. After the inevitable delay, the same voice came back on the line. 'Mr Fabian said I was to take any message you've got. He's too busy to talk to you.'

Overworked though he knew Fabian must have been, Webb was irritated by his friend's response.

'All right,' Webb replied, 'tell Bob that if he wants Walsh, he's at his home in Plumstead.'

'Yeah, when did you hear of a wanted man living at home? That was the first place we'd look if we thought he was there.'

Without saying another word, Webb hung up in disgust.

❖

Former Detective Sergeant Jack Morris, a chubby man with the beginnings of a double-chin, had retired from the Met three years earlier. He'd since taken a job with the Royal Marine Police, based at the Woolwich Arsenal garrison, conveniently close to his house on Tormount Road.

Just after 2:00pm on Friday 16 May—the approximate time of Webb's phone-call to Fabian—Morris was driving home with some freshly purchased shopping. His route took him along Plumstead Common Road. This skirted the western half of the Common, a long, thin stretch of parkland, formerly used for tethering barrage balloons. At that end, late Victorian houses had encroached onto the Common. These looked dismal in the steady rain drumming on the roof and windscreen of Morris's car. Through the downpour he noticed a lone figure sheltering under a tree at the junction between Herbert and Plumstead Common Roads. As the car approached it, Morris—who had, when he'd been on the beat, learned never to forget a face—recognised the man standing beneath the tree. He was a professional criminal, familiar to Morris and his erstwhile colleagues in the CID Office at Plumstead Police Station.

Despite having retired from the Met, Morris found it impossible to resist visiting his former workplace where he'd spent fourteen of his twenty-six years in the police. While he was there, he couldn't get out of the habit of perusing the *Police Gazette*. Only serving officers were meant to have access to it, but nobody had the heart to snatch it from Morris's grasp. During a recent flick through the *Gazette*, Morris recalled seeing a mug-shot of the man ahead of him. In one of the many improbable twists of fate punctuating the story of the Antiquis case, that man was none other than Bill Walsh.

Dabbing the brake-pedal, Morris slowed down and pulled up next to Walsh who was clad in a grey pinstripe suit with padded shoulders. Even though he and Morris were on different sides of the law, the two men got on well. Morris wound down the window and said, 'Hello, chum. How's it going?'

He and Walsh exchanged pleasantries. Then Morris stepped out of his car and, playing for time, continued the conversation. He talked about everything he could think of—the weather, the state of the country, the people of Plumstead. After around ten minutes' of this, he saw a uniformed policeman cycling towards them. The cyclist was a middle-aged, off-duty Constable named Frank Farthing, who was on his way home for a late lunch. Morris caught Farthing's eye and surreptitiously pointed at Walsh, who had his back to the Constable. Farthing realised that the man ahead of him was Walsh. Like Morris, he had come across Walsh in the past.

Walsh didn't notice Morris signalling to the cyclist. Hastily dismounting from his bicycle and leaning it outside the local Conservative Club, Farthing sneaked up behind Walsh and trapped him in an arm-lock. At the same time Morris moved forward and gave Walsh a bear-hug.

'This is the man you want,' Morris said to Farthing.

Wedged between the two bulky officers, Farthing's misshapen nose hinting at pugilistic experience, Walsh made no attempt to resist. 'I didn't think you'd do a thing like this to me, Jack,' he said to Morris.

Together with Farthing, Morris manouevred him over to the parked car. 'There's no need for you to hold me like this,' Walsh said to the Constable. 'I haven't got any guns.'

Mention of guns reminded Morris to frisk Walsh. Just as Walsh had said, there were no firearms concealed in his clothes.

❖

At approximately 4:00pm that day, Fabian heard what had happened on Plumstead Common. He and Higgins set off for Woolwich Police Station where Walsh had been detained. The journey took them at least half-an-hour.

When they confronted Walsh, he greeted them with a wary smile. 'What d'you want me for?' he asked. 'Not all this fuss for dodging my ticket of leave, surely?'

Fabian told him that he was being transferred to Tottenham Court Road Police Station for questioning about his suspected involvement in an armed robbery and the sale of stolen property. Walsh was then cautioned.

'Tell me exactly what you're talking about?' he asked.

He was informed that Fabian and Higgins were conducting enquiries into the robbery of a jeweller's shop in Bayswater on 26 April 1947. The detectives also announced that they were investigating another matter which involved murder.

'I can see it's serious,' Walsh replied. 'I'll tell you my part in the Queensway job, but I have nothing to do with the other matter.'

❖

160 miles away in the Yorkshire town of Goole, the local police were following up a report that Doris Hart had been seen there the previous night. Apparently waiting for someone, she'd been spotted on Boothferry Road, near the picturesque jumble of nineteenth-century buildings jostling for position beside the canal.

Before the police could make much progress verifying the story, she walked purposefully towards West Riding Constabulary Headquarters. It was a large redbrick building on Gladstone Terrace which branched off the market square. Clasping a newspaper with a photograph of her on the front-page, she went up the steps. At that moment—around the time Walsh was being interviewed at Woolwich Police Station—a uniformed Constable came out of the front-door. She buttonholed him, waved the newspaper in front of him and said, 'D'you want to see me about this?'

Even though her blonde hair made her look different from the woman pictured in the newspaper, the Constable realised who she was.

'I don't know what all this is about,' she added, 'but I thought I'd better come to a police station as soon as I could.'

She was taken inside and questioned by Detective Chief Inspector Stubbs of West Riding CID. At his prompting she provided valuable information about Walsh and also revealed how she'd ended up in Yorkshire. She said she'd been staying with Walsh in a Southend lodging house until three days ago. When they'd parted, she had travelled to Goole where she'd arranged to visit a man by the name of George Pollard. The two of them had met in Southend the previous summer. Pollard, who lived on Third Avenue, had just got home on leave from a stint with the British army in Palestine.

Arrangements were made for officers from the Met to catch the train to Goole and escort Hart back to London for questioning by Fabian and his team. News of her sudden appearance at the police station had, meanwhile, spread round the town. A small crowd, eager to catch a glimpse of her, gathered outside.

❖

The squad car carrying Walsh drove along Whitfield Street and into the spacious, covered yard at the back of Tottenham Court Road Police Station. To conceal his identity from at least two waiting press photographers who had been tipped-off about his impending arrival, he borrowed one of the detectives' hats to cover his face. The hat was soon replaced by a jacket placed over Walsh's head. With Fabian bringing up the rear, a pipe clenched between his teeth, Walsh was guided across the yard and up the steep flight of steps leading to the station's back entrance.

When interviewing a violent suspect like Walsh, there was a danger that he might use an ink bottle or steel ruler as a weapon, so detectives were advised to clear the surface of the desk at which they sat. Even for such experienced detectives as Fabian and Higgins, interrogation remained the most testing of all the varied tasks that they were expected to perform. No aspect of the job required greater subtlety and psychological insight. The Interviewing Officer's approach and language had to be tailored to the personality of the suspect. However uncooperative or hostile the interviewee was, detectives were taught to remain calm and civil. Above all, suspects were not supposed to be browbeaten into making confessions. Any hint of irregularity or attempted coercion was liable to be exploited by the defending counsel in a bid to discredit the circumstances of the interrogation and, by extension, the contents of the defendant's statement.

In compliance with Judges' Rules, Walsh was cautioned for a second time before being asked about his role in the Antiquis murder and the raids on A.B. Davis Ltd of Queensway and Jay's Ltd of Tottenham Street. He was also questioned about the raincoat which Jenkins had claimed to have lent him.

At first he said nothing. He just paced up and down, chain-smoking cigarettes. That gave Fabian and Higgins a chance to observe his behaviour and gestures. For a suspect to become so unnerved during an interview was sometimes perceived as a sign of innocence. Guilty interviewees tended to be undemonstrative or else to treat the whole thing as an absurd misunderstanding.

After a while, Walsh requested a glass of water. No sooner had one been fetched for him than he agreed to make a written statement about his involvement in the Queensway robbery and with the Jenkins family whom he'd known for the past five years.

The detectives provided him with some foolscap statement forms. Wreathed in dense cigarette-smoke, he sat down and began to write, his fountain-pen scratching the surface of the paper. He proceeded to describe how, sometime towards the beginning of April, he had gone round to Weller House where Jenkins's parents lived. While he was there, he'd heard that Jenkins was due back from borstal on Wednesday 23 April.

'I was living at home at this time,' Walsh wrote. 'But soon after—I think it was on 10 April—I walked out of my home because my wife was carrying on with other men.' He added that he'd stayed with a friend named Charlie Strong in Southend until the day Jenkins had been released. That day, his statement declared, he had returned to London. During the evening, he had called round to see Jenkins. The two of them had gone for a drink, after which Walsh had stayed with Jenkins at Weller House. 'The next day we went to a café in Aldgate and met a chap. I think his name is Joe.' From Aldgate, he explained, they had made their way to Kilburn, where Joe had gone into a house on Princess Road and emerged roughly half-an-hour later with a fellow they called Chris.

Walsh put down on the statement form that he, Chris and the others had ended up in a Kilburn pub. 'They had beers and I had orange squash. I mostly sat on my own, and the three of them were talking together but I don't know what about. The only part of the conversation I did catch was from Chris, who said he had been waiting in for the Borstal Association man to call all day.'

Fabian and Higgins already knew enough to make an educated guess: that 'Chris' was Chris Geraghty.

Carrying on with his rambling statement, Walsh described how they'd moved from the pub in Kilburn to one in Aldgate. 'I can't think of the name of the pub but there are knives and daggers hanging up on the walls—also an elephant's foot. We had one drink, then came out. Me and Harryboy left the other fellow and went home to the Jenkins' place.'

After another night spent at Weller House, Walsh wrote, he and Jenkins had gone to the café in Aldgate to meet Chris and Joe. 'The four of us had some breakfast there together and I listened to the conversation, which was more or less about a job they was going to do at Queensway, Bayswater. The man called Joe seemed to have most to say about the job. Joe said it was to be a stick-up and they would have a car handy and ditch it after the job was done.'

Evidently striving to downplay his own role in the Queensway robbery, Walsh added that Jenkins and Chris—who had agreed to be the driver—had clarified their plans over breakfast. Walsh declared that he and the three others had then left the café and taken the underground from Aldgate to Bayswater. He claimed that he had, while they were on the train, tried to talk Jenkins out of going ahead with the robbery.

When they had reached Baywater, Walsh revealed, he'd been asked to go round to A.B. Davis, the jeweller's shop on Queensway which the others were planning to rob. 'I went into the shop and asked if they had any horseshoe-shaped earrings. They had none and pointed out another shop to me. I then came out and saw the others waiting by the station. I told them that there were only two men in the jeweller's, and the four of us had a stroll round. The others were looking for a suitable car to use on the job. Before they found their car, Harryboy said to me, "Go home to Wapping and wait for me." '

Why Jenkins would have chosen to sideline an experienced armed robber like him, Walsh failed to explain. He wrote that he'd followed Jenkins's instructions and headed over to Wapping where he had waited at Riverside Mansions. He added a sentence about Jenkins joining him later that afternoon. Once again trying to portray himself in a more favourable light, Walsh went on to describe how he'd immediately quizzed Jenkins about the robbery and whether they had used their guns. 'Harryboy said there had been no shooting. I was a bit dubious. I asked him where his gun was. He showed me a .32 automatic pistol.' Walsh claimed to have picked up the gun with a handkerchief—obviously to avoid leaving fingerprints—and inspected it.

Next, Walsh offered an account of how Jenkins had shown him the proceeds of the robbery. 'We counted out the value of the things, which amounted to nearly £4,000. We got the value off the tickets. There was bracelets, watches, rings, and other jewellery. I put the stuff in my pocket.'

He continued with a description of him going with Jenkins, plus Jenkins's wife and baby, to Southend. According to his statement, they had a drink in a local pub, then took a taxi to Westcliff-on-Sea where Mr and Mrs Birchall lived.

Arthur Birchall had, of course, already been interviewed in connection with the investigation. Contradicting Birchall's story of how Walsh had sold him a wristwatch in a Southend café, Walsh wrote that he'd given Birchall the watch from the cache of stolen goods. He also wrote—even less plausibly—that he'd presented Birchall's wife with a diamond ring. 'After this I had a wash and shave and, whilst shaving, Harryboy told me to give the stuff to his wife. I finished my shave and walked out the back, saying I was going to the lavatory.' But Walsh admitted that he'd never returned. Instead, he had taken the opportunity to sneak off with the rest of the jewellery and wristwatches.

'That night I walked round Southend and, the next morning, I met a fellow in a café near the Labour Exchange. This man had been pointed out to me by Charlie Strong and I was told he could get rid of good stuff.' Walsh stated that he'd let the man examine some of the stolen items. Soon afterwards another man had entered the café and started talking about horse-racing, but there had been something suspicious about him. 'The other fellow seemed to smell a rat and showed out to me to drink up and get out of the café. We walked round the corner and got on a bus going up the London Road.' He added that, as the bus had pulled away, he'd looked out of the back window and seen the suspicious man running after it. Walsh described how he'd got off the bus, hung round the sea-front for a while, then taken a coach back to London, where he had stayed with Johnny Gardner, an old schoolfriend who lived in Abbey Wood, a district adjacent to Plumstead. 'I showed him one of the rings and asked him whether he knew anyone who would buy it. He said, "Not here, but there is someone over at Stratford." '

On the afternoon of Sunday 27 April, Walsh's statement went on to explain, the two of them had travelled to Stratford in east London, where the landlord of the Abbey Arms pub inspected the stolen goods. Walsh wrote that the landlord had arranged for someone to meet them in his pub at noon the following day.

By that stage, Walsh's statement had covered seven sides of the forms he had been given. He then launched into a lengthy and irrelevant digression about a mix-up with the taxi firm which had taken him and Gardner back to Abbey Wood.

Picking up the central thread of his story, Walsh revealed that he had, as arranged, returned to the pub in Stratford on Monday 28 April. There he'd met Ashley, the man summoned by the landlord. In the privacy of the gents' toilet, he had shown Ashley the items from the Queensway robbery. But Ashley had only wanted to buy the rings. They had haggled over a price, eventually settling on £500. Ashley had, Walsh stated, mentioned someone who might be interested in buying the stolen wristwatches and bracelets.

Walsh wrote that, having accepted the offer, Ashley had driven him over to Aldgate. There, Walsh had sold the wristwatches and bracelets. As a postscript to his account, Walsh declared that Gardner had provided him with a bed for the night. And on the morning of Tuesday 29 April—the day of the Antiquis murder—he had taken a taxi to Dagenham where he'd lodged with Gardner's mother-in-law for nearly a fortnight before returning to his wife and family on Monday 12 May. Stretching credibility, he added that, when ex-Detective Sergeant Morris had arrested him on Plumstead Common Road, he'd been on his way to Woolwich Police Station where he had intended to turn himself in.

At this point Walsh supplemented his statement with an extra paragraph, addressing the question of the raincoat that Jenkins had allegedly lent him—the raincoat later abandoned at Brook House by one of the gang who'd raided Jay's. Walsh testified that Jenkins hadn't lent him the coat. Jenkins had, instead, handed it to him on the day of the Queensway robbery and asked him to take it back to Wapping. Both Fabian and Higgins believed his story—or, at least, this element of it—and felt certain that Jenkins was attempting to frame Walsh.

Rounding off his statement, Walsh wrote: 'I want to say that I know nothing at all about the Charlotte Street shooting and have never heard it discussed with anyone at all and do not know who was responsible. All I do know is the girl, Doris Hart, whose photo has appeared in the press, was an acquaintance of mine whilst I was in Southend. I have not seen her since 23 April.'

But Fabian knew that she and Walsh had been together until at least 14 May, the day of the raid on the Southend lodging house. Presumably, Walsh was trying to protect her.

Each page of his statement was now ready to be signed by both him and one of the senior detectives. It could then be typed up in preparation for the inevitable court case.

❖

In his statement Walsh had twice referred to someone named 'Joe', who had been part of the gang responsible for the Queensway robbery. On examining the statement, Fabian and Higgins realised that Joe could be Michael Joseph Gillam, whose name had featured in the Occurrence Book which they'd inspected at Southend Central Police Station. Their suspicion was strengthened by the discovery that Gillam's home address was 61 Princess Road, Kilburn, a north London address that chimed with Walsh's account of the evening before the Queensway robbery.

The decision was taken to haul Gillam in for questioning. At 11:45pm Hodge and eight other detectives left the CID offices and piled into a couple of squad cars. The quickest way to get to Kilburn was by going down Oxford Street, past the huge 1930s Cumberland Hotel and the Marble Arch Pavilion Cinema, then up Edgeware Road. As the squad cars approached Kilburn, which was about three miles from the investigation headquarters, the buildings became more run-down.

Gillam lived on one of a tangle of streets just beyond Paddington Recreation Ground. The house, which he shared with his father and ailing mother, was part of a two-storey Victorian terrace. Like the neighbouring properties, it had a basement and steps up to the front door. When the police were let into the Gillams' home, Joe Gillam was, precisely as they had planned, asleep upstairs in his bedroom. Hodge woke him and said, 'We are police officers enquiring about an armed hold-up at a jeweller's shop at Queensway, Baywater on 25 April 1947. I am going to take you to Tottenham Court Road Police Station pending enquiries.'

Probably identifying himself by flourishing his warrant-card, Hodge cautioned Gillam who still appeared to be half asleep.

'I don't know what you're talking about,' Gillam replied. 'I'll wait and see what you've got on me.'

It was a response hardly calculated to convey the impression that he was innocent of any involvement in the Queensway robbery.

After a lengthy pause during which Gillam started dressing, Hodge repeated the caution, along with what he had said previously. Gillam carried on dressing. Meanwhile, Gillam inadvertently confirmed Jenkins's involvement by asking whether he'd been arrested as well.

Gillam was driven over to Tottenham Court Road Police Station where, at 2:00am, he was brought face to face with Hodge's boss who said, 'I am Chief Inspector Fabian. You will be detained here while enquiries are made as to your movements on 25 April, the day on which a robbery took place at Davis, the jeweller's at Queensway, Bayswater.'

'The inspector who brought me here told me that,' Gillam replied before being locked up for the rest of the night.

❖

Whether or not Gillam had been mixed up in the Queensway robbery and Charlotte Street shooting remained open to question. There was no doubt in Fabian's mind, though, that Jenkins and Geraghty had been involved in the latter. Despite their youth, he realised that both men were tricky customers who might easily slip through the net which was beginning to close around them. Alert to that danger, he and Higgins debated how best to handle the case.

If they arrested Jenkins first, Fabian knew that Jenkins possessed the cunning to fend off their questions. Geraghty seemed to be the weakest point in the chain. Hard-bitten though he was, he didn't possess his friend's coolness under pressure. And the pressure was certainly mounting now that Walsh had implicated him in the Queensway job.

To authenticate and expand upon what Walsh and the others had told them, the police initiated what a Fleet Street reporter would describe as 'one of the biggest information hunts of recent years.' Across the capital, clubs, billiard halls, houses and all-night cafés were raided and scores of people interviewed.

❖

Next morning—Saturday 17 May—the newspapers carried yet more stories about the investigation. Visible on the display-racks that hung outside most newsagents, there were several related headlines, the most prominent of these being the *Daily Telegraph and Morning Post's* 'GUNMAN HUNT: MAN QUESTIONED'.

In the magazine sections of many of those same newsagents, there was the latest issue of *Picture Post*, its boxy red logo standing out against the photo on its cover. Inside there was a four-page feature about the reporters covering the Antiquis investigation. Entitled 'Fleet Street's Murder Gang', it was illustrated with nine of Bert Hardy's dramatically lit black and white pictures, among them a shot of reporters at a briefing. 'When not out of town,' the article proclaimed, 'crime reporters gather in the Press Room at Scotland Yard, doing menial jobs such as a suicide in Chelsea or a black market theft of dried eggs—"Who on earth wants that stuff?" '

❖

Later that morning Detective Sergeant Richard Lewis, one of many CID officers under Fabian's command, was ordered to bring Geraghty in for questioning. When Lewis arrived at the address he'd been given, he found Geraghty at home.

'I'm a police officer,' he said to him. 'Chief Inspector Fabian wants to see you again to clear up one or two points about the Charlotte Street affair.'

'All right,' Geraghty replied as he accompanied Lewis out of the house.

On his return to Tottenham Court Road Police Station, Lewis guarded him while he waited for his next interview with Fabian. Geraghty virtually admitted his guilt by saying, 'I hope he doesn't think I'm going to open up and get a gun in my back. Anyway, I'll wait and see what he's got to say...'

The young suspect was kept hanging round until about 1:00pm before Lewis was instructed to take him through to the Interview Room. There Geraghty was faced by the intimidating triumvirate of Fabian, Higgins, and Hodge. Fabian noticed that Geraghty couldn't stop fiddling with his lank, fair hair. Other than that, he gave a convincing performance as a man with nothing to fear.

Fabian told him that he was being detained in connection with the Queensway robbery and with the attempted robbery and shooting in Soho on 29 April. Then Fabian cautioned him, prompting Geraghty to say, 'I suppose someone has been chatting since you saw me. You've got them all in, I hear. What I've got to say takes some thinking about...'

❖

Confined in a cramped cell at Tottenham Court Road Police Station, Geraghty was left with nothing to do but sleep, pace round the green asphalt floor, listen to the tantalising rumble of traffic, and brood over his predicament. At around 5:00pm he was peering through the barred window of his cell-door when Hodge walked past. Geraghty called out, 'Can you get me something to read?'

The good-natured detective replied, 'Yes. What would you like?'

Geraghty told him that he fancied some magazines.

But Hodge was unable to find anything suitable lying round the offices: a stray copy of, say, *Film Fun* or *Football Monthly*. All he could provide was a selection of books. As Hodge delivered these, Geraghty said he'd been mulling things over and wanted to make a statement.

Hodge promised to set up an interview with Fabian.

The best part of an hour later, Hodge reappeared and escorted Geraghty up to the CID offices where Fabian intended to conduct the promised interview.

When Fabian casually mentioned Jenkins's name, he saw the way Geraghty's eyes became defiant. Fabian sensed that whatever else may have been sinful and rotten in their young lives, these two ex-borstal boys would die for each other.

In preparation for Geraghty's statement, Hodge filled in the blank spaces on the opening page of a sheaf of witness forms.

'Would you care to make a statement as to your movements on 25 April?' Fabian asked Geraghty.

'You mentioned the Queensway job to me. I know something about that,' Geraghty replied. He then agreed to tell Fabian what he knew.

Once Fabian had cautioned Geraghty, Hodge wrote, 'I have been cautioned that I need not make a statement unless I wish to do so, and that anything I do say will be taken down in writing and may be used in evidence.'

Hodge left a space for Geraghty to sign this. Geraghty's signature was compact and legible.

He began his statement by outlining the background to the Queensway robbery. From about Tuesday 22 April to Monday 5 May, he said, he hadn't turned up at the building site where he'd been working. 'There was no particular reason. I just felt like staying away.'

Clutching a fountain pen, Hodge scribbled down what he was saying. As he did so, Hodge corrected most of the inevitable contractions, lending the statement a formal, slightly stilted quality. 'On Thursday 24 April 1947,' Hodge transcribed, 'I went to the Three Horseshoes Public House near Clerkenwell Green at about eleven o'clock in the morning. I had arranged to meet Harry Jenkins and Joe Gillam there. I had known Jenkins for about a year.'

Geraghty said Jenkins and Gillam had become friends of his while they were at Sherwood Borstal. Before he was freed in November 1946, they had, according to Geraghty, made arrangements to meet him when they, too, were let out on parole. As planned, he had been waiting for them at St Pancras Station on the day of their release—Wednesday 23 April 1947. Geraghty told Fabian and Hodge that he and his friends had gone for a drink the following lunchtime in the Saloon Bar of the Three Horseshoes. When he'd got there, he said, Jenkins had introduced him to Bill Walsh. They had stayed there for about three and a half hours, during which he recalled that Walsh had suggested they collaborate on 'a stick-up'.

Already there was a conspicuous discrepancy between this version of events and the one offered by Walsh. Each of the suspects was, predictably, portraying someone else as the instigator.

'After a little discussion, me and Gillam agreed to go in with him,' Geraghty said. 'Harry Jenkins turned it down. Bill Walsh then told us he had a place to do somewhere in Queensway, Bayswater. I asked him what sort of place it was and he said a jeweller's.' Geraghty mentioned previously checking that Walsh had a gun. 'Walsh said he had one, an automatic. I said I'd got a gun and told him it was a .45 revolver. Walsh asked Gillam if he had got a gun and he said "No". Walsh then said, "Well, you had better

*Chris Geraghty with a police escort. (Copyright: Mirrorpix)*

do the driving." We all agreed that we should wear caps and masks, which we intended to get rid of as soon as we had done the job.'

Prior to leaving the pub at closing-time, Geraghty explained, they'd arranged to meet the following day—Friday 25 April. Geraghty said that they had, as intended, met at lunchtime in the Saloon Bar where Jenkins had unexpectedly joined them for a quick drink. 'Walsh, Gillam, and I left at about half-past one,' Geraghty continued. 'Us three went straight by tube to Queen's Road Underground Station, got out and went and had a look at the jeweller's. I don't know the name of the shop.'

He went on to itemise the clothes worn by him and the gang. 'I was dressed in a blue overcoat, blue serge suit, and I had a blue cap in my pocket. I was also wearing a white silk scarf. Walsh was dressed in a raincoat, I think, a grey chalk-striped suit and a cap. I think he had a scarf as well. Gillam had a blue raincoat and a green trilby.'

Geraghty described how, when they had arrived at Bayswater Underground Station, Walsh had told them to wait while he sized up the shop they were planning to rob. 'I saw him walk into the jeweller's and come out after a few minutes. When he came back to us at the tube station, Walsh said, "There are only two men in there. It's easy." The three of us then walked around a square nearby to sort out a car to do the job with.

In a back street we came across an unattended car, and Gillam unlocked the car door. He already had the keys to fit. Walsh and I got in and Gillam drove us up to outside the jeweller's shop we'd sorted out. Walsh asked me if I had my gun on me and I said "Yes." It was already loaded. I had the gun since last December. Walsh told me he had his gun ready, and I think he said it was loaded.'

Geraghty recounted how he, Gillam, and Walsh had already worked out what they were going to do once they were inside the shop. 'Me and Walsh had put on our masks before going in. I mean we used our scarves as masks. As we got into the shop, I saw two customers inside—a man and a woman. They were being attended to by an assistant.' Geraghty described how he and Walsh had pulled out their guns and threatened the customers and staff. He added that Gillam had, in the meantime, gathered up the jewellery in the shop window, transferred it into a paper bag and walked back to the getaway car. Geraghty explained that Gillam had honked the car horn twice in a pre-arranged signal for the others to leave the shop. They had, he said, run out of the shop, then driven off at high speed and abandoned the car near a railway bridge.

'We all three jumped on a bus, took three halfpenny fares and, I think, got off somewhere near Maida Vale. There were some public lavatories where we got off the bus, and Walsh and I went inside. Gillam waited outside.' Geraghty stated that while they were in the basement lavatories Walsh had transferred the contents of the paper bag into his shirt. 'Then he asked me for my gun and said he was going to dump it. I gave it to him. We went up into the street and joined Gillam and then we all three got on a bus and went to Victoria. We went into the buffet and Walsh said we had better wait there for a couple of minutes. The time then would be just turned four o'clock. We had a lemonade. Walsh left us in the buffet and said he was going out to phone the buyer.'

Echoing Walsh's otherwise contradictory statement, Geraghty revealed that the older man hadn't returned to the buffet. Walsh had, instead, double-crossed them by absconding with the proceeds from the hold-up. On realising what had happened, Geraghty said, he and Gillam had gone over to Riverside Mansions to see Jenkins. Geraghty offered no explanation for this, creating a suspicious gap in the story. It implied that Jenkins had been involved in the robbery and that Geraghty was trying to shield him.

'When we got there, we saw a sister of Harry Jenkins's wife and she told us that Walsh and Harry Jenkins and his wife had just left for Southend,' Geraghty said. 'Gillam then left me and I think he went home. I told him I was going to try and find out the address where Walsh had gone to in Southend. I went to Harry Jenkins's mother's address. It was somewhere in south London, but I don't know the exact address. I could take you there. I saw Harry Jenkins's sister Mary there. And she said that Harry had phoned her and told her he was off to Southend but she didn't know exactly where.'

Geraghty mentioned staying the night with another of Jenkins's sisters, Mrs Kemp, and her husband, then going back to Riverside Mansions the following day, by which time Jenkins had returned home. 'I asked him where Walsh was, and he said he had blown from Southend and didn't know where he was.' Geraghty went on to describe meeting Gillam the next day and talking over what had taken place. 'That's all I can tell you about the Bayswater job. I never had any jewellery or anything out of it and I am pretty certain Gillam didn't.'

There was, it seemed, nothing more for Geraghty to tell Fabian and Hodge. All of a sudden, though, he started talking again. 'I would like to say from the start of the planning of the job I had no intention of firing my gun at anybody in the shop but, if I had to, I would have fired at the ceiling just to frighten anybody.' He said he hadn't seen Walsh or Gillam since the events he had spoken about. In addition he trotted out his alibi for the day of the Charlotte Street shooting when he claimed he'd been bedridden with a bad attack of boils. To emphasise the severity of his illness, he assured the detectives that he hadn't been out of his house until Sunday 4 May or Monday 5 May.

He was then shown the raincoat found at Brook House and asked about it. He replied that it was his coat, though Fabian knew that it belonged to Jenkins's brother-in-law, Tom Kemp. Geraghty assured the detectives that he'd worn it on the afternoon of the Queensway robbery. He said he'd later left it behind at the Kemps' flat when he had stayed there.

Before Fabian brought the interview to a close, Hodge displayed an assortment of revolvers and automatic pistols obtained in the course of the investigation into the Queensway robbery. Hodge asked Geraghty if any of the guns belonged to him. Geraghty pointed to a .45 revolver in a homemade holster. Tape had been wrapped round the butt. 'It's the one I used in the hold-up,' he told Hodge.

❖

Around the time Geraghty was making his statement, a crowd of press photographers, representing publications as varied as the *News of the World* and the *Sunday Dispatch*, had formed on one of the platforms at King's Cross Station. They'd been tipped-off that the train carrying Doris Hart would be arriving shortly. When it pulled into the station, brakes hissing, smoke billowing, she was escorted from a reserved compartment by two police officers, one male, the other female. Embarrassed by her predicament, she held a handkerchief over her face as she was led through the gauntlet of photographers taking flashlit pictures. She wore a tightly belted, three-quarter-length camel-hair coat, her wavy blonde hair brushing its padded shoulders. From under her coat, a grey dress with a stripes round the hem protruded.

Still hiding her face behind her handkerchief, she was taken to a waiting squad car. She was then driven to Tottenham Court Road Police Station where Fabian and Higgins questioned her for three hours about her involvement with Walsh.

❖

During what remained of that evening, Fabian and his team had a chance to go through Geraghty's signed statement in search of discrepancies and aspects of it that would need verifying. The inconsistencies centred on three areas.

First, Geraghty and Walsh disagreed on the identity of the three men who had carried out the Queensway robbery. Geraghty had insisted that the gang had comprised himself, Walsh and Gillam. But Walsh had named himself, Geraghty, Gillam and Jenkins as the culprits. Not that the police believed him.

The second major discrepancy concerned the immediate aftermath of the robbery. In Walsh's account, the gang had gone to Southend to sell the stolen goods to Mr and Mrs Birchall. Geraghty had, on the other hand, concocted a story that avoided any mention of the Birchalls. What's more, it contradicted the evidence that he and Gillam had been in Southend on the night of the robbery.

A third even more significant area of doubt involved Geraghty's alibi for the day on which Antiquis had been murdered. Near the end of his statement he had declared that he'd been housebound and off work on Tuesday 29 April due to illness. Earlier in his testimony, though, he had referred to how he'd failed to turn up to work because he 'just felt like staying away.'

❖

At midnight Fabian shifted the focus of the investigation onto Gillam who, after twelve hours languishing in the cells, was brought up to the CID offices. Fabian questioned him about his movements on Friday 25 April.

'I suppose someone has talked about the job at Queensway,' Gillam replied. 'I didn't get anything out of it but had better tell you what part I took in it.'

Before Gillam said anything else, Fabian cautioned him. Fabian then asked Gillam whether he'd like to make a written statement.

'Yes, you write it down and I'll tell you.'

Detective Sergeant Lewis was sitting nearby, ready to transcribe whatever Gillam said.

Gillam embarked on a self-serving preamble about how, in June 1945, he had been sent to Sherwood Borstal where he'd struck up a friendship with Jenkins and Geraghty. 'I did this mainly because Harryboy was the guvnor up there and he had a certain amount of persuasion with the other boys and I didn't want to get in his bad books.'

He said that he and Jenkins had taken the train back to London together after they'd been released from borstal. Confirming what Geraghty had already told Fabian, Gillam described the encounter in the Three Horseshoes pub and the subsequent discussion about the proposed robbery. Like Geraghty and Walsh, he presented himself as a bit-part player in the Queensway raid—in his case someone who had been bullied into it by Walsh and Jenkins.

*Doris Hart arrives at King's Cross Station on Saturday 17 May 1947. (Copyright: N.M.S.I.)*

Fabian and Lewis were then treated to Gillam's detailed account of the run-up to the robbery, of how the gang had walked round Bayswater looking for a car to steal. Contrary to Walsh's statement, Gillam claimed not to have been carrying a gun.

For the next few minutes he talked about what had occurred inside the shop. His portrait of events differed from Geraghty's in certain crucial respects, namely the involvement of Jenkins and the absence of any reference to Walsh. If Gillam was to be believed, Jenkins and Geraghty had burst into the shop, masks over their faces, guns drawn. He said that he remembered them announcing, 'This is a stick-up' and 'One squeal and you've had it...'

Striving to win the detectives' sympathy, Gillam mentioned how he had pleaded with Geraghty not to kill one of the shop's staff. 'I ought to say that the reason I said, "Don't kill him, don't kill him", was because I knew that they would stop at nothing and I didn't want any shooting or bloodshed.'

Lewis had, by then, covered three-quarters of the seventh page of a stack of statement forms. As Gillam moved on to outline their getaway, in the process substantiating Geraghty's account, Lewis began to fill the remaining lines. Gillam said that he, Geraghty and Jenkins had ended up in the buffet at Victoria Railway Station. He described how Jenkins had left them, ostensibly for a brief appointment at the nearby Borstal Association headquarters, from where he had failed to return. In the hope of tracking down Jenkins, Gillam said he and Geraghty had gone over to Riverside Mansions that evening, only to hear that Jenkins and Walsh had just left for Southend with the proceeds from the robbery. Gillam admitted that he and Geraghty had followed Jenkins and Walsh.

'I ought to say we had no address to go to in Southend, only a phone number that Chris had in his pocket. We arrived at Southend round about 10:00pm. We came out of the station and took the second turning right, I think, to the phone box. Chris asked me to ring the number, but after trying several times the operator said there was no such number.' On emerging from the phone box, Gillam added, a Police Constable had approached them and enquired what they were doing. That was the moment, recorded in one of the Southend Occurrence Books, when the Constable had asked to see their identity cards. 'We both produced our cards and Chris explained that we were trying to get in contact with some friends of ours down there. The Constable was satisfied with our cards and the story. We walked down the road a little bit further and Chris then said to me, "I don't like the look of it down there. It looks too hot. Let's get back to the Smoke." I have an idea that Chris ditched the gun down there, but I am not sure about this. We then caught about the last train back to London. We arrived at Fenchurch Street around twelve o'clock and Chris asked me if he could come and stay at my place for the night. I didn't really want him to come, but he was in a bad mood and I eventually let him. When I got home, my father wouldn't let him stay, as he didn't like the look of him, but eventually we slept out in the back garden.'

Gillam declared that he didn't see Jenkins again until he and Geraghty paid a visit to Riverside Mansions on the afternoon of Sunday 26 April. 'Harry was in a raving temper, saying that Bill Walsh had turned him over for the gear. This really didn't concern me much. All I wanted to do was break away from them and get a job and go straight.'

He maintained that he hadn't seen either of them since. As if he was already in front of a jury, pleading for a lenient sentence, Gillam went on to set out a few mitigating factors. 'I would like to say that I have been driving for a firm of haulage contractors for the past fortnight and when I left Sherwood I made my mind up to keep out of trouble and run straight, but I am afraid that I was not strong-willed enough to turn down the job at the jeweller's, owing to the fact that those two people had me in their clutches.'

❖

After Gillam had been returned to his cell at about 1:00am, Fabian and Hodge switched their attention back to Geraghty. This time they concentrated on questioning him about the raid on Jay's and the Antiquis murder.

At length he admitted that he'd been part of the gang. He agreed to make another statement, but he had to be cautioned again before they allowed him to go ahead. With that formality out of the way, he was asked how the gang had obtained the guns used in the raid.

He said that he and Terry Rolt and another fellow he didn't want to mention had, late on the night of Saturday 26 April, burgled a gunsmith's on Union Street. 'I don't know the name of the place. We climbed over a back wall and broke in through the roof. We stayed in the premises all night and came out at roughly eleven o'clock Sunday morning with a quantity of guns and ammunition. We all three separated and I went home on Sunday night. I was carrying two of the guns we had stolen. One was a .45 and the other a .32. Before separating, we all made arrangements to meet on the following Tuesday.'

Geraghty told the detectives that he and the others had met outside Whitechapel Tube Station at about eleven o'clock that morning. He said they'd taken a train to Goodge Street where they had got out and looked at various jeweller's shops before earmarking Jay's as their target. To avoid the lunchtime rush, they had killed time by going for something to eat first. 'We went into a café and had a meal and, when we came out, Rolt and the other fellow went to look for a car. I looked at the jeweller's shop—I mean Jay's—and decided it could not be done because there was too many people in the shop and too many doors.'

The sound of Geraghty's voice was accompanied by the frantic rasp of Hodge's pen on the statement sheets. Geraghty added that, about a quarter of an hour later, they had gone back to Jay's. 'As we were walking, I said to the other fellow, "Walk straight past. It's too big for us to do." He just said, "Okay." Meanwhile, Rolt drove the car up the road—I mean

Tottenham Street—pulled up outside Jay's, got out, and before we could get to him, he walked straight in. Of course we had to back him up then and couldn't leave him on his own.'

All three of them, he explained, had been carrying loaded guns, stolen from the shop on Union Street. He claimed that they had only planned to shoot in the air to scare anyone who got in their way.

He said, 'The other fellow run into Jay's after Rolt, with the intention of dragging him out. I run round the other door—I mean the side door—and Rolt and the other fellow, seeing me go in, they went in by the Pledge entrance. I was wearing my silk scarf as a mask and I know the other two had masks on. When I got in the shop, I heard a scuffling from the Pledge side and a lot of people ran out of the offices and came straight at me. I fired one of my guns up into the air and the people stopped. Then I heard someone say, "Get out into the car!", from the Pledge side, so I run out into the street and we all three got into the car. As we got in, a van drew up in the middle of the road, stopping us from going forward. Rolt was too flustered to reverse...' Geraghty allowed the sentence to trail off. 'Me and the other fellow got out of the car and Rolt was halfway across Charlotte Street by the time we reached the corner. A motorcyclist—I don't know whether he was riding it or pushing it... I think he was riding—got in our way and I fired my .32 off, intending to frighten him. I saw him drop off the motorbike and fall in the gutter.'

Geraghty's uncertainty about the details suggested that he might be telling the truth. For experienced detectives like Fabian and Hodge, a suspect's ability to recall every little incident tended to undermine credibility.

'I was so frightened I ran off down Charlotte Street towards Euston Road,' Geraghty admitted. 'I don't know which way Rolt and the other fellow ran. I turned first right and stopped running and I got on a bus in Tottenham Court Road, going towards Camden Town. At Camden Town I got on the tube and went to Wapping, where I threw both guns in the river on the foreshore.'

The detectives asked him what he'd been wearing that afternoon.

'A grey pinstripe suit.' He told Fabian and Hodge that he'd worn it in combination with a cap and blue RAF raincoat, all of which he had burnt. 'I also got rid of the ashes.'

Here was the final element necessary to confirm that Jenkins had left the raincoat at Brook House. Geraghty's earlier insistence on being the owner of the coat must have been nothing more than a misguided attempt to shield his friend, his loyalty towards whom was unshaken by the aftermath of the Queensway robbery. As Fabian knew by then, Jenkins had joined

Walsh in double-crossing Gillam and Geraghty, then been double-crossed himself. Somehow Jenkins had succeeded in persuading the stalwart but gullible Geraghty that his sudden disappearance wasn't an act of betrayal.

In a panicky epilogue, Geraghty declared that he hadn't seen either Rolt or the 'other fellow' since the day of the shooting. This was, however, patently untrue. A surveillance officer had, after all, reported to Fabian about a meeting between Geraghty, Rolt and Jenkins during the first weekend in May.

'Nobody tackled me when I was running away, except the motorcyclist who swerved towards me,' Geraghty informed the detectives. 'I didn't mean to injure him. My sole purpose in firing was to frighten him. I only fired two shots, one in Jay's and one in Charlotte Street.'

This was the cue for him to be shown the two revolvers found on the Thames foreshore. These, he acknowledged, were the guns that had been stolen from the shop on Union Street and carried during the raid on Jay's. 'I haven't got anything else to say...'

❖

Fresh from interviewing Geraghty, Fabian left the investigation headquarters at 2:00am on Sunday 18 May. Along with Higgins and Hodge, he was chauffeured round to Rolt's home in Bermondsey, a district where the V-2 rockets fired by the Germans had wrecked dozens of homes. On confronting Rolt, who had just got out of bed, Fabian said, 'Since we saw you before, we have made further enquiries and wish you to come along with us to Tottenham Court Road Police Station, respecting the murder and armed hold-up at Charlotte Street on 29 April. I'm not satisfied with your explanations of your movements on that day.'

The ashen-faced Rolt was promptly cautioned.

'I'll come along,' he replied. 'Don't wake mother...'

With the detectives loitering in the flat, Rolt put on some clothes, topped by a raincoat. Next to the CID men, all old enough to be his father, he looked small and child-like: scarcely the obvious candidate for involvement in a murder and armed robbery.

Fabian had heard a great deal of talk about why youngsters had, over the past few years, been committing so many violent crimes. All sorts of credible explanations had been put forward. There was the disruption to the education system caused by evacuation from the cities and by bomb damage to schools. There was the shortage of playing fields and other healthy alternatives to hanging round on street corners. There was the possible influence of violent crime movies. And there was the inevitable cheapening of life inherent in wartime. Fabian could see why some people, who believed in birching as a deterrent, were arguing for the ban on it to be lifted. But he felt that the best cure for the problem would be to restore the number of constables on street patrol to its pre-war level.

When Fabian and the other detectives got back to the police station shortly before 3:00am, they were quick to apply psychological pressure on Rolt. They informed him that Geraghty had made a statement implicating him. This revelation didn't, however, precipitate an instant confession.

Rolt was taken to a room adjacent to where his brother, Ted, was also being held for questioning. For the next three hours Fabian and Higgins, who seemed tired and irritable, appear to have cross-examined Rolt about his suspected involvement in the Antiquis killing. Given that Rolt had not yet been charged with any crime, this would have been a breech of Judges' Rules, significant enough to shed doubt on the contents of his subsequent statement.

With dawn breaking over the West End, Rolt's resistance finally subsided. 'I knew it must come out,' he said. 'I see you've got Chris. I bungled it. I'll tell you what happened. Chris never meant to kill that man...'

Fabian interrupted the boy's confession and asked if he'd care to have it written down.

He agreed.

This time Higgins adopted the secretarial role, pen poised over the first page of a statement form.

Before the detectives permitted Rolt to resume his confession, he was cautioned again.

Rolt began his statement by recounting the genesis of his friendship with Jenkins which dated back nearly two years. Through Jenkins, he said that he'd 'met a fellow named Walsh.' He also said that Jenkins had, on a different occasion, introduced him to Geraghty. In describing a drink he'd had with Jenkins and Geraghty the day before the Antiquis murder, Rolt added, 'I heard Chris say he would like to get his hands on someone for turning him over. I understood from the conversation that someone had taken money or stuff belonging to them. They were talking about where the man might be, and I thought they were talking about the man Walsh.'

He went on to tell the detectives how he had joined Geraghty and Jenkins that evening for a drink in a local pub. 'We were talking of the money situation and asked one another how each was fixed. We didn't have much between us and, while talking, I said I wouldn't mind getting some money either one way or another. We went on drinking until nine o'clock when I left and went home, arranging to meet Harry and Chris the following day—29 April.'

On the morning of the robbery, he explained, he'd gone round to

Riverside Mansions, where the possibility of staging a hold-up had first been discussed. 'I turned round and said that I would try anything once,' Rolt admitted. He revealed that he'd suggested they use some guns he had previously stolen from a shop in Southwark. He neglected to mention that the raid on the gunsmith's had been committed with the help of Geraghty and Jenkins.

Ready for the hold-up at Jay's, Rolt said, they'd decided to steal a car which they could abandon later. 'I was to drive the car and, when Harry and Chris had held the shop assistant up, I was to clear the window out. Harry told me it was a jeweller's shop we were to hold-up. I left them some time that morning and arranged to meet them again at Riverside Mansions with the guns. Chris told me to put some shots in the guns just to frighten anyone.'

Rolt described how he'd gone round to a derelict house on Fair Street in Bermondsey where he had hidden the stolen guns and ammunition. He said that he'd returned to Riverside Mansions at about midday and handed a .32 to Jenkins, plus two of the other revolvers to Geraghty. He had kept a .38 for himself. From Riverside Mansions, he told the detectives, the gang had travelled to Jay's. Their plan had been to speed away from the scene of the crime in a stolen car, park it outside Goodge Street Underground Station, and catch the tube home. He said that once they'd taken a look at the shop they had nipped back to Goodge Street and bought three homeward-bound tickets. 'We then returned to the jeweller's and found there were too many people about to do the job then. Harry and Chris had not then had their dinner, so they went into a restaurant a couple of turnings away from Jay's shop. Harry Jenkins told me to go round to the shop to see how much jewellery there was in the window and find the amount it would come to. I left them in the restaurant and went alone to Jay's and looked in the window. I had a quick reckoning up and it came to £2,000 or just over.'

Fabian and his colleagues were given an account of how the gang had stolen a Vauxhall Saloon. 'Harry then told us what to do. Him and Chris were to walk down to Jay's. Chris was to go into one entrance, and me and Harry in the other. I was to take the Vauxhall car and drive to Jay's, where they would be waiting to go into the shop as soon as I arrived.'

Following these instructions, Rolt said, he'd parked the car on the corner opposite Jays. He explained that Jenkins and Geraghty had soon walked into view, but they'd disappeared by the time he had started the engine. Here Rolt's version of events diverged from Geraghty's which had tried to shift some of the blame onto Rolt.

'I drove the motor to outside Jay's, jumped out and went into the entrance,' Rolt said. 'But I couldn't see Harry or Chris and everything was quiet. I was just going to leave the shop entrance when Harry came rushing in. He said, "Chris is round the other entrance." I could see three or four cubicles inside the shop and, after opening one of the cubicle doors, I went inside with Harry and jumped over the counter. There was a young fellow and an old man there behind the counter. I told the young fellow not to make a sound and pointed my gun at him. He then said, "Okay, chum" or words to that effect.

'Harry then pushed the young fellow through a door into another room. The old fellow, who was deaf, didn't seem to know what was happening, so I poked him one and said, "Get over there", pointing to the other room. I had them covered with my gun. The old man then went out of my way and I then heard a commotion in the shop near the door where Chris had come in.'

Rolt recounted hearing a gunshot, heralding the appearance of another old man who had rushed through from the same part of the building as Geraghty. All of this tied in with what Fabian and his officers already knew. So did Rolt's ensuing account of how he'd vaulted the counter and climbed into the getaway car, only to find a lorry had just blocked the road.

Fabian had never been able to work out why the gang had abandoned the car instead of putting the gears into reverse and speeding away. The explanation would have been amusing were it not for the tragic consequences. Rolt was such a novice driver that he hadn't known how to put the vehicle into reverse.

'I then got out of the car and started running,' Rolt said. 'I could see Harry just in front of me, and Chris was by my side. We ran to the corner and saw a motorcyclist driving his motorcycle towards us. There was a lot of shouting at this time. The motorcyclist missed me and I ran on. I could see he was trying to trip us up. After running a few yards I heard a shot.'

Rolt proceeded to tell the detectives about the moment when a passer-by had attempted to stop him from escaping. Probably out of pride, he omitted any mention of being rescued by Jenkins. He merely said that he'd managed to retrieve the gun before he had continued running in the same direction as Jenkins. Together, he told the detectives, they had fled into an office block—Brook House. Rolt described going into an upstairs store-room where Jenkins dumped his cap and raincoat.

As they were on their way down the staircase, he said, they had crossed paths with an office boy. 'Harry Jenkins and I then went out of the block and walked round until we found a main road. We jumped on a bus and went to a tube station. I think it was the Strand. Harry then bought two tickets for Liverpool Street Station and we both went to that station. From there, I caught a 78 bus, leaving Harry to make his own way. He told me to go home and not to call on him until he sent for me. I went home and changed my suit, then went and flung the car keys, guns and bullets into the Thames at the pier by the Tower of London.'

Higgins's wrist must have been aching from the effort of transcribing Rolt's statement which had started a quarter of an hour or more earlier.

'I didn't see Harry again until the Saturday morning,' Rolt said. 'He told me Chris was all right, that he hadn't heard anything from the police and he thought it would die down after a while. I forgot to mention that while we were in Jay's shop Harry dropped his gun, or so he told me. When I met him on the Saturday following the affair, he said he didn't know for sure how the motorcyclist had got killed.

'After the job at Jay's I went to the empty house in Fair Street and took all the guns and ammunition I had hidden there and threw them in the Thames.' He added that he had stolen three shotguns and some boxes of cartridges during the raid on the gunsmith's. These had been too heavy for him to carry, so he'd buried them under some rubble on a bomb-site. Anxious to make a good impression, he completed his statement by saying to Hodge, 'I would like you to put down that I was desperate for money when I went on the job at Jay's, otherwise I wouldn't have dreamt of doing it.'

Once Rolt had read and signed Hodge's transcript, he said, 'About those guns I told you about. If you like, I'll take you and show you where I put them.'

❖

Shocked by what she'd heard about Walsh's ruthless associates, Doris Hart had been terrified that they'd seek retribution against her for cooperating with Fabian's investigation, so she had demanded police protection. Overnight she'd been allowed to stay at Tottenham Court Road Police Station. The following morning—Sunday 18 May—she was told to go home, but she refused because her fears hadn't been allayed. The police had to arrange for an Essex hospital to provide her with a safe haven. When she was driven there, reassurance was offered by a police escort, comprising a Woman Police Constable and two other officers.

❖

Along with a handful of reporters, Higgins was standing on Tower Bridge Pier. They were watching a boat from the Met's Thames Division perform an underwater search known as 'a magnet drag'. This technique, utilising a powerful electro-magnet, had first been tried almost two years earlier

*Officers from the Thames Division magnet-drag the Thames.*
*(Copyright: Metropolitan Police Historical Collection)*

during the hunt for the killer of Frank 'The Duke' Everitt, a London taxi-driver and small-time blackmarketeer whose bullet-holed body had been abandoned on Lambeth Bridge. Though the operation had lasted six days, the murder weapon had never been found.

The current magnet drag was equally unproductive. Despite Rolt's claim that he'd dumped some of the stolen guns in that stretch of the river, none of them had surfaced. Perhaps Rolt hadn't been telling the truth. Perhaps he had kept the guns and secreted them somewhere. Perhaps he hadn't thrown them very far into the river and they'd been exposed at low tide and fished out by someone else. Or, perhaps, the river's current, sufficiently powerful to make swimming hazardous, had washed them away. If that had happened, the guns wouldn't, at least, have fallen into the wrong hands. They would, instead, have been lying safely on the riverbed with all the other rusting detritus.

❖

On the strength of the evidence and statements obtained by the investigation team, a warrant had been issued for Jenkins's arrest. Later that Sunday, Rolt asked to see Charles O'Connor, the solicitor acting on behalf of both him and Jenkins. In an infringement of Rolt's legal rights, Higgins refused. The detective had good reasons for this, though. He feared that O'Connor would tip-off Jenkins, making him even harder to find.

At roughly 3:45pm, Higgins spoke to Rolt, who was still being held in the cells at Tottenham Court Road Police Station. The detective raised the subject of the stolen shotguns and asked Rolt whether he was still in the same cooperative frame of mind.

Rolt said that he was.

'I'll take you out, and you can show me where you hid them,' Higgins replied.

Not long after that, Rolt was en route to the spot where he claimed to have buried the guns. He was accompanied by Higgins as well as a couple of other officers, recruited to deter him from trying to escape.

The police vehicle in which Rolt was travelling drove down Union Street, a busy road lined with small shops. F. Dyke & Co., the gunsmith's that had been robbed by Rolt and Geraghty, was close to the junction with Redcross Way. The bomb-site named by Rolt was next-door. Gesturing towards a pile of bricks and rubble in the corner of the wrecked building, he said that was where he'd hidden the guns. Higgins noticed that the rubble showed some signs of recent movement. But the guns were no longer there.

❖

It was three days since Walsh had been arrested. During that time he had been allowed to stew over the grim prospect of a long spell in gaol. On top of the likely indictment for his role in the Queensway robbery, he now faced six more charges. These were for burglaries he had committed in Southend and surrounding villages, crimes that had netted him over £500 worth of goods: everything from a Smith & Wesson revolver and a set of War Savings Certificates to valuable clothing coupons and rolls of material.

He'd clearly reached the conclusion that the judge might not give him such a stiff sentence if he cooperated with the police and told them what he knew about the raid on Jay's. With that incentive, he volunteered to make another statement.

'I have decided to tell the truth, so far as I know, about the hold-up at a jeweller's shop not far from Goodge Street Tube Station,' he informed Higgins, who was writing down what he was saying. 'I don't know the name of the shop or even the name of the street, but what I do know is this...' Walsh paused before describing how, on Thursday 24 April, he had been with Jenkins in a Clerkenwell pub—the Three Horseshoes. While they were there, he explained, Jenkins had introduced him to Geraghty and Gillam whose nickname was 'Handy'. This was consistent with what the investigation team had already heard. True to form, Walsh did his best to deflect the blame by claiming that it wasn't his idea to carry out the stick-up job at Jay's.

Together with the others, Walsh said, he'd left the pub and gone over to Whitechapel before heading back to Clerkenwell for dinner in a local café. 'The four of us—Harry Jenkins, Chris, Handy, and myself—then went to Goodge Street Station. We came out of the station, turned left, then left again. We were then looking round for a likely place I understood they wanted to stick-up. Chris and I walked along one side of the street behind the other two. When they reached a jeweller's and pawnbroker's which is on the corner of a street on the righthand side, Harry and Handy stopped outside the jeweller's shop, looking in the window. Chris and I met them there and we all looked in the window at the display. I remember the shop because it is a double-fronted place.'

He said that he and the rest of the gang had walked a short distance down the street before discussing what they'd seen. 'One of the others, I am not sure which, said there was some good stuff in the shop window.'

Walsh launched into an account of how they had boarded a bus, disembarking at an underground station where he and Jenkins had parted from Gillam and Geraghty. He added that he and Jenkins had later met up with Geraghty in a café near Farringdon Road Underground Station in Clerkenwell. 'I should mention this is the café I thought was in Aldgate and which I mentioned in my previous statement. I get mixed up between Farringdon Road and Aldgate.' Walsh said that the three of them had gone from the café to the house in Kilburn where Gillam lived. 'I have already told you what happened after that,' he said to Higgins.

The detective showed him the grubby coat and cap which had been found at Brook House. Quizzed about these items, Walsh declared that Geraghty had been wearing them on the day of the Queensway robbery. 'I can say that I have never been lent any coat or mackintosh by Harry Jenkins or anyone else in London.'

Higgins also showed him both the jewelled bracelet that he'd given his wife and the raincoat that Rolt had been wearing on the afternoon of the raid on Jay's. Walsh said he didn't recognise the raincoat, but he confessed to stealing the bracelet. 'It came from the Queensway job,' he admitted.

❖

On weekdays Robert Churchill, who lived with his doting second wife in the Kent town of Crayford, always followed the same early morning ritual. He liked to head over to his shooting-range where he'd switch on his clay-pigeon trap. As the targets were sent spinning into the air, Churchill—who was a crack shot—unleashed volley after volley until he'd exhausted his supply of 150 cartridges. So regularly was he required to cushion the butt of his shotgun against the recoil that the muscles in his left arm bulged if he clenched his fist.

This cacophonous overture to the day completed, Churchill caught the 8:15am train to London, usually boarding it at the last moment, breathless from the rush. The train took him to Charing Cross Station, which was within easy walking distance of his shop. Most afternoons he'd leave Jim Chewter in charge and return to his shooting-range, where he instructed pupils in marksmanship. Whenever the police phoned him at home about an urgent case, he'd return to London, not by train but by car, impatiently piloting his gargantuan old two-seater Buick.

That weekend's developments in the Antiquis case prompted the police to contact him again. To verify what both Geraghty and Rolt had claimed about the robbery of the gunsmith's on Union Street, Churchill was asked to go round to the shop and examine its stock. He compared the cartridges sold by F. Dyke & Co. with the ammunition that had been found in the revolvers linked to the Antiquis case. All the ammunition in those three handguns, he was able to confirm, matched ammunition stocked by the shop.

❖

Seeking to consolidate the evidence against Walsh, Gillam, Rolt and Geraghty, Fabian and his team organised the biggest series of identification parades so far staged in London. These were held at Tottenham Court Road Police Station. More than two dozen witnesses to the Charlotte Street or Queensway robberies attended them. The parades lasted several hours, yet the police were unable to secure a positive identification of any of the suspects.

A meeting was arranged at Scotland Yard, enabling Fabian, Sir Ronald Howe and Commander Hugh Young to discuss whether there was sufficient evidence to proceed with legal action against the four men already in custody. Despite the failure of any of the witnesses to pick out the suspects, Fabian and his colleagues decided to press charges as soon as Jenkins was arrested.

Towards the end of that afternoon, the police heard that Jenkins was hiding at Tom and Vera Kemp's flat on Paradise Street. Not the most obvious hideout, bearing in mind its proximity to Rotherhithe Police Station.

At about 6:00pm a squad car pulled up outside 23 Paradise Street, the plain, triple bay-fronted early nineteenth-century building that housed the local police station. Fabian and Hodge were in the car, together with a couple of other detectives.

While Fabian and Hodge waited near the car, a junior officer— Detective Sergeant Percy Woollway—walked past the Queen's Head pub and into the block of flats where the Kemps lived. Woollway was soon talking to Jenkins. 'Chief Inspector Fabian wants to see you respecting certain matters that have come to light since he last saw you.'

As they walked to the squad car, Jenkins said, 'What is it? D'you know?'

Eager to demonstrate how composed and unflappable he was, Jenkins started crooning the incongruous opening lines of *Sentimental Journey*, the lilting song that had scored a hit for the young Doris Day a few years earlier.

With Jenkins safely stowed in the squad car, Woollway fetched Fabian and Hodge who had disappeared into the police station. When they reappeared, Fabian spoke to Jenkins. 'As a result of further enquiries and investigations made, I shall now arrest you for being concerned in the Charlotte Street murder and attempted robbery.'

Fabian then cautioned him.

'I don't know what all this is about,' Jenkins replied. Evidently taken aback by what had just happened, he protested that he hadn't been picked out at the identification parade. He seemed to assume that this had rendered him immune from arrest.

❖

Less than an hour after he'd left the Kemps' flat, the car carrying Jenkins drove into the back yard of Tottenham Court Road Police Station. The press had got wind of the fact that the police were poised to charge Jenkins, Geraghty and Rolt for the Antiquis murder, so the entrance to the yard was crowded with reporters and press photographers, whose presence had attracted inquisitive passers-by. Police officers continually tried to disperse what was fast becoming a sprawling crowd, but it kept regathering. Jenkins eyed the waiting throng haughtily through a side window like a movie star arriving at a film première, his impassive features betraying nothing more than mild curiosity.

From the car, he was shepherded through the station's rear entrance. This opened straight into the Charge Room, a large, cheerless room traversed by a sturdy, pine counter, known as the 'Charge Desk'.

Under the satisfied gaze of Fabian and Higgins, Jenkins was lined up alongside Geraghty and Rolt. The prisoners were facing the counter, manned by the Station Sergeant.

'As a result of enquiries made,' Higgins said to the prisoners, 'you are now going to be charged with the murder of Alec de Antiquis at Charlotte Street on 29 April.'

Higgins cautioned them.

Jenkins didn't reply, but his companions couldn't resist filling the awkward silence.

'I've already made a statement,' Geraghty declared.

'I've told you the truth,' Rolt assured everyone.

At 7:20pm, the Station Sergeant read out the Charge Sheet compiled by Fabian. It featured their full names, as well as the charge of 'feloniously, wilfully and of malice aforethought killing Alec de Antiquis on the 29th day of April 1947 at Charlotte Street, London W1.'

This was a charge which carried the death penalty, though Rolt could not be hanged because he was under eighteen, the age at which people were regarded as adults. If found guilty, he could nevertheless be gaoled for an indeterminate period.

He and the others also faced a charge of 'being armed with offensive weapons to wit, loaded firearms', used to 'feloniously assault Alfred Ernest Stock, director of Jay's the Jeweller's Ltd, with intent to rob him, contrary to the Larceny Act 1916, Section 23 (1a).'

Once these charges had been read out, the Station Sergeant cautioned the three prisoners. None of them said anything this time. Rolt and Jenkins were led away, their places immediately taken by Gillam and Walsh.

Geraghty and the two new additions to the line-up were now informed by Higgins that they were about to be charged with carrying out the armed robbery at Messrs A.B. Davis Ltd of Queensway on 25 April. Though Jenkins had, in all likelihood, been involved in the crime, he dodged this charge, thanks to Geraghty's insistence that he had nothing to do with it.

Higgins went on to address Walsh who faced a further charge of 'feloniously receiving' part of the proceeds of that robbery. For the third time in the space of a few minutes, the formal caution was recited. On this occasion Higgins did the reciting. When he had finished, Walsh said, 'I only stood outside, and that can be proved.' Fear scrambling his train of thought, he added, 'I took the stuff—you already know—off Jenkins...'

By 7:30pm, the last of the charges had been read out and the prisoners had been taken back to their cells. Commander Hugh Young, who had been waiting upstairs, came down and congratulated Fabian and his team.

Exhausted by the investigation which had lasted twenty days, Fabian signed off duty and went home. At last he was free to see his wife for more than a few hurried moments, free to go for a day at the races, free to play some snooker, free to catch up on his gardening, and free to enjoy a decent night's sleep, uninterrupted by phone-calls or urgent messages.

V

# ECHOES
# OF A
# GUNSHOT

The charges brought against Jenkins, Geraghty, Walsh, Gillam, and Rolt provoked a slew of headlines in both that evening's papers and the following morning's editions. These ensured substantial public and press interest in the men's first court appearance, scheduled for Tuesday 20 May, the day after their arrest. Defendants in such major criminal cases at that time faced a preliminary trial in front of a magistrate who had to decide whether the evidence warranted a full jury trial.

Once again, a sizeable crowd had assembled around the back of Tottenham Court Road Police Station, where the alleged gunmen had been held overnight. Uniformed and plain clothes officers mingled with the crowd to prevent it from coalescing into a lynch mob.

At brief intervals each of the accused was led down the steps into the yard, loaded into a waiting squad car and driven away. By splitting them up like this, the police aimed to deter any of their associates from staging a rescue attempt.

Jenkins and the others were driven to Marlborough Street Court which handled crimes committed in North Soho, Mayfair, Chelsea and Hyde Park. With the same perversity that renders English spelling so inconsistent, the court was located not on Marlborough Street but on *Great* Marlborough Street. Built in 1900 to a design by a specialist police architect, the three-storey building, adjacent to the London Palladium Theatre, featured a wide stone façade, its ground-floor punctuated by tall, bow-fronted windows. The impression of grandeur was accentuated by the royal coat of arms carved into the stonework above the entrance.

In preparation for the arrival of the five squad cars, the roads within half a mile of the court had been sealed by the police. Yet more officers were posted on the roof and in the windows overlooking the court. A further thirty detectives were stationed inside the building. And there was a line of uniformed officers guarding its entrance. They examined the identity cards of everyone entering, among them a queue of people anxious for seats in the Public Gallery. Many of those people had been standing outside for nearly three hours. No such inconvenience awaited Fabian, Higgins and Hodge whom a lurking cameraman photographed swaggering down the pavement, three abreast like a trio of dapper Hollywood gangsters.

For reasons of discretion and security, prisoners were driven round to the rear of the building, sturdy gates screening their arrival from the street. One by one, they were taken down the long corridor that led to the cells. It had a stone floor, high ceiling and tiled walls.

Prisoners were locked in separate cells, empty apart from a stark wooden bench and half-partitioned toilet. They remained there until it was time for them to appear before the magistrate who began with the so-called

*Uniformed officers and CID men surround Harry Jenkins as he is led out of the back entrance to Tottenham Court Road police station, ready for his first appearance at Marlborough Street Court.*

'night charges'. These involved people making their first court appearances, having been arrested the previous night. Cases were heard in ascending order of complexity and seriousness. The earliest appearances invariably featured a cast of beggars, vagrants, French or Belgian prostitutes, drunks, shoplifters, and street-traders who dealt in black market goods. Restauranteurs, accused of flouting the rationing system, also formed a regular component of the stream of defendants that flowed through the court, seldom pausing to utter a defiant 'Not Guilty'.

Eventually Jenkins, Geraghty and Rolt were led into the courtroom, the walls of which were lined with dark panelling. A large, expectant audience had formed in the Public Gallery and in the seats set aside for members of the press. The audience included Sir Ronald Howe and Commander Hugh Young, plus Fabian and his two righthand men.

Each of the defendants was accompanied by a young detective, gripping him by the arm or wrist. The prisoners and their escorts filed alternately through the gate into the dock, once occupied by Oscar Wilde. The dock consisted of a wooden bench with a chest-high metal ballustrade round it. In case the prisoners attempted to escape, packed rows of police officers were positioned behind them. These officers and the prisoners faced the built-in table at which Charles O'Connor, the solicitor acting for Jenkins and Rolt, was sitting. As yet, Geraghty didn't have any legal representation.

From a raised desk opposite the dock, just beyond O'Connor's seat, the magistrate, J.B. Sandbach, presided over this preliminary hearing. A former barrister and Deputy County Court Judge, Sandbach was a sixty-nine-year-old with a tolerant, kindly manner that belied his fondness for waspish asides. He'd been a Metropolitan Magistrate since 1934. In that period he had sat in every London court. He regarded Marlborough Street as the pleasantest of the lot. During his time there, he'd acquired a reputation for leniency towards young offenders. Lately, though, his patience had been tested by the flood of petty criminals who made Marlborough Street one of the busiest magistrates' courts in the capital.

The hearing was prefaced by an announcement that this was the case of 'Rex versus Charles Henry Jenkins, Christopher James Geraghty and Terence John Peter Rolt.' Then the first set of charges, relating to the raid on Jay's and the Antiquis murder, was read out.

When Sandbach spoke to the defendants, he had trouble distinguishing them from their youthful guards. Despite the gravity of the situation, Jenkins was amused by the magistrate's confusion. Turning to the detective standing next to him, Jenkins whispered, 'Better stand down, chum, or they'll be topping you by mistake.'

After the charges had been read out, Sandbach moved on to the next stage in the process. He asked Higgins, who was now in the witness-box, to take an oath before addressing the court. Higgins then trotted out the required account of how he had, in the company of Fabian and other officers, witnessed the prisoners being charged and cautioned the previous evening.

Like every other member of the Met, he'd been drilled in the necessity of testifying in a precise, factual manner, highlighting the date, time and location of what was being described. With its supposed adherence to the facts, its preference for certain stock expressions, this ritualised manner had been developed to help policemen under cross-examination, yet it left them vulnerable to ridicule by comedians who mimicked their stilted accounts of 'proceeding in a northerly direction'.

Higgins concluded his spell in the witness-box by submitting a formal application for the prisoners to be held on remand.

Further court appearances looked inevitable, prompting O'Connor to request that the magistrate grant certificates entitling his clients to legal aid. Sandbach agreed to this before remanding the three defendants into police custody for a week, during which the prosecution case could be finalised.

The defendants were ushered from the dock and out of the courtroom by their escorts. But Geraghty was immediately brought back to face the next batch of charges. For these, his co-defendants were Gillam and Walsh. Like Geraghty, they had no legal representation. The charges against them were prefaced by a list of their full names, addresses and occupations. Walsh and Geraghty were described as 'labourers' while Gillam was listed as a 'lorry driver'. All three defendants were accused of carrying out the Queensway robbery. Walsh faced the supplementary charge of 'receiving with a guilty knowledge part of the property, valued at £2,437 16s'—a figure equivalent to about £69,000 in 2007 currency.

Called to the witness-box again, Higgins testified that Gillam, Walsh, and Geraghty had all confessed to their involvement in the Queensway robbery. Gillam nevertheless had the temerity to apply for bail, but Sandbach refused to authorise it.

As Walsh turned to leave the dock, he glanced at a group of women standing in the entrance to the courtroom. From this group, there were shouts of 'Bill! Bill!'

Soon afterwards Walsh and the four other accused men, all of them being held on remand, were ushered singly down the long flight of steps at the back of the building. Rolt looked tearful, the palm of his right hand cupped over his eyes in an anguished gesture. He was braced by three detectives, one of whom had a cigarette dangling nonchalantly from his lips.

Their court appearance completed, the prisoners were driven back to Tottenham Court Road Police Station in separate squad cars. A crowd of men and women waiting in the street surged forwards and surrounded one of these cars, delaying its short journey across the West End.

❖

Being under eighteen, Rolt found himself separated from the others while they awaited their next court appearance. He was probably held in a borstal. Jenkins, Geraghty, Gillam and Walsh were, on the other hand, taken from Tottenham Court Road Police Station to HM Prison Brixton in south London. It was a formidable nineteenth-century building with wings that radiated out from the central block. These dwarfed the terraced houses in the surrounding streets.

As a veteran of the penal system, Walsh would have found nothing to surprise him within its walls. For Jenkins, Geraghty and Gillam, however, this was their first experience of an adult gaol. Once they had been driven through its immense gates and hustled out of the vehicles used to transport them, they went through the prison's depersonalising induction process which could take up to five hours.

Supervised by prison officers who often tried to scare new prisoners into an attitude of cowed acquiescence, the latest arrivals were marched

*Terry Rolt being led down the back steps of Marlborough Street Court after his first appearance in court.*

over to the reception area where their civilian clothes, wristwatches and other property were taken from them, itemised and packed away. Then the newcomers were fingerprinted, herded into baths and inspected by Dr Taylor, the Prison's Medical Officer. During the examination, he noticed that Geraghty was in an extreme state of nervous tension. This manifested itself not in frenzied behaviour but in an attitude of apparent boredom, accompanied by continuous yawning.

At length, each new arrival was given a freshly disinfected prison uniform and a pillow-case stuffed with other prison-issue items. Now wearing coarse-textured clothes that seldom fitted properly, they were handed some food which they ate while they waited until cells were found for them in the main body of the prison. But Dr Taylor arranged for Geraghty to be taken to the prison hospital instead. There he was placed under continuous observation.

The prisoners were shepherded out of the reception area and through a series of heavy, steel doors by a couple of warders, their progress counterpointed by the jangling of keys. On reaching the prison's dimly lit central hall, the prisoners had a startling view down each wing of the building. Like some exercise in perspective, long vistas of asphalt were flanked by cell doors and iron walkways, divided into sections known as 'landings'.

One by one, new prisoners were led to their cells, the syncopated rhythm of footsteps echoing round the building, along with the sound of voices and remote doors being slammed. Until more suitable accommodation became vacant, freshly arrived inmates were often

*Harry Jenkins is escorted down the back steps of Marlborough Street Court.*

allocated cells swarming with lice. Apart from that, the cells—none of them larger than seven feet by thirteen feet—were hard to distinguish. As the studded doors swung open and the prisoners stepped into these stuffy cubicles, they faced the same bleak view.

Set high into the white-washed wall, there was a small, barred window. If it overlooked the adjoining streets, the window was fitted with opaque glass. The cell's only furnishings were an unyielding bed, a wooden table and stool, a small wall-mirror, a chamberpot and a corner shelf. Hanging from the wall were a couple of cards that listed the prison rules. Sometimes there was also a washstand where the prisoner could leave his enamel water-jug, washbasin and plate.

From when the doors banged shut behind them, prisoners were alone until the following morning. At 6:30am next day, inmates were woken by an alarm-bell. The cells were unlocked a few minutes later.

Together with the fifty or sixty other prisoners on their landing, Jenkins, Gillam and Walsh were expected to hurry to the nearest 'sanitary recess' where they could 'slop out'. For newcomers this was the most odious of the many squalid aspects of prison life. Crowded into a miniature bathroom, they were supposed to refill their water jugs from the sink and empty their chamberpots down the toilet, but the toilets were frequently out of order, forcing prisoners to pour urine and excrement down the sink. So foul was the smell that few prisoners exchanged more than the odd passing word before returning to their cells.

Warders then came round, closing the cell-doors. The noise of doors crashing shut merged with the metallic clatter of pots and pans in the downstairs kitchen where breakfast was being dished up. With the stench of slopping out hovering in the air, the warders delivered a slice of bread and margarine, a mug of tea and a pint of porridge to each prisoner. After the cell-doors had been locked, the warders went for their own breakfasts. During the ensuing hour, prisoners were required not only to eat their porridge but also to work their way through a standard cleaning routine, listed on the rule cards. Besides using their jugs of water to wash themselves, they had to clean their plates and scrub the floors of their cells with it. Their plates had to be laid out with their other prison-issue equipment, ready for inspection. Failure to comply with this or other rules resulted in punishment, the commonest forms of which were solitary confinement and the imposition of an even more restricted diet.

Released from their cells once the warders had completed an inspection tour, the prisoners were taken for an hour's exercise in the adjoining yards. Younger inmates such as Jenkins and Gillam spent half the time performing military-style exercises, coordinated by a drill instructor. Meanwhile, grouped in twos or threes, prisoners of Walsh's age and upwards trudged in a circle round the prison grounds. Midway through the exercise session, this joyless procession was swelled by the arrival of the younger convicts.

The inmates were now ready for a three and a half hour shift in the prison workshops. Originally built to house treadmills, these were filled with men sewing mail bags by hand, making brushes and performing other repetitive tasks. Even though conversation between prisoners was permitted, warders were prone, at regular intervals, to order them to 'Stop talking!'

*A group of women watch the accused men leave Marlborough Street Court.*

Their morning shift finished at noon when they had to return to their cells where they were issued with their main meal of the day, often comprising salted fish with potatoes and cabbage, steamed into a soggy, vitamin-free mess. At the conclusion of an hour and a half lunch break, the prisoners were sent back to the workshops for the afternoon shift which lasted until 5:00pm.

Back in their cells, the inmates were served a paltry supper consisting of eight ounces of bread, a pint of cocoa, an ounce of margarine and a slice of cheese. Experienced prisoners didn't eat everything at once, preferring to save some bread until just before they went to bed. If they did that, there was less likelihood of them waking in the night and being too hungry to get back to sleep.

Between supper and dusk when the lights in their cells were turned off, prisoners had to perform two hours' more work, usually sewing mail-bags. Deprived of the snatched conversations that helped to pass the time in the workshops, many inmates found this final session hard to endure. Unless they fulfilled the minimum level of productivity during these unsupervised evening shifts, they could be sentenced to solitary confinement on a diet of bread and water.

Dusk on Tuesday 20 May wasn't until 10:51pm, so Jenkins, Gillam and Walsh had almost four hours to spare after they'd finished their work and eaten their supper. To fill this time, they were permitted a magazine as well as a maximum of two non-fiction books per week from the prison library. Along with visits from their solicitors and the offer of a weekly evening class, those were the only distractions from the tedium of life behind bars.

Late on the afternoon of Thursday 22 May, while the prisoners at HM Prison Brixton were nearing the end of their final stint in the workshops, the Home Secretary made an announcement in the House of Commons. Bowing to the pressure exerted by Parliament and the newspapers, he declared that he'd decided to make ex-gratia awards to Mrs de Antiquis and her children. She'd receive £100 a year, topped up by £18 a year for each of the children until they reached the age of sixteen.

Chuter Ede's announcement triggered a spate of favourable press articles. For the government, which had been the butt of countless critical newspaper stories about its perceived mismanagement of the economy, these were especially welcome.

❖

The monotonous prison routine endured by Antiquis's alleged killers continued until that weekend. Immediately the Saturday morning shift in the workshops was over, the prisoners were locked in their cells. They remained there for most of the next thirty-one and a half hours leading up to the alarm-bell that greeted another working day.

Their next court appearance wasn't until the day afterwards: Tuesday 27 May. Mimicking the previous week's travel arrangements, Jenkins, Geraghty, Walsh, Gillam and Rolt—who had all swapped their prison uniforms for civilian clothes—were picked up and driven to Marlborough Street Court in separate squad cars. The police took the added precaution of handcuffing them.

Both Rolt and Jenkins covered their faces as they arrived at the court. Verging on hysteria, Geraghty was laughing and joking with his escort. He and the other accused men were soon facing J.B. Sandbach, who recited the familiar litany of charges against them. Still handcuffed, Geraghty kept looking over his shoulder towards the back of the court, hoping to see friends and relatives.

After Sandbach had run through the charges, Higgins entered the witness-box and requested to have the prisoners' remand period extended. He justified their protracted detention by explaining that the case against them was still being prepared and that several of the witnesses had been unavailable over the Bank Holiday weekend.

No sooner had Higgins returned to his seat than A.C. Protheroe—the solicitor hired to defend Walsh and Geraghty—applied on their behalf for legal aid. Besides sanctioning the application, Sandbach gave permission for Protheroe to obtain copies of the statements that his clients had made to the police.

When Gillam, who still didn't have legal representation, followed his friends' example by requesting legal aid, Sandbach granted it. The magistrate enquired whether Gillam would be willing to use Mr Protheroe, but Gillam said he'd rather have his own solicitor. Emboldened by his success in obtaining legal aid, Gillam made another application for bail. Again, it was refused.

Sandbach then remanded him and the other accused men into custody for an extra week. The entire hearing had taken no more than a few minutes. It concluded with the men's next court appearance being set for Tuesday 3 June.

❖

In the week leading up to that Tuesday, a few more acres of newsprint were expended on the preliminary stage of the trial process. And Higgins carried on marshalling his evidence, due to be submitted to Maurice Crump, the lawyer appearing on behalf of the Director of Public Prosecutions.

For the third consecutive Tuesday, Jenkins, Rolt, Walsh, Gillam and Geraghty were ferried over to Marlborough Street Court. Members of the public, who had been waiting hours to get seats in the Public Gallery, listened to Sandbach reading out the charges again. Then he invited Crump—a middle-aged man with close to twenty years' experience as a barrister—to put forward the evidence supporting the accusations against the defendants.

Crump said that he wasn't ready to proceed with the armed robbery case against Walsh, Gillam and Geraghty. In view of this, Gillam's recently appointed solicitor asked the magistrate to grant his client bail. Sandbach refused, but he gave permission for Gillam to be visited in prison by his parents.

These legal niceties out of the way, Crump was free to outline the grounds for the murder charge faced by Jenkins, Geraghty and Rolt. The prosecution lawyer augmented his account of the raid on Jay's and the Charlotte Street shooting with incriminating extracts from the statements made by Geraghty and Jenkins. Sandbach was sufficiently impressed by the strength of the case to order Antiquis's alleged killers to be detained, along with Walsh and Gillam, until the following Friday. Geraghty, meanwhile, remained under observation in the hospital at HM Prison Brixton.

As the prisoners were driven away in the usual squad cars, a gaggle of well-dressed young girls, hair teased into modish styles, hung round outside the court like autograph-hunters loitering next to a stage door. A press photographer took a picture of them peering through the window of one of the squad cars.

❖

At a time when newspaper circulation figures were much higher than they are today, few people in the country would have been unaware of the Antiquis murder and the subsequent investigation. As the case moved ponderously through its final phase, it continued to receive plentiful coverage. Another round of newspaper reports on the case preceded the accused men's next trip to Marlborough Street Court.

That day Fabian and Hodge were sitting near the dock. Exhibits 9, 10 and 11—three of the revolvers allegedly used in the robbery of Jay's—had been arranged on a table in front of them.

Consolidating his case against the men in the dock, Crump called the first in what would become a parade of prosecution witnesses which lasted throughout that day's hearing. Robert Churchill and Sir Bernard Spilsbury were among those who testified. Through their work for the police, these two most authorative of expert witnesses had often crossed paths since their initial encounter at a trial in January 1913. Opposites in physique, manner and education, the overweight, barely educated gunsmith's bluff charm contrasting with the lean, erudite pathologist's aloofness, they'd established an improbable friendship.

The parade of police witnesses resumed the following week. These included George Mizon and Edward King, the children who had found two of the guns presented as evidence. King was so short that he was barely able to see over the rim of the witness-box.

Even though there were additional hearings on Tuesday and Friday of that week, the court still hadn't worked its way through the lengthy roster of prosecution witnesses. In keeping with what had become a laborious routine, further court sittings were held the next Tuesday and Friday.

Before the process could be completed, the court had to convene once more. This final sitting took place on Tuesday 24 June when Higgins was called as a witness for the prosecution—a role he didn't relish. Courts were, he thought, places where one could easily make a fool of oneself by quite inadvertently saying the wrong thing in response to sarcastic, forceful questioning.

On behalf of Rolt, Charles O'Connor began to cross-examine Higgins. First, Higgins was asked whether Fabian had been present throughout the interview with Rolt.

Higgins, who was envious of what he regarded as his friend Spilsbury's composure and winning manner under cross-examination, agreed that Fabian had left the room on one occasion.

O'Connor focused on that period. 'Did you pick Rolt up by the lapels of his coat and shake him against the wall? Did you do that?'

'No,' replied Higgins. He was accustomed to the way that criminals put forward the most far-fetched defence to their solicitors, a regular feature of which was an attack on the police and their methods.

'Did you say, "If you have forgotten, there are ways and means of making you remember"?'

'Certainly not.'

'Did you say, "We may not be able to get you hanged, but we can put you away for a long time"?'

Annoyed, Higgins replied, 'I did not say that.'

'Did one or other of you say that "If you don't tell us everything it will be worse for you"?'

'I have no knowledge of that being said.'

'While all this was going on, was Rolt's brother detained in another room?'

'Yes.'

'On hearing you shouting at Rolt, did he jump up, bang the wall and say something like, "Stop bullying the boy!"?'

'I never heard anything of it.'

'Did one or other of you say, "We have been given this case to crack. We are going to crack it. You know something about it, and we mean to get it out of you?"'

'No.'

'All this is sheer fiction...?'

'Yes, as far as I am concerned.'

A little later in the cross-examination, O'Connor suggested Higgins had questioned Rolt like that for two hours after Rolt had said he knew nothing about the incident in North Soho.

'That is entirely wrong. At that stage he was not even suspected of being concerned in it,' Higgins replied, a denial calculated to conceal a breach of Judges' Rules.

'Did either of you say, "If you don't open up and tell us what you know, you will find the case pinned on you"?'

'No.'

Quoting a statement supplied by Fabian, O'Connor said that Rolt had been taken to the police station on two occasions before he was arrested. 'On those occasions Rolt stated quite definitely he knew nothing whatever about this case...?'

'That's right. Yes.' Asked about the statement that Rolt had made, Higgins said Rolt had written at the end of it, 'I have read the statement and this is true.'

'Did you ask him to write that sentence?'

'I told him to write at the bottom if it was true and if he had read it.'

'Were you anticipating some objection to this statement?'

'I never know what will happen. There's always that possibility.'

'Did Chief Inspector Fabian say to Rolt, "Two men have made a statement implicating you: you tell us what you know"?'

Higgins denied this.

'Did one or other of you say, "Chris Geraghty and Harry Jenkins have implicated you in this"?'

The truth was, of course, that Higgins had put pressure on Rolt by letting him know that Geraghty had already made a statement implicating him. Had Higgins told the truth, he'd have been admitting to a contravention of Judges' Rules. An admission of that sort was serious enough to weaken the case against Rolt and, possibly, to invoke disciplinary procedure against Higgins. Mindful of his own career prospects and the case against Rolt, Higgins chose to perjure himself for the second time that day, countering O'Connor's question with an emphatic 'No'.

O'Connor continued probing for a weak point in the detective's testimony, for a means of forcing Higgins into a damaging admission. 'Geraghty was in another room...?'

'Yes.'

'Did you take Rolt into a position where he could see Geraghty?'

'No.'

'Did you say, "There's Chris. He said you were there"?'

'No.'

Relentless in his attempt to undermine the credibility of Rolt's confession, O'Connor asked Higgins whether Rolt had been told that 'if he played ball, the guvnor would make it easy for him.'

Again, Higgins denied the accusation.

'Was it said to him, "You may be taking the rap for murder"?'

'No.'

'You were trying to frighten him...?'

'No.'

O'Connor said he 'would further suggest that the statement was made by Rolt as a result of persuasion and threats and never read over to him at all, and that he was not even cautioned.'

'That is entirely wrong. He was not persuaded. He was not threatened. He was very composed and he made it quite voluntarily,' Higgins said in reply to these allegations of further breeches of Judges' Rules.

After Higgins had left the witness-box, Sandbach informed the defendants that it was their right to call witnesses and, if they desired, give evidence on their own behalf. 'Do you wish to say anything in answer to the charge?' he asked. 'You are not obliged to say anything unless you desire to do so, but whatever you say will be taken down in writing, and may be given in evidence upon your trial.'

Responding to Sandbach's earlier question, Jenkins said, 'No.'

Geraghty said, 'I plead not guilty and reserve my defence.'

Coached by his solicitor, Rolt said, 'I plead not guilty and reserve my defence and call no witnesses.'

Sandbach then announced his decision that the evidence heard over recent weeks justified the five accused men being committed for trial.

❖

The notoriety of the Antiquis case ensured that it would be heard in London's most prestigious trial venue: Number One Court at the Central Criminal Court. In readiness for the trial, due to begin on Monday 21 July, the Clerk of the Court wrote to the Borstal Association, requesting background information on Jenkins and Geraghty. The Association obliged with a typewritten report that summarised not only their character and prospects but also their lives after they'd been discharged from Sherwood Borstal.

Under the terms of their parole, the Association had continued to monitor them. The report revealed that the Association had helped the two former borstal boys find work. And, in Geraghty's case, it had provided him with financial assistance.

Jenkins was described in the report as 'hasty tempered, adventurous and irresponsible, mature and suspicious of authority.' According to the warders at Sherwood Borstal, 'his future was doubtful.' The prognosis for Geraghty turned out to be every bit as bleak. He was characterised by the staff at Sherwood as 'a very mature young man, quick tempered, with no moral sense and one who would not let anything stand in his way.' Even before his latest brush with the law, he had already been tagged as 'a potential gunman doing smash and grab raids.'

❖

Since March 1935, a militant campaign against capital punishment in Britain had been running alongside the more conventional campaigns mounted by the Howard League for Penal Reform and the National Council for the Abolition of the Death Penalty. This radical branch of the movement was the creation of an eccentric sixty-five-year-old former skullery maid named Mrs Violet Van der Elst.

Usually clad in black, a fur stole draped round her shoulders, she had a matronly figure and dark, curly hair, cut into a shortish style. One side of her face was slightly swollen, the result of a botched facelift. Vestiges of her native Cockney were discernible through her affected upper-class accent and fondness for mock-aristocratic exclamations of 'By Jove!'

Almost five decades earlier, she'd escaped a life of domestic service by marrying a prosperous engineer and inventor. Craving the freedom conferred by wealth, she had set up a business manufacturing face cream. Purportedly made from an old Venetian recipe, it was sold as 'Doge Cream'. To promote the brand, she had dressed in eighteenth-century Venetian-style clothes and toured London in a gold coach drawn by a team of six handsome horses. From her seat inside the coach, she had proferred jars of the cream. Quick to recognise the power of publicity, she had spent lavishly on advertising space, marketing it as the 'Marvellous Complexion Restorer'. Its popularity had led her to expand her range of products. These would soon earn her such immense wealth that she could afford to purchase a 300 carat diamond necklace, indulge her ambitions as a composer of music, and drive around dispensing pound notes to tramps.

When her husband had died, she'd remarried with unseemly haste. Her second spouse was Jean Van der Elst, an impecunious young Belgian. But their happy marriage had been brought to a premature end by the fatal illness that had struck him in July 1934. Thrown into despair, his widow had tried to contact him via seances and had refused to relinquish his corpse. Until the local council had forced her to cremate it, she'd kept the body in a lead-lined coffin, stored in the basement of their London mansion.

Within a few months, she had, however, found a constructive outlet for her grief. Among her late husband's papers, she'd come across an essay in which he had railed against capital punishment. The foundation of his argument was that murderers were insane at the time they committed their crimes, so they shouldn't be held responsible for their actions. Less contentiously, his essay highlighted the fundamental flaws in the legal system that sent people to the gallows. Chief among these was the fact that alleged murderers stood little chance of obtaining an acquittal unless they could afford to hire a top barrister, capable of matching the legal expertise deployed by the state. Mrs Van der Elst's second husband had also been critical of the power bestowed on potentially ill-educated and unbalanced jurors.

As a memorial to his conviction that the government was hanging the innocent and insane, his widow had launched her crusade against what she termed 'legalised murder'. Her beliefs had been reinforced when, in March 1940, she'd purchased a selection of stolen post mortem reports on hanged men. One of these documents referred to an occasion when the condemned man's heart had continued beating long after his execution.

Inspired by the attention-grabbing tactics of the suffragette movement, Mrs Van der Elst had gone on to stage numerous noisy demonstrations outside prisons where hangings had been about to take place. She had hired planes to fly overhead, towing giant banners with the words 'STOP THE DEATH SENTENCE' written on them. She had frequently been arrested and received court summonses, often on spurious charges of breeching London's traffic regulations. She had organised petitions that she'd presented to the House of Commons. She had made speeches to packed meetings. She had penned letters to the press, written on notepaper bearing the Van der Elst family crest, its motto of 'Pitié avec Justice'—'Compassion with Justice'—apt for the circumstances. She had stood for Parliament three times without success, most recently as an independent candidate in the 1945 election. And she had hired barristers on behalf of alleged murderers unable to afford top-flight legal representation.

Whenever a murder trial was imminent, her assistant would contact the defendant's family. If necessary, he'd hire suitable legal counsel for the accused and make subsistence payments to their dependents and to those of the victim.

Jenkins and Rolt were, in all likelihood, beneficiaries of Mrs Van der Elst's largesse. With their trial looming, they each acquired teams of two barristers whose fees would not have been covered by the legal aid they'd been granted. Why Geraghty didn't follow their example remains a mystery. Perhaps he was too stubborn to accept help from someone whom he might have mistakenly regarded as an establishment figure.

While Geraghty hired Paul Wrightson, a mere solicitor, to handle his defence, Jenkins and Rolt were represented by Russell Vick and Richard O'Sullivan, experienced barristers, each of whom had an assistant. In the build-up to the trial, the lawyers evolved widely varying defences against what seemed, on the surface at least, an impregnable prosecution case.

❖

Geraghty's extended sojourn in the prison hospital at Brixton had led to concerns on the part of the Director of Public Prosecutions that he'd be declared unfit to face the charges. The Prison Medical Officer was duly asked to provide a formal evaluation of his patient's state of mind.

A week before the trial, Dr Taylor submitted his assessment. 'I have interviewed him, received reports from officers concerning him and have studied the depositions,' the doctor wrote. 'He states that his brother and sister died of tuberculosis; there is no other morbid family history. He has no serious illnesses and is above average intelligence... Whilst under observation his conduct has been exemplary; he has been quiet, well-behaved and clean and tidy in person. At interview he has been coherent and well-orientated. Insight is excellent. He exhibits a cold, callous attitude and shows little concern for the person or property of others. From his story he has been utterly reckless in his behaviour for many years... I have elicited no evidence of mental disease and in my opinion he is not insane or mentally defective. He is fit to plead to the indictment.'

❖

On the opening day of their trial, Jenkins, Geraghty and Rolt were driven to the Central Criminal Court, widely known as the 'Old Bailey'. Since their arrest, new parking restriction signs—bright yellow bands round lamp-posts and broad arrows on the kerb—had appeared en route.

As a result of the heavy wartime bombing, the view of St Paul's

Cathedral from the Old Bailey was less obstructed than it had been. In between the court and cathedral, rows of publishers' warehouses had previously stood. These had been destroyed by a single air-raid, incinerating an estimated six million books. Bombing had also inflicted severe damage on the Old Bailey, which had had one of the smaller of its four courtrooms destroyed. Occupying the site of the notorious eighteenth-century Newgate Gaol, from where condemned prisoners used to be transported in open carts for public executions at Tyburn, it was a substantial, four-storey Edwardian building, fronted with Portland stone. At the summit of its verdured copper dome, there was a gilded statue of a woman symbolising justice. In her right hand, she held a sword. Hanging from her left hand, there was a set of scales.

After Jenkins, Geraghty and Rolt had been delivered to the Old Bailey, they were taken down to the basement where prisoners awaiting trial were kept separately in row upon row of cells. The stout door of each equally spartan cell was fitted with a spy-hole. The cells all had a wooden bench, a table screwed to the floor, and a small rear window covered by an iron grille. Tiles protected the lower parts of the walls. Above that, the walls were whitewashed, boredom and anger spawning graffiti, some of it wryly amusing such as the line, '145,152,000 seconds, THEN I'M OUT!'

Prisoners weren't released from the miserable confines of their cells until minutes from the start of their trial. Under escort from a detachment of prison officers based at the Old Bailey, Jenkins, Geraghty and Rolt were led up a flight of stone steps connecting the basement with Number One Court. These emerged in the same spacious dock where Neville Heath and the wife-murderer Dr Crippen had sat.

The three defendants took their places in the dock, separated by low wooden partitions. Sometimes referred to as the 'bar', it was flanked by seating for relatives and reporters. From the dock, the defendants were able to survey the grandeur of the huge, oak-panelled courtroom. Opposite them was the judge's raised desk and high-backed chair where Mr Justice Hallett sat. He wore one of the anachronistic grey wigs integral to British legal tradition. Known as the 'genial Cockney judge', Hallett was an unhealthy-looking sixty-year-old with dark circles round his eyes. These weren't his most prominent feature, though. That dubious honour belonged to his jutting chin.

In front of the judge was a box-seat for the Clerk of the Court, with a long table set aside for the ushers occupying the valley between that and the dock. At an oblique angle to the prisoners' left were the empty benches reserved for the jury. On separate benches to their right, the prosecution barristers and a platoon of newly appointed defence lawyers—

*Number One Court at the Old Bailey*

all of them male and all of them wearing grey wigs—were arrayed.

Anthony Hawke, an eminent barrister who held the post of Senior Prosecuting Counsel to the Crown, was handling the case against Jenkins, Geraghty and Rolt. Now in late middle-age, his hair almost blended with his wig. Behind thick glasses that had heavy, oval frames, his much-magnified eyes possessed a predatory quality befitting his surname.

Henry Elam, Hawke's usual assistant, was next to him. Together they formed a successful partnership which had, six months earlier, secured a conviction in another prominent case, dubbed the 'Chalk Pit Murder' because the killers had hidden their victim's corpse in an old chalk quarry.

Close to the prosecution counsel, the five defence lawyers, including Russell Vick, Richard O'Sullivan and Paul Wrightson, were lined up. They had to communicate in whispers to prevent their opponents from eavesdropping on them.

Above the rival legal teams was the Public Gallery from where a closely packed crowd watched the trial unfold. It began with the Clerk of the Court reeling off the charges against the three defendants. He asked how they pleaded. As expected, Jenkins, Geraghty and Rolt each pleaded 'Not guilty' in response to the charges of assault, armed robbery and murder.

Moments after the prisoners had submitted their pleas, the jurors were shown to their seats by an usher. They comprised nine men and three women who were, one by one, sworn in by the Clerk of the Court. Next, he had the task of informing them of the accusations made against the defendants.

Before the prosecuting counsel could embark on his preliminary speech, Jenkins's lawyer, Russell Vick, intervened. An ambitious, fifty-three-year-old Yorkshireman, he'd once been a keen rugby player. He possessed a polished, witty manner, honed during a legal career that stretched back almost three decades. Rising to his feet, he spoke to the judge, whom lawyers had to address as 'My Lord'. He requested permission from Hallett to speak to the court in the absence of the jury. Hallett agreed to his request, temporarily dismissing the jurors. While they were gone, Vick asked Hallett to make arrangements for Jenkins to be tried separately. Vick justified this on the grounds that his client had not been present at the scene of the shooting.

Sharing his thoughts with the court, Hallett replied, 'I think where three men are alleged to be members of a gang carrying out an outrage as a result of common design, to try them separately would be a travesty of justice from the point of view of the community, although it might be very desirable from the point of view of the man whom Mr Vick represents.'

Once the jurors had been shown back to their seats, Hawke opened the case for the prosecution. His speech outlined the events of Tuesday 29 April 1947. He told the court that Jenkins, Geraghty and Rolt had been armed with revolvers when they'd staged the robbery at Jay's. 'You will not be surprised to hear that not one of these men was identified by any of the people who witnessed this wild affair,' he said. 'For one thing they all wore masks for the purpose of avoiding identification.'

Hawke then described how Antiquis, 'an ordinary citizen on his ordinary occupation', had been murdered in the course of trying to thwart the gang's escape. The most important question for the jury was, he explained, 'Who fired the shot that killed Mr de Antiquis?'

He said that Geraghty and Rolt had made extensive statements admitting their involvement. In support of what he had just told the court, Hawke read out a long extract from Geraghty's statement, labelled 'Exhibit 20'. The extract culminated in an account of the shooting and how Geraghty had only intended to frighten Antiquis.

'Members of the jury, I do not know whether Geraghty is going to invite you to take the view that that is a true statement of fact,' Hawke added. 'If that is so, on his own confession, he is the man who fired the shot that resulted in Mr de Antiquis's death.'

Turning to the question of the alleged complicity of Jenkins and Rolt in the murder, Hawke said, 'If two or three or more men go out on a common enterprise—in this case the common enterprise of robbery—and these three men, before starting out, provide themselves with guns which they carefully load... it matters not which of them fires the gun which causes death or grievous bodily harm. It is the same as if every one of them had his finger on the trigger and pulled it.'

To reinforce his argument, Hawke read out Rolt's statement. With the foundations of the prosecution case already laid, Hawke called the first witness for the Crown.

An usher was responsible for summoning the witness from one of the four waiting-rooms, two of which were reserved for men and women of 'a better-class'. The witness was Charles Herbert Grimshaw. Under cross-examination, he told the court what had happened to him on the afternoon of Tuesday 29 April. He said that he'd tripped the smallest of the fleeing robbers and had then been kicked in the head by a taller member of the gang. Hawke congratulated him on his 'very valiant attempt' to foil the getaway of the men who had murdered Antiquis.

Grimshaw's reference to the height of the accused led Hallett to ask Jenkins, Geraghty and Rolt to stand up, so that the jury could see their relative stature.

But Vick protested on behalf of Jenkins. 'I object that a man whose case is that he was not there should be pointed out to the jury that one is taller than the other.'

'If you object to the jury seeing that your client is taller than Rolt, your objection shall prevail,' Hallett replied, in the process negating Vick's minor success.

No sooner had Grimshaw completed his testimony than Hallett adjourned the case until the following day.

Even though there was stiff competition from other domestic news stories, primarily the derailing of the Euston to Liverpool express train and the death of five passengers, the first day of the trial received abundant attention from the press. As innumerable commuters headed into work next morning, into offices, shops and factories rendered uncomfortable by soaring temperatures, many of them must have pored over accounts of what had happened at the Old Bailey.

❖

When the trial resumed on Tuesday 23 July, Hawke summoned Higgins to the witness-box and asked the detective to read out Rolt's statement.

This was sufficient to make Vick jump up and lodge another objection.

The judge said he presumed the objection was based on the fact that the statement contained references to Jenkins. Overruling Vick's objection without even waiting to hear the reasons for it, Hallett added that he would 'tell the jury at the proper time that the statement was not evidence against Jenkins.'

'If your Lordship rules that, I bow to that ruling,' Vick replied, 'but not one word in this statement is one word against Jenkins.'

Hallett informed Vick that duplicates of the statement had already been distributed to the jury.

'I have never known copies of a statement of this character being made for a jury, and I object to the jury being handed them,' Vick said.

'Very well. No doubt your objections will be recorded.'

Higgins then read out Rolt's statement and was quizzed about aspects of it. Once the interrogation was over, the prosecuting barrister called Hodge to answer questions about the statement made by Geraghty, sections of which were also read out.

Hodge confirmed that Geraghty had confessed to the theft of guns from a shop on Union Street, and to being part of the gang that had raided Jay's. According to Hodge, the defendant had admitted to firing a shot intended only to frighten Antiquis. Hodge added that Geraghty had described throwing his guns into the Thames.

The reference to firearms heralded the usher's familiar cry of 'Call Robert Churchill...' Over the past forty-five years, Churchill had appeared as an expert witness at most prominent murder trials involving guns. Though the date of this particular hearing was inconvenient for him because it clashed with the season when he travelled all over Britain attending shooting parties, he'd agreed to testify on behalf of the Crown.

Like his friend, Sir Bernard Spilsbury, he cut a conspicuous figure whenever he arrived at the Old Bailey, dressed in a dark, three-piece suit and rakishly angled bowler-hat. Entering the court, he always carried a black morocco briefcase containing his notes. To a layperson, these resembled some abstruse code.

Just prior to him mounting the steps up to the witness-box, it was standard practice for his professional credentials to be established. This was done by reciting his qualifications as a gunsmith. His expertise had recently been endorsed by the awarding of an OBE in the first post-war Honour's List.

At least one impatient judge had cut short the customary listing of his qualifications with the line, 'Never mind that. We all know Mr Churchill....'

After Churchill had taken the oath, he was asked to examine the three revolvers, the ammunition and the spent cartridge cases linked to the Charlotte Street shooting.

Hawke questioned him about each of the exhibits, including the mangled bullet that had killed Antiquis. It was sealed inside a transparent paper envelope.

Churchill said the bullet was fifty-years-old. He disliked this stage of the process because the prosecution lawyers sometimes inadvertently wrong-footed him by deviating from the pre-arranged list of questions. That's why he preferred cross-examination by opposing lawyers, whose angle of interrogation was consistent—consistently unpredictable. Despite finding the life or death drama of murder trials a grim business, the combative Churchill enjoyed the tense atmosphere, the head-to-head clash with the defence lawyers.

When Hawke had finished questioning him about his findings, the cross-examination began. But Churchill was immune to the type of bullying that sometimes undermined the evidence given by expert witnesses. Instead, it was the defence lawyer, Paul Wrightson, who allowed himself to be overawed by the occasion. He asked Churchill how rapidly the alleged murder weapon could be fired. Since the case involved only two shots, fired with a significant interval between them, Wrightson's question served no purpose.

On being presented with the empty .320 revolver, Churchill pointed it at the ceiling and pulled the trigger eight times in rapid succession, the dull click of the pistol's hammer audible across the hushed court. Lowering the weapon, he told Wrightson that each shot might have taken only one and a half seconds to fire.

Wrightson asked him to repeat the exercise. The gunsmith raised the revolver and pulled the trigger a few more times. He said that, on reflection, two and a half seconds were needed to fire each shot.

Leaving the prosecution case looking even stronger, Churchill was allowed to step down from the witness-box. Not that he would have been confident in the trial achieving what he regarded as an equitable outcome. During recent years he'd been appalled by the meekness and mildness which, he felt, had crept into sentencing policy.

❖

So often the trump-card in court cases, Spilsbury's arrival usually provoked an expectant rustle. Smartly dressed as ever, he wore a light grey three-piece suit, an old-fashioned round-collared shirt and dark, formal tie. He was soon standing in the witness-box which he had, as a young man, first graced thirty-seven years earlier. In what had been his debut appearance in a murder trial, he'd testified against Dr Crippen. His skilful testimony had not only helped to secure a conviction but had also marked him as a future star of his profession.

He was shown the transparent envelope previously examined by Churchill. Questioned by the prosecuting counsel, he identified the piece of twisted lead as the murder bullet. He also disclosed his findings from the post mortem on Antiquis.

Spilsbury's courtroom manner barely diverged from his gentle and measured everyday manner. Whenever possible, he avoided medical jargon, preferring to use simple phrases that wouldn't confuse the jury.

The lawyers representing Jenkins, Geraghty and Rolt now had their chance to cross-examine him. Even the most

*Sir Bernard Spilsbury on his way to testify at the Old Bailey.*

distinguished of barristers found the prospect intimidating. Besides being hard to lure into verbal traps, Spilsbury had a such an impressive reputation that juries tended to believe what he was saying, his demeanour and obvious sincerity bolstering their instinctive trust.

Wrightson stood up and, undeterred by the fruitless cross-examination of Churchill, began to question Spilsbury about the range from which the fatal bullet had been fired. To lend credibility to Geraghty's claim that he'd only been trying to frighten Antiquis, Wrightson had to demonstrate that his client hadn't shot the motorcyclist in the head from point-blank range. Wrightson started by saying, 'If a shot is fired very close to a person, there are usually powder burns…?'

'It may be so. It depends on the gunpowder.'

'That is one of the ways you can tell how close the shot was fired…?'

'Yes.'

'In this case there were no powder burns…?'

'No.'

Geraghty's lawyer then asked Spilsbury whether the shot had been fired from close range.

'It may have been fired within a yard.'

'You cannot say from what distance it was fired?'

'No.'

❖

The prosecution held back three key items of evidence until then. These consisted of the raincoat left at Brook House, the stock ticket inside its lining and the scarf found in one of its pockets.

Hawke sought to establish the connection between the coat and the accused men through the testimony of Arthur Amos, manager of the Deptford High Street branch of Burton's. Shown the raincoat and stock ticket, Amos confirmed that he'd sold the garment to Thomas Kemp of Park Buildings, Rotherhithe.

Patiently constructing his case, Hawke also showed the raincoat to Kemp's wife, Vera. She said it looked like the coat that belonged to her husband and that she had, the previous April, given to a man brought round by her brother, Harry Jenkins. 'He was introduced to me as Walsh, but since this case came on I found out he isn't.'

As a means of cementing the link between the men in the dock and the items found at Brook House, Hawke summoned the office boy, Brian Cox. For his day in the limelight Cox was wearing a double-breasted suit, cut from dark material. He recalled that one of the gunmen, whom he'd seen at Brook House, had been wearing 'a white scarf, like Exhibit 3, when I first saw him.'

❖

Towards the end of that afternoon, Hawke sent for the final prosecution witness, Chief Inspector Robert Fabian. Hawke, who admired Fabian's mastery of his job, had worked with him on numerous occasions, these dating back to when Fabian had been a Detective Sergeant.

Hawke asked him about the raincoat found at Brook House.

Fabian testified to Jenkins's cagey reaction when questioned about the coat.

Before Fabian was permitted to exit the witness-box, he was cross-examined by Vick and O'Sullivan, the barristers representing both Jenkins and Rolt. In response to a question by O'Sullivan, Fabian gave details of Rolt's arrest. His account, garnished with remembered dialogue between himself and Rolt, was interrupted by the judge. Hallett told Fabian to read the exact words recorded in his police notebook.

'I don't need your Lordship's assistance to cross-examine Mr Fabian or any other witnesses,' Vick snapped.

'When you are irregular, I shall stop you, even if it enables you to make a tactical scene,' Hallett said, displaying none of his trademark geniality. 'Now please go on. I think you try to manufacture these in the hope it will get sympathy...'

Hallett was still speaking when Vick said, 'My client needs no sympathy, only justice. If you will allow me, I shall ask my next question.'

'If a question is irregular, I shall interrupt you again.'

Vick completed the cross-examination without further provoking the judge.

Bringing both the prosecution case and the second day of the trial to a close, Hawke read out the statement made by Rolt.

Soon the reporters who had been sitting near the dock were on their way out of the court. Like the two other courts housed on the first-floor of the Old Bailey, it was reached via the cavernous Great Hall, directly beneath the dome. Over the next few hours, the reporters filed their accounts of the trial.

❖

The third day's proceedings began with Hallett issuing legal guidance to the jury. He remarked that it was everyone's duty to prevent the escape of a felon fleeing from justice. 'For at least 273 years,' he added, 'it had been the view of every court that those performing that duty were entitled to a very special protection, because it was a duty that could only be performed at risk to themselves. If the felon used some violent measure to prevent the private person from stopping him, the felon did so at his own risk and was guilty of murder if that violent measure resulted, even unintentionally, in the death of the other person.'

Hallett's advice was followed by a successful request from Wrightson for the jury to be asked to leave the room. In its absence, Wrightson made a two-hour speech arguing that the evidence didn't prove that Antiquis had tried to prevent his killer from escaping. Wrightson insisted that this meant the murder charge against his client should be dropped in favour of a manslaughter charge.

To that, Hallett responded by saying, 'Why did Geraghty fire to frighten the motorcyclist unless he thought the motor-cyclist was trying to stop him? Geraghty himself said that this man, the deceased, got in their way and that he fired to frighten him. Are not the jury entitled to take the view, if they think it proper, that Geraghty himself regarded this man as a man who was trying to stop them, to impede their escape, and then fired in order to make Antiquis desist?'

Hallett rejected Wrightson's appeal and recalled the jury. Deprived of his client's sole defence, Wrightson conceded defeat. He announced that he wouldn't be calling Geraghty as a witness, nor would he be presenting any evidence on his behalf.

❖

Richard O'Sullivan, Rolt's barrister, was next to offer the case in defence of his client who maintained that he'd been placed under duress while being interviewed by Higgins. But O'Sullivan didn't risk putting Rolt in the witness-box where he could be grilled by the prosecuting counsel.

Attempting to repair some of the damage caused by Rolt's confession, O'Sullivan summoned Captain George Rogers to provide evidence. Rogers, who ran a boys' club in Bermondsey, obliged by giving Rolt a flattering character reference.

When O'Sullivan had finished his presentation of Rolt's case, Vick took centre-stage. Jenkins's barrister said that his client had 'always denied that he had anything to do with the affair. He was not present at the time, and his defence is an alibi.'

Called to give evidence, Jenkins replied to Vick's questions with disconcerting bursts of speech. These were so full of slang that Hallett translated some of them into formal English for the benefit of the jury. 'I am a fellow Londoner, born and bred, and he is talking in a language which perhaps comes easier to me than to some people,' Hallett explained.

On resuming his evidence, Jenkins was instructed by his barrister to speak louder and at a slower pace. But he persisted in talking so quickly that the court's shorthand writer, responsible for making a transcript of the trial, couldn't keep up with him.

Jenkins claimed that he hadn't been in North Soho at the time of Antiquis's murder. Referring to the identification parade, attended by all the witnesses, he said, 'Well, I was not picked out. I wasn't there.' He declared that he'd had nothing to do with the robbery apart from persuading his sister, Mrs Kemp, to lend Geraghty a raincoat. He told the court that he'd been with his other sister, Mrs Mary Burnham, on the afternoon of 29 April 1947. In the hope of finding him a job, she had, he said, taken him to the Wentworth model-making factory in Clerkenwell. They'd stayed there until 2:30pm, then moved on to a café, after which they'd visited another potential employer before going home to Wapping.

Cross-examining him about this, Hawke prefaced a question with the words, 'If you are telling the truth…'

Vick rose to object to Hawke's heavily weighted phrasing just as Hallett also began to remark on what had been said.

'Will you please not interrupt me when I am speaking?' the judge told Vick. 'You have been doing it for several days and I shall not let it continue.' Hallett asked Vick if he wished to reply.

'I was only going to say that for once I was very good and haven't said a word.'

This triggered laughter among the watching crowd.

'I do not like laughter in these cases,' Hallett declared.

'I did not laugh.'

In support of Jenkins's alibi, Vick called both Mrs Burnham and a work colleague of hers to the witness-box. Mrs Burnham, who had been waiting apprehensively outside the courtroom throughout the trial, said that she and her brother had been together from 10:00am until 4:00pm on the day of the shooting. Her story was backed up by Robert Rabiotti, a paint-sprayer at Wentworth's. Asked how he could be so certain about the date on which Jenkins's visit to the factory had taken place, Rabiotti said, 'It was the first day of the Newmarket races and the week of the Two Thousand Guineas. It was Tuesday 29 April. I often have a flutter on a horse and that was the only day I did not have a bet. I was held in conversation by Mrs Burnham and her brother and did not have time to put on a bet. If I had been able to, I would have won on "Wings of a Song". I remember it from that day to this. It was an outsider and won at 20-1.'

Rabiotti's gambling misfortunes provoked another ripple of laughter across the courtroom.

Hallett turned to Jenkins's barrister and said, 'I am sure you are not responsible but I regard a murder case as most unsuitable for comedy.'

Powerless to restrain himself from sniping at the judge, Vick returned to this theme later in the afternoon. His comments directed towards the jury, he said, 'If I appeared to have upset the quiet demeanour of his Lordship, I know you and he will forgive me because of the responsibility on my shoulders. This is not a game of cards. Lives are at stake.'

❖

Since the beginning of the trial, the weather had been improving. That trend continued the following day. Despite the lure of bright, warm sunshine, a large crowd once again packed into the viewing gallery of Number One Court, where the efficient ventilation system ensured a refreshingly cool temperature.

When the trial restarted, Vick delivered his closing speech to the jury. He began by urging them to question their preconceptions about what the judge had described as 'the outrage' on Charlotte Street. 'You must put out of your minds this starting point—that Jenkins was there at the outrage,' he said. 'That is one of the things which is in serious dispute in this case.' The prosecution had, he argued, failed to prove their case against Jenkins. 'They may have caused grave suspicion in your minds, but it is laid down by judges at all times that suspicion is not enough. It must be proven.'

Vick then switched his attention to the main element in the case against his client, namely the alleged statement made by Rolt. 'That statement, which is not evidence against Jenkins, which Rolt has not sworn to by going into the witness-box so that I could cross-examine him upon it, you are being asked to put completely out of your minds when you are considering the case of Jenkins.'

In a speech that lasted for an hour and forty-five minutes, Vick continued to chip away at the evidence against his client. To round off his oration, he turned to the jury and said, 'Taking a broad view of this case before the evidence was called—and it is easy to sneer at an alibi—are you sure, are you certain, are you convinced that Jenkins was there?'

The defence case having drawn to a close, Hawke was free to embark on his final, lengthy speech for the prosecution. He reminded the jury that the raid on Jay's had been carried out by three men and that the central question was one of identification. 'I imagine that you will have no doubt who two of these men are. Indeed, as I understand it, you are not invited to come to any other conclusion but that two of the men are Geraghty and Rolt. These two have made statements which set out in the clearest possible terms their part in the matter.' He went on to stress that all the evidence, not least the statement made by Rolt, demonstrated that Jenkins had been the other gunman. In a reproachful coda to his speech, Hawke observed that 'the time, to our shame, is apparently not yet past when certain criminal people range the streets of London armed with guns, and hold up places where there are valuables to be obtained.'

Before bringing that afternoon's instalment of the trial to a close, the judge announced that he wanted to spare the jurors the inconvenience of spending the weekend deliberating on their verdict. He'd therefore taken the decision to adjourn proceedings until Monday morning.

❖

The temperature in London had soared to 29°C by midday on Friday 25 July. For Jenkins and his fellow defendants, the ensuing long weekend, spent waiting for the trial to reach its climax, must have been unbearable. The contrast between their wretched circumstances and the holiday atmosphere prevailing elsewhere in London could scarcely have been more conspicuous.

Coinciding with the start of the school holidays, thousands of people flocked to the mainline railway stations, intent on travelling to the seaside. At Waterloo Station alone, 3,500 holidaymakers slept on the platforms just to ensure that they'd be able to catch an early train. And, despite petrol rationing, traffic on the southbound side of the London to Brighton road was measured at 2,000 vehicles per hour: heavier than at any point that year.

By 9:00am on Monday morning it was already apparent that another hot day was imminent in central London. The court was due to convene just after lunch. Reporters, members of the public, plus relatives of Jenkins, Geraghty and Rolt poured into the Old Bailey, aware that they might be about to witness the climax of the legal battle.

In readiness for the resumption of the trial, Hallett asked the ushers to close the doors and not allow anyone to enter or leave Number One Court while he was speaking. He then embarked on the traditional summing up and guidance for the jurors. To help them reach correct decisions on the charges against the defendants, he provided them with a resumé of the questions fundamental to the case.

'It is not every day, thank God, that innocent people are shot down in the streets of London in circumstances such as occurred here. It is not every day that hold-ups by three men armed with guns occur in London, though naturally this case has attracted a great deal of public notice. I described the affair as an outrage—what else could it be called?'

He said that the case could be broken down into three principal areas of debate. Firstly, 'What was the crime committed by the man who killed de Antiquis? Was it murder, anything short of murder, or manslaughter at least?' Secondly, 'Were his two companions either or both of them responsible for what he did?' And lastly, 'Was it established to the jury's satisfaction that the third man was Jenkins?'

The first two areas of discussion, he explained, primarily concerned legal questions, about which he would issue guidance. The third point was, he said, almost entirely a question that had to be answered by the jurors.

'There was no suggestion from first to last that the gun was accidentally let off. We start with this: a man was killed by a bullet wound in the head from a gun fired intentionally and without provocation. What would you have called that if you had been asked the question ten days ago. I think you would have called it plain, stark, staring murder. Of course you might be wrong. At the end of the hearing, this case of crime against the community has to be decided by the common sense of the jury.'

To find someone guilty of murder, he informed the jurors, they had to be satisfied that the defendant had, 'without lawful excuse, intentionally and without provocation committed a cruel act of such a nature that death or grievous bodily harm was likely to result.' The judge reminded the jury that Geraghty had no lawful excuse for shooting Antiquis. Moreover, there was no doubt that Geraghty had fired the fatal shot, a shot that had been fired without provocation. 'The only point which emerges upon which there can be any shadow of doubt is this: can it be said that Geraghty was not attempting to discharge his gun at Antiquis? If he *was* shooting at Antiquis with intent to resist lawful apprehension and killed him unintentionally, I say that it is murder and nothing else. Have you any doubt that he was intending to resist lawful apprehension? Geraghty says that he shot into the air, but can you believe that? Geraghty said that he intended to frighten people by firing into the air, but did he? Is it true or just a plain lie?'

Hallett dismissed the suggestion that Antiquis, far from trying to stop the gang from escaping, had merely got in the way. After all, Grimshaw had heard the 'hue and cry'—the shouts of 'Police! Police! Stop them!'—from much further down Tottenham Street. 'Don't you think that Antiquis would have heard it, too?' Hallett asked the jury.

In a similarly sceptical assessment of Jenkins's defence, he said, 'You may have come to the conclusion that Jenkins is a quick-brained, clever man. But clever men sometimes make fatal slips, and you may think that Jenkins's remark to Chief Inspector Fabian when told he was to be put up for identification was such a slip. He said, you will remember, referring to the coat one of the men was seen to be wearing, "I suppose it's because I had the coat." ' Hallett also quoted Jenkins's remark that 'I'm not a grass but I'm not having this on my own.' Was there any possible explanation for that, Hallett asked, except that he was one of the gunmen?

Moving on to the armed robbery charge faced by the defendants, Hallett warned the jury that a guilty verdict couldn't be reached if they had 'the slightest doubts' in their minds over the following points: 'that the intention of these men was robbery; that they were armed with offensive weapons; that they were acting together; and that one or the other—or all of them—in the course of the scene committed an assault with intent to rob.'

At 5:05pm, three and three-quarter hours after he'd started speaking, the judge concluded his summing up. He directed the jurors to swap the courtroom for the privacy of the Retiring Room where they could consider their verdict.

❖

About forty-five minutes afterwards Jenkins's sister, Mary, tried to relieve the tension by venturing outside. Juries sometimes took days to reach a decision, so she was uncertain how long she would have to tolerate this psychological torture. She'd only been gone for a few minutes before the jurors trooped back. In line with normal procedure the doors to the court were then locked.

Prior to the start of the trial, the jury had elected a Foreman. Just before 6:00pm, the Clerk of the Court turned to him and said, 'Members of the jury, are you agreed upon your verdict?'

'We are.'

The Clerk of the Court read out the full names of each defendant and asked the Foreman of the Jury whether they had found him guilty or not guilty of each offence. On all three occasions that Geraghty's name was read out, the Foreman said, 'Guilty.' The same happened with Rolt and Jenkins.

In the Public Gallery, where relatives of Jenkins and Geraghty were sitting among the rapt audience, a disbelieving silence greeted the verdicts. This silence was broken by the sound of several of those relatives bursting into tears.

On Hallett's instructions, Rolt was temporarily removed from the dock and taken down the steps to the basement. Swivelling to face the remaining prisoners, Hallett said, 'The jury have in my judgement merely done their duty, a duty which they owe to the community whose representatives they are. For the crime of which you have been found guilty, there is only one sentence known to law… Prisoners at the bar, you severally stand convicted of murder. Have you anything to say why the court should not give you judgement according to the law?'

Neither of the defendants appear to have taken the opportunity to reply.

One of the court's ushers then stood up and made an announcement. 'My Lords the King's Justices do strictly charge and command all persons to keep silence while sentence of death is passed on the prisoners at the bar, upon pain of imprisonment. God save the King!'

Just then Jenkins's sister, Mary, returned to Number One Court, only to discover that she'd been locked out. As she stared desperately through the glass panel in the door, she saw Hallett place a square of black silk on top of his wig. She knew that this signified the passing of a death sentence.

Seconds later Hallett spoke to Jenkins and Geraghty who were standing in the dock. 'The sentence of the law upon you and each of you is that you be taken from this place to a lawful prison and thence to a place of execution, and that you be there hanged by the neck until you be dead; and that your body be afterwards buried within the precincts of the prison in which you shall have been confined before your execution. And may the Lord have mercy on your souls.'

Jenkins and Geraghty maintained blank expressions as the judge declaimed these dreaded words. Turning as sharply as soldiers on parade, the two men hurried down to the cells. Before disappearing, Jenkins glanced towards his relatives in the Public Gallery and smiled at them.

❖

A pair of horn-rimmed glasses conferring on him a studious appearance, Rolt was soon back in the dock. Like Jenkins and Geraghty, he was asked if he had anything to say.

He said that he hadn't.

'By reason of your age, it is not permissible to pass upon you the sentence which has been passed on your companions. The order with regard to you is that you will be detained in custody until His Majesty's pleasure is known'—a quaint euphemism for an indefinite period of imprisonment. 'When you will be released rests with the authorities, not with me. Having regard to the grave facts of this case and the necessity of making an example to others, I think it my duty to express my opinion that you ought not to be released from custody until at least five years have expired.'

Rolt showed no reaction to the sentence. When he was ushered out of the dock, he looked straight ahead like a tightrope-walker. His lack of apparent emotion contrasted with the reaction of several of his female relatives. On their way out, they were so distraught that they had to be comforted by court staff.

Joe Gillam, meanwhile, took Rolt's place in the dock. Gillam was charged with being part of the gang that had carried out the Queensway robbery. Bill Walsh should have appeared alongside him, but a doctor testified that Walsh was unable to attend because he was currently in St Giles Hospital, Camberwell waiting to have his appendix removed. Geraghty— the other defendant in the Queensway case—was also absent, his impending execution prompting the police to drop the charges against him.

Hallett said that he didn't think 'it would be in Gillam's interests for him to be tried separately', so the trial was postponed until September. The judge assured Gillam that the period he spent in prison would be deducted from any sentence that might be passed.

Within a few hours of the judge wrapping up that day's proceedings, Stanley Firmin and other reporters were composing excited accounts of its dramatic conclusion for the front-pages of their papers. These were destined to carry headlines such as 'DEATH FOR TWO ANTIQUIS MEN'. Firmin had witnessed innumerable death sentence dramas without suffering one disturbing thought, except perhaps for an involuntary flicker of pity. In his piece for the following morning's *Daily Telegraph and Morning Post*, he sounded a triumphant note. 'The end of the trial,' he wrote, 'brings to light one of the most remarkable pieces of detection work of recent times.'

❖

Newly sentenced prisoners were taken from the cells under the Old Bailey and loaded into one or more armoured black police vans, known as a 'Black Marias'. Each prisoner was marched down the van's central aisle and locked in separate compartments on either side. The absence of windows in these ensured that travelling in them was an unpleasant, often nauseating experience.

Whilst Rolt was taken to HM Prison Wormwood Scrubs in west London, Jenkins and Geraghty were driven just over two miles from the Old Bailey to HM Prison Pentonville. Nicknamed 'the Ville', this forbidding, purpose-built Victorian gaol was situated in a solidly working-class district near to where Geraghty had been living. The entrance to the prison comprised a pedimented gateway set back from the righthand side of Caledonian Road. Facing the gateway was a café, as well as a fish and chip shop.

Through the gates, Jenkins and Geraghty were confronted by a building with a layout that would have carried unwelcome reminders of their stay in Brixton. The prison was made up of five tall wings, radiating like the spokes on a wheel. These were bounded by an impenetrable-looking hexagonal wall, punctuated by watch towers. Inside the main building, its immense structure skewered by an equally immense chimney, there were four floors with cast-iron walkways, linked by spiral-staircases.

The two new prisoners underwent an induction process similar to the one they'd experienced at Brixton. To prevent them from committing suicide or strangling a warder, the laces were removed from their prison-issue shoes, lending them a shuffling walk redolent of novice skaters inching round the edge of an ice-rink.

They were now ready to be placed in the condemned cells, reserved for prisoners awaiting execution. These were entered from a first-floor corridor, leading to the execution chamber. Each of the cells allocated to Jenkins and Geraghty had a barred window with wire netting stretched across it. The windows overlooked an exercise yard so bleak that it made the cells appear welcoming in comparison. Both cells were equipped with a bed, together with a table and three chairs, arranged in the centre. They also had bathrooms, housing a toilet and washbasin. Against the dividing wall of these back-to-back bathrooms was a wardrobe that took up a substantial portion of the room, lit by a single electric bulb which burned continually, making sleep difficult.

Jenkins and Geraghty had to share their cells with two warders at a time. Those warders—the so-called 'death watch officers'—usually coaxed condemned men into games of cards, chess and dominoes, designed to take their minds off their fate. Newspapers and books served a similar purpose.

Allowances of ten cigarettes or half-an-ounce of tobacco, not to mention a pint of beer or stout every day, provided additional diversions. So did a succession of visitors.

Condemned prisoners received obligatory twice daily visits from the prison's Chief Officer, Medical Officer, and Governor. Friends and relatives were allowed to see them as well. Geraghty had no religious convictions, yet he sought further solace from a Roman Catholic priest.

Through their lawyers, who were allowed to visit them too, he and Jenkins joined Rolt in lodging appeals against their murder convictions. The grounds for each of the appeals differed. Jenkins's was based on his dogged insistence that he had nothing to do with the murder, but the appeals lodged by Geraghty and Rolt rested on a legal technicality. According to their lawyers, the judge should have given the jury the option of finding them guilty not of murder but of manslaughter, which didn't carry the death sentence.

The outcome of these legal manoeuvres was due to be decided at a hearing of the Court of Criminal Appeal, timetabled for Thursday 3 September.

❖

Even though the trial had finished, the Antiquis case continued to spark occasional newspaper stories over the ensuing days. To start with, the *Evening Standard* carried an article announcing the Met's creation of its first medal. In honour of Captain Binney, the man killed by Jenkins's brother, this opportunistic annual award was named the 'Binney Memorial Medal'. The article revealed that it would be bestowed to the member of the public who demonstrated the greatest bravery in upholding law and order. Courtesy of an obvious leak from the police, Antiquis was confidently tipped as its inaugural winner.

Four days after the *Evening Standard* article, a more substantial, even more opportunistic story appeared in the downmarket *Sunday Pictorial*. Headlined 'A Gangster—By His Mother', it was an exclusive, presumably ghostwritten article that promised to reveal how Rolt, 'a high-spirited boy who started life with bright prospects, ended up in the dock at the Old Bailey charged with the gravest offence in the criminal code.'

'The worst thing Terry did at school was to stick a pin in the boy sitting in front of him at prayers,' the article began. 'He is not much more than a schoolboy now—seventeen and a half. Yet today he is branded a gunman.

'Is it my fault that Terry Rolt is a boy gangster?

'Is it the fault of the army authorities who turned him away, only six months ago, because they said he was too young to enlist?

'Or is this wretched mess he is in just another war casualty—something that might happen to any little Bermondsey boy brought up in the hysteria of wartime Britain?

'Terry was born in Tooley Street—a sturdy, sporting little chap and the apple of his father's eye. My husband, Henry, was a great man around here. He was a Sergeant-Major in the first big war. He spent his nineteenth birthday in the trenches and won the Military Medal in 1918—he was also a fine amateur footballer, cricketer and boxer.

'I remember how proudly he watched young Terry's punching muscles grow, and how they pranced about the kitchen as Terry learned the ring tricks that were to make him as good a man as his father. In the house the boy was up to all kinds of tricks, washing the greens in soap, smothering the furniture with polish and even locking us out and laughing in the face of the policeman who tried to get him to unfasten the door.

'Then, in 1938, our world went to pieces. My husband was a docker: he had been at the wharf nineteen years and we were happy and moderately prosperous. One day he had to open a barrel of wet skins for Customs examination, and the following Sunday morning when he got up to make a cup of tea and go to church there was a tiny spot on his neck with a black ring round it. Eight days later he died in agony. I heard them say at the hospital that it was a "beautiful" case of anthrax, the only one found in this country for years.

'I got £547 10s compensation and a letter of condolence. We had three children and a little girl born six month's after her father's death. It was plain that life on our own, with my widow's pittance, was going to be a struggle. But there was more bad luck to come. Seamus, the youngest boy, was accidentally killed when a roof collapsed. We lost everything when our house in Maltby Street was bombed.

'When war broke out we evacuated to Hailsham, Sussex, and Terry who had been going to Dockhead Roman Catholic School continued his studies at Dicker Village School.

'He wasn't a good scholar—we often tell him he is as ignorant as the pigs of Ireland—but he made a lot of friends, learned to climb trees and became quite a good little countryman. He was happy, too, at Battle Road School, Hailsham, and at a school run by nuns at Hayle in Cornwall.

'We came back to London just in time for the flying bombs.

'He thought he would like to learn carpentering, so between us we bought him a set of tools and found him a job where he earned about £1 a week as a learner. But the sawdust damaged his health, so he took a job as a warehouseman at £2 10s a week, not a bad wage at fifteen.

'The mistake I made, as I see it now, was in letting him stop work. He wanted to change to building work, but the best wage he was offered was

11 ½ d an hour. and after the inflated earnings a boy could make in wartime that didn't seem much.

'My mother was ill and needed an attendant. Terry was earning less than any other member of the family, so we let this adventurous, active boy stay at home to look after her.

'We made sure that he was never without money. But he had no regular wage. Maybe that was the big mistake.

'He was always busy, looking after granny and going to the Downside Boys' Club most nights of the week. He played football and cricket for the club and boxed for them and was even on the organising committee. I have a medal which he won there for table tennis, and they say that at camp he was a tower of strength.

'The neighbours like him because he was genuinely thoughtful, carrying old people's coal for them in snowy weather, mending their gramophones, making toys for children and generally doing any good turn that he could.

'He never had any girls; he never drank anything stronger than shandy; and he seldom smoked.

'How could a boy like that get into trouble?

'I think it was through meeting boys of his own age already schooled in crime at coffee stalls and cafés. No matter how many good boys' clubs there are in a neighbourhood they will always gravitate to a coffee stall on the way home. And Terry was restless and adventurous.

'But it would never have happened if he had been able to get into one of the services. Last year, when he was sixteen, he wanted to join the Merchant Navy, and for weeks he haunted the offices in Leadenhall Street. I agreed to find £25 for a training course. But he was turned down because his eyes weren't good enough.

'So he tried for the army, going to every recruiting office in London. He even went as far as Maidstone because he thought they might take him there. But always the answer was the same: "Come back when you are seventeen and a half."

'He was seventeen and a half at the end of June. By then he was awaiting trial—as a gangster and a murderer.'

❖

Over the thirty-five days leading up to the hearing of the Court of Criminal Appeal, Jenkins and Geraghty must have found it impossible not to fret about the outcome. Their predicament was made even more tortuous by the continued heatwave, the temperature hovering around 32°C during mid-August.

In the absence of fresh news on the Antiquis case, the press turned its attention to other major stories. And there were plenty of those both at home and abroad. The two dominant foreign stories centred on inter-communal tension in British-occupied India and Palestine. While India was about to be carved into two independent states, Britain was struggling to contend with Zionist and Arab terrorism in Palestine, destination for boat-loads of Jewish refugees from Europe. When a couple of soldiers from the occupying forces were kidnapped and murdered by a Zionist group, anti-Semitic riots broke out across Britain. Coverage of these was juxtaposed with reports on what were seen as bigger domestic stories, on the collision between two express trains near Doncaster, on the death of over a hundred miners in an accident at Whitehaven Colliery, on the heatwave and accompanying drought, and on the intensifying economic crisis afflicting the country, a crisis so deep that Parliament was about to be recalled to discuss proposed emergency measures.

For many people, Jenkins and Geraghty aside, respite from the gloom was offered by the impending marriage of Princess Elizabeth—the future Queen—and Lieutenant Philip Mountbatten, as well as by a memorable second half to the cricket season. Watched by crowds of 30,000 or more on some days, the England team trounced their South African rivals. Victory was achieved with the help of Denis Compton, a swashbuckling batsman who also sustained a career as a top footballer. Young, handsome and flamboyant, he was one of the great sporting heroes of that era. As the blazing summer neared its inevitable conclusion, the sports pages carried regular bulletins on his quest to break the record for the number of runs scored in a season. But there was a strong possibility that Jenkins and Geraghty might not live to discover whether or not he claimed this seemingly unassailable record, which had stood for forty-one years.

❖

By English standards, the temperature was still uncomfortably hot when the lawyers representing Jenkins, Geraghty and Rolt made their way into the Central Criminal Court on Thursday 3 September. They were, once again, confronted by Anthony Hawke, representing the Crown. Their appeal was heard by three judges: Mr Justice Morris, the elderly Mr Justice Croom-Johnson, and Mr Justice Oliver who acted as chairman.

Explanations as to why Jenkins, Geraghty and Rolt shouldn't have been convicted on a murder charge were soon being set out by their lawyers. Speaking on behalf of Jenkins, Russell Vick stressed that his client, unlike Geraghty and Rolt who had confessed to their roles in the robbery, had not been present at the scene of the crime. 'I asked the judge for a separate trial for Jenkins,' Vick said, 'but he acted against my application, and all three men were tried together.' Vick added that, from the outset, there had been a danger that the jury would treat Rolt's statement, implicating Jenkins, as evidence against his client.

But Croom-Johnson waved away this complaint by saying, 'The trial judge referred to that half a dozen times and gave the jury explicit warning.'

Vick reminded the court that Jenkins possessed an alibi, though Mr Justice Hallett had swayed the jury by ridiculing it. In a dramatic announcement, Vick asked for permission to call a supplementary witness, a man who would confirm the alibi. That witness, he explained, had been in court throughout the trial but had only contacted Jenkins's relatives afterwards. Vick said that the man had been having lunch with Jenkins in a Clerkenwell café at the time of Antiquis's murder. The man was confident about the date of their lunch because it had coincided with his godchild's birthday. But the chairman of the court denied Vick permission to summon this new witness.

Satisfied that the case against Jenkins had already been explored in sufficient detail, Oliver didn't invite Hawke to present any counter-arguments. Instead, he wound up the hearing. Together with the two other judges, he retired to discuss the arguments put forward by the defence lawyers.

Oliver and his colleagues didn't take long to reach a conclusion. Returning to his seat on the bench, he announced their verdict. He started by summarising the law in relation to the three defendants. 'If a number of men set out to commit a felony of violence,' he said, 'and there was evidence to show that they all intended to carry through that felony at all risks and, in pursuit of the design, one of these men killed someone, then all three were guilty of murder.'

The judge moved on to assess the validity of each appeal. There was, he observed, ample evidence to support the jury's belief that Jenkins's story about being elsewhere at the time of the shooting was untrue. 'With regard to Geraghty and Rolt,' the judge added, 'the complaint was made that there was no direction to the jury on the question of manslaughter. On the facts of the case, this court did not think that any direction as to manslaughter was necessary. There was no ground on which the verdict of the jury could be impugned, and the appeals must be dismissed.'

❖

Rolt accepted the court's ruling, but Jenkins and Geraghty—for whom there was far more at stake—pursued the next stage in the appeals process. This involved their lawyers applying to Sir Hartley Shawcross, the Attorney-General, for permission to present their case to the House of Lords.

Jenkins and Geraghty subsequently had a tense thirteen day wait, during which Denis Compton passed his cricketing milestone with an atypically tentative innings of 86, scored against a South of England Invitation IX. Neither the heatwave nor the drought, in the meantime, showed any sign of abating.

On Tuesday 16 September—nearly five months after the Charlotte Street shooting—Jenkins and Geraghty received the news that the Attorney-General had refused to grant them permission to take their case to the Lords.

Emphasising the significance of Shawcross's decision, a date was promptly set for the execution of the convicted men. That date was a mere three days away.

Only one legal avenue remained open to Jenkins and Geraghty. Via their lawyers, they appealed to the Home Secretary, for clemency. Chuter Ede had the authority to commute their sentences to life imprisonment, but the politicised nature of the appeal system meant that the chances of him granting a reprieve were slim. He was, after all, a staunch believer in the deterrent value of the death penalty. By commuting the sentences passed on Jenkins and Geraghty, he'd have risked alienating the police who also supported capital punishment. Besides, the government needed to demonstrate that it was taking firm action against the post-war crimewave in general and gun-toting criminals in particular.

Even though Jenkins and Geraghty had not yet exhausted the available legal options, arrangements were made for their execution. Albert Pierrepoint, who had just returned from Hameln where he'd dispatched ten more Nazi war criminals, was asked to carry out the hanging. For that he would receive £15, half of it payable on completion of the job, the balance two weeks afterwards. On being appointed Number One Official Executioner, Pierrepoint had negotiated a fifty-percent pay rise on the standard fee, which had remained unaltered since his father's day. But he still felt that the authorities were, unlike their counterparts in other countries, getting the services of hangmen on the cheap. He considered the five guinea fees paid to his assistants scant compensation for taking as long as two days off work.

Prior to each hanging, it was customary for Pierrepoint and other senior executioners to be allocated a qualified assistant. Pierrepoint had noticed that names frequently dropped off the list because many of the people on it found their duties too upsetting. At the start of his career Pierrepoint had, in between working 'as a delivery driver, performed those duties for his Uncle Tom.

When a double execution was scheduled, two assistants were employed. Pierrepoint knew from experience how tricky it was to hang two people at once because there was greater potential for confusion. In the interests of efficiency, he liked to have three assistants for these occasions, but the authorities were unwilling to incur the added expense.

Harry Critchell and Harry Allen, two experienced assistants, were assigned to help him with the execution of Jenkins and Geraghty. He'd worked with them several times before. Allen—an exuberant Mancunian—had once worked alongside him on another multiple hanging. Through bitter experience, however, Pierrepoint had learnt to be wary of his assistants, many of whom had tried to discredit him in the hope of usurping his cherished job. He could even recall an occasion when acid had been applied to the rope chosen for a hanging, the intention being to cause it to snap when the condemned man dropped through the trapdoors. Had the sabotage achieved its objective, Pierrepoint would probably have been removed from his duties by the Home Office, ending a family tradition that stretched back almost half a century.

❖

Hollinwood was a typical Lancashire mill-town, its factory chimneys sprouting from a network of terraced houses and cobbled streets that had long since merged with neighbouring Manchester. A little over a year earlier Pierrepoint and his wife, who had previously run a grocer's shop together, had taken on the tenancy of one of the town's pubs. Part of the reason for their change of business was that Pierrepoint knew that by switching jobs he would have fewer problems obtaining time off whenever he was asked to carry out a hanging.

Why his pub wasn't called the White Horse or the Nag's Head or anything conventional, nobody had ever been able to explain to him. Instead, it revelled under the bizarre name of Help The Poor Struggler, often abbreviated to the Struggler. Regular newspaper stories about the jovial executioner moonlighting as a publican had played a role in ensuring that the pub had prospered in spite of its name. Groups of ghoulish sightseers made long, circuitous journeys there simply to shake hands with Pierrepoint or obtain his autograph, dispensed with a friendly smile. Every now and again, they even attempted to bribe him to let them watch an execution.

Alongside the sightseers, there were numerous regulars who didn't seem to mind having their pints poured by someone equally accustomed to tying nooses. A blackly humorous reminder of their host's parallel career was provided by a notice on the counter reading 'NO HANGING ABOUT THIS BAR'. Yet the bar was routinely occupied by a talkative gaggle of regulars who often enlivened the atmosphere with communal renditions of traditional ballads and Irish songs.

Pierrepoint was obliged to report to HM Prison Pentonville by 4:00pm on Thursday 18 September. On the day before an execution, he usually caught an early train to London, early enough for him to enjoy a lunchtime drink with Fabian and the Allchilds at the Fitzroy Tavern.

The first signs of autumn were tangible when he presented himself at Pentonville that day. Not only had the unrelenting heat of recent weeks been replaced by much cooler temperatures, but the drought had also ended, a thunderstorm and torrential overnight rain leaving the streets wet.

Visitors to Pentonville were expected to hammer on the gates with an oversized door-knocker. For Pierrepoint, the prison had powerful associations. It was there, during the winter of 1932, that he'd been trained in what he called the 'craft', the fundamentals of which he had learnt by repeatedly hanging a dummy known by the prison officers as 'Old Bill'. And it was there, almost nine years later, that he'd made the transition from being a mere assistant to being in charge of an execution. He still had a crisp memory of that morning, of swiftly dispatching Antonio Mancini, the

*Christmas card sent by Albert Pierrepoint.*

gangster who had murdered 'Little Hubby' Distelman. Since then, Pierrepoint had taken charge of 238 more hangings.

Discreet though he was, the reason for his arrival wasn't hard to guess. So regular were his visits, many of the prison officers had got into the habit of addressing him by his christian name. A few had even adopted the affectionate northern custom of calling him 'Our Albert'.

Sometimes he reached the venue for an execution only to be informed that a reprieve had been granted for the person he was scheduled to hang. In these circumstances, the authorities had occasionally left him out of pocket by with-holding his fee and failing to compensate him for either his travel expenses or the hours he'd wasted. But he was spared any such irritations by Chuter Ede's decision to turn down the appeal for clemency from Jenkins and Geraghty.

Immediately Pierrepoint arrived at Pentonville, he had to report to the Governor, W.J. Lawton, whose large, well-heated office and imposing desk reflected his pre-eminence in the prison hierarchy. Though Lawton was on cordial terms with the senior warders, even pausing to share stilted witticisms with them, he could be patronising in his treatment of hangmen and other subordinates.

The main purpose of this potentially awkward meeting was for Lawton to hand over a sheet of paper with the height and fully clothed weight of Jenkins and Geraghty written on it. These figures enabled the executioner to work out the drop required to hang them. The list revealed that Jenkins was five feet, nine inches tall, and weighed 146 pounds. Geraghty was half an inch taller and 35 pounds heavier.

❖

Until the execution had been carried out, neither Pierrepoint nor his assistants were permitted to leave the prison. From the Governor's office, he was always shown to the room where he'd be spending the night. He had to share the same accommodation as the assistant executioners, over whom he exerted effortless authority.

His assistants had to accompany him when the Prison Engineer Officer took him over to the execution chamber. In the meantime the condemned men had, as a rule, been escorted down to the exercise yards. That way, they wouldn't have to suffer the horror of listening to the executioners' preparations.

Instead of being the dark, messy dungeon that Pierrepoint had once imagined, the execution chamber was clean, light and tidy, its bright colour-scheme further defying expectations. The walls were painted green and the two double doors were bright yellow.

Where the ceiling of the room above had been, there were a couple of sturdy beams. Three thick chains were stretched across them. Below the beams were the hinged trapdoors through which the condemned men would plunge. The trapdoors, suitable for hanging three people at once, were two and a half feet wide and eight and a half feet long. A sizeable grey metal lever, jutting up from the floor like a lever in a railway signal box, operated them. Against the wall opposite was a narrow flight of stairs down to what was known as the 'pit'—an identically proportioned room beneath the trapdoors. These were connected to the side of the pit by four massive springs. In an incongruously thoughtful touch, the springs prevented the trapdoors from swinging back and hitting the condemned man after the hangman had pulled the lever.

This lethal mechanism provided a tangible link between Pierrepoint and his late father. Albert was only seventeen when his father died, so he treasured such connections. As Albert already knew from studying his father's memoirs, the scaffold at Pentonville had previously been installed in Newgate Gaol where his father had first worked. Pierrepoint senior, who regarded it as the best scaffold in Britain, had written so vividly about his work that Albert felt as if he too had witnessed the scenes described.

Except for two large black chests, two bulging sandbags, and a board the size of a stretcher, the prison authorities tended to keep the execution chamber empty. Fitted to the board were leg and arm straps. Pierrepoint was proud of the fact that he had never yet required this device, built for hanging unconscious prisoners. He had, however, made frequent use of the contents of the chests which he was responsible for inspecting.

These chests, which the Home Office dispatched to prisons where a hanging was imminent, contained leather wrist and arm straps, white cotton hoods, as well as four lengths of rope, two of them old, two of them new. Knowledgeable as he was about every aspect of his craft, Pierrepoint was aware that the ropes, each of them approximately six feet long, had been supplied by John Edgington & Sons, a tentmaker's shop on the Old Kent Road. Besides selling execution equipment to the whole of the British Empire, the shop hired out marquees for university balls and debutantes' dances.

Pierrepoint made a habit of running his fingers all the way along the four ropes, starting with the top end and finishing with the noose. Unlike the Americans who favoured a coiled hangman's knot, the British used a noose formed by threading one end of the rope through a pear-shaped metal eye woven into the other end. Pierrepoint liked to check that the friction of the metal on the ropes hadn't weakened them, leaving them liable to snap at the crucial moment. Invariably, he selected the old ropes.

Next, he had to test the mechanism that operated the trapdoors. To avoid these being accidentally opened, the control lever was secured by a pin that slotted into its base. Once the pin had been removed, Pierrepoint was able to push the lever, releasing the heavy bolts that held the trapdoors shut. Unless the mechanism was faulty, the springs yanked the trapdoors open with explosive force. The noise must have been audible throughout that wing of the prison.

The assistant executioners were sent down to the pit to close the trapdoors. Pierrepoint could then pull the lever that slid the bolts back into position. Now he was ready to fasten the ropes to the chains stretched across the overhead beams. This was done by hooking the metal eyes at the top of each of the ropes onto shackles which, in turn, could be fixed to the chains.

With the help of his assistants, Pierrepoint routinely checked that the two sandbags left in the execution chamber, were slightly heavier than the condemned men. Both sandbags had to be manoeuvred into position on the trapdoors, at which point the nooses were fastened round them and pulled tight. When Pierrepoint wrenched the lever again, the sandbags plummeted into the pit where they were suspended in midair.

Leaving the ropes to stretch overnight, he and his assistants vacated the execution chamber. At that point—between about 5:00pm and 6:00pm—Pierrepoint was taken to a position from where he could observe Jenkins and Geraghty without them seeing him. The intention was for him to study their musculature and the strength of their necks: factors that had to be considered when calculating the drop appropriate for both men. By looking at the condemned men, he also hoped to get an impression of how they might be expected to react en route to the scaffold.

If the prisoners were still in the exercise yard, he had to peer at them through a window. Alternatively, if they were back in their cells, he had to inspect them through the spy-holes in each of the doors. Not that it was always possible to obtain a good view of prisoners through these. He remembered once trying to look at a condemned man who would not get up off his bed, placing him partially out of sight. At the suggestion of a prison officer, Pierrepoint had gone into the cell pretending to be a member of staff inspecting the plumbing. But he had emerged with the unnerving impression that the prisoner had sensed the real reason for his visit.

Of the two condemned men, Geraghty was the more muscular. Even so, he didn't possess the type of bull-neck that required Pierrepoint to make substantial adjustments to his calculations. That evening Pierrepoint consulted the *Home Office Table of Drops* which ranged from five feet to eight feet six inches. First produced in 1888, thanks to a gruesome process of experimentation that had involved an accidental decapitation at HM

Prison Norwich, the table was based on the principle that heavier people required a shorter drop. Though a refined edition had been issued in 1913, Pierrepoint had been taught by his uncle to treat it as no more than a guide to the perfect figure. Perfection, in this case, was a drop that caused instant death by severing the spinal cord between the second and third vertebrae. To obtain that ideal measurement, Pierrepoint drew on his experience, adjusting the recommended figure to allow for the prisoner's age, height and musculature, along with any pertinent information relayed by the Prison Medical Officer. On the night before many previous executions, the young Pierrepoint had listened to his uncle Tom talk through these subtle calibrations, sharing the insights accrued by his father who had been Tom's tutor in the hangman's craft.

For Jenkins, Pierrepoint decided on a drop of seven feet, seven inches. Being a much heavier man, Geraghty was assigned a six feet, three inch drop. These figures were submitted to the Governor. From time to time, prison governors had given Pierrepoint useful comments on the figures, but his calculations had only once been disputed, leading to a tense stand-off.

Following the example set by his father, he jotted down the length of the drop, plus the name, age, height and weight of the condemned prisoners in an execution diary. He also used this cheap pocketbook to record the identity of his assistants, as well as the date and location of the execution.

Now that the bulk of the preparatory work was completed, Pierrepoint and his assistants could spend the rest of the evening trying to relax before they went to bed. They did this by chatting, playing dominoes and quaffing their pre-execution allowance of two pints of beer. Pierrepoint banned any reference to the reason why they were there.

Despite his matter of fact attitude towards his duties, he admitted to feeling tense during the run-up to an execution, though he tried not to let this show. But most people who knew him well could tell when he was nervous because he had a habit of frequently straightening his jacket by tugging on the lapels. Of course, he had far less reason for anxiety than the two men he was scheduled to execute at 8:00am the following day.

❖

Over in one of the condemned cells, Geraghty was composing a long valedictory letter to his parents, from which remorse was noticeable by its absence. He explained to them how his ambition to become a professional criminal dated back to 1946 when he'd just been sent to Sherwood Borstal. 'With that idea in my mind, I formed associations at borstal,' he wrote. 'In the view of most of the other boys I was already a "big-timer". In borstal my friends and I talked of little else except the jobs we intended to do when we were out in the world again...

'I was frightened at borstal, but within a month I was one of the "wolves"—the boys who are the terror of the others. In my first week I was in a fight and had my nose broken by a kick to the face. That taught me a lesson. I knew I could be as vicious as any of them. I decided that I would show them. I did, and from that time onwards I was left alone and admitted as one of the "heads".

'At borstal there are only three subjects of conversation: what you have done and are in for; what you are going to do when you get out; women and girls. Boys who are experts in one type of crime hold "classes" of their own for other boys. There is a good deal of boasting. Friendships are struck up and gangs are formed of boys who are likely to be released about the same time.

'The idea of going straight is laughed at. Arrangements are made that "X" will call at a certain café or public house in London on certain days of the week, so that when his friends "Y" and "Z" are released they will be able to team up at once...

'Within a week of being freed in November 1946 I had renewed all my old contacts. I had talked with "fences" and visited certain underworld "drums". I was also in touch with the men who will size up a job and give one a working plan of the interior of a shop. They take a mental note of the premises when making a simple purchase.

'During that same week, I had obtained a pair of guns. I was not yet ready to start off on big-time jobs so I contented myself with stealing a car, which I sold, and with stealing small stuff. I was waiting for my friends from borstal and, meanwhile, I would not even let my left hand know what my right was doing.

'Then came the day when Jenkins, whom I trusted above all, was released from borstal. I received a message about the time he would be in London. I met him as he came off the train at St Pancras. There was little to explain to him except the place which I intended should be held up. It was a carefully planned job. A planner had taken sights. We knew the layout. We had the guns and a driver. We knew in advance where we would dispose of the stuff. It looked as if we were onto a good thing. Then, as all the world knows, our plan went wrong. I had thought, after the many times it had been discussed in borstal, that nothing could go wrong. But it did.

'I had studied the lie of the land. I knew the area well. Those in the know had described the place carefully. I was to be the "minder"—the one who protects the "grabber". We had planned what we would do if things went wrong, but at no time was there any discussion about shooting. I think we were satisfied that the guns alone would scare off any opposition. There was never any agreement to shoot our way out.'

Geraghty described the brawl that had erupted inside Jay's and the gang's subsequent escape. He went on to articulate what he described as 'my feelings and thoughts while standing trial for my life'.

'I am not religious and I am quite easy in my mind and conscience...,' he informed his parents. 'On the eve of departing this life, my only regret is that I have wasted twenty years of my life and I have thrown away the other fifty. My early environment taught me that you have to fight or go under. I fought for things which I could never have got any other way.'

In an aside from his main theme, he asked his parents to pass on his thanks to the priest who had visited him in prison. Referring to 'tragedies like mine', he then addressed some of the social problems which, he felt, had pushed him towards a life on the wrong side of the law. 'One does not peck at the problems with boys' clubs, Sunday schools and such like things,' he declared. 'You have to go to the whole root of the trouble— the slums... I am not gloomy over my going like this and I don't want you to be. Goodbye. Look after yourselves. Love, Jim.'

Last thing that night, Geraghty received the normal farewell visit from the Governor. Since taking over at Pentonville early the previous year, W.J. Lawton had carried out this duty on several occasions. It provided Geraghty with the opportunity to relay the letter to his parents, who weren't above passing it on to the *News of the World*.

❖

The unvarying execution morning ritual required that a prison warder was sent to wake Pierrepoint, Critchell and Allen at 6:00am on Friday 19 September. Before they could have their leisurely breakfast, they had to complete the final arrangements for that morning's hangings.

While the condemned men were safely out of earshot in either the chapel or, more likely, taking a few minutes' exercise, Pierrepoint and the others were escorted to the execution chamber. There they performed the most strenuous aspect of their preparatory work. This entailed hauling up the two sandbags which had been dangling overnight in the pit, where two stretchers awaited the bodies of Jenkins and Geraghty. Once the nooses had been removed, the sandbags could be stowed out of the way. The trapdoors were then closed, the lever pulled back into position and the safety catch reinserted at the base of it.

As the hangmen ploughed their way through this checklist of final tasks, Pierrepoint liked any conversation to be whispered, just in case the condemned men had returned to their cells, from where the voices would have been audible. Terrible though the crime committed by Jenkins and Geraghty was, he felt that they still warranted mercy. Being a committed Christian, he thought of each of his victims as his brother or sister to whom something dreadful must be done.

One of the first things he did on execution mornings was to climb a ladder, propped against the higher of the two overhead beams. By adjusting the position of the chains stretched across them, he could raise or lower the ropes shackled to the outermost chains. If necessary, he could alter the height of the noose by as little as half an inch, so it hung at just the right height to slip over the condemned man's head. To ensure that the rope hung vertically and didn't twist out of position, Pierrepoint and his assistants wrapped and then fastened twine around all but the bottom part of the noose which was sheathed in soft leather.

Continuing the meticulous preparation, Pierrepoint liked to chalk a white T-shape on the trapdoor beneath each of the nooses, denoting where the condemned men had to stand. On either side of these marks, a single plank had to be laid across the width of the trapdoors.

Only one thing needed to be done before Pierrepoint, Critchell and Allen left the execution chamber. That consisted of partially removing the safety catch on the lever operating the trapdoors, an adjustment which Pierrepoint regarded as important because it shaved a fraction of a second off the execution process. Out of a mixture of professionalism and a desire to avoid prolonging the prisoner's misery, he'd always sought to match the speed and efficiency of his father. By reputation Pierrepoint senior had been capable of leading prisoners from the condemned cell as the clock had struck and dispatching them before the last of the chimes had sounded.

❖

During the three hours prior to the execution, euphemistically known by police and criminals as the 'eight o'clock walk', a subdued crowd had formed outside the front of the prison. Anticipating the usual anti-capital punishment demonstration led by Mrs Van der Elst, uniformed policemen had been positioned along the driveway and plainclothes officers had been posted in the crowd.

As 8:00am approached, however, there was no sign of Mrs Van der Elst's familiar advance guard of sandwich-board men, their placards bearing slogans such as 'STOP CAPITAL PUNISHMENT' and 'MERCY IS NOT WEAKNESS'. Nor was there any sign of their leader whose chauffeur-driven black Rolls Royce invariably headed a slow-moving procession of vans with tannoys mounted on them.

The crowd consisted of about a hundred men, women and children who had gathered at both ends of the driveway. They included friends and family of the condemned men, plus a press photographer and a couple of reporters from the London evening newspapers. The occasion had also attracted an assortment of onlookers, among them a glamorous young woman and her husband who had travelled there from Kentish Town. Approached by a reporter from the *Evening News*, she explained that they felt a particular connection with the Antiquis case because they'd been sitting in a café near Jay's only about fifteen minutes before the shooting.

When a group of Geraghty's friends tried to stand outside the prison gates, the police forced them back. A silent huddle of Jenkins's cronies, meanwhile, waited elsewhere in the crowd which spilled across the pavements on either side of Caledonian Road. His eldest sister joined them. Like so many people in the crowd, she was smartly dressed, a light biscuit-coloured coat worn with brown slacks and a grey pullover. She paced nervously up and down, taking frequent drags on a cigarette.

❖

After a quick breakfast, Pierrepoint and his assistants were escorted back to the condemned cells. As the three men headed there, they would have heard the everyday noises of the prison where the inmates were already on their work details, intended to dissipate the atmosphere of tension that foreshadowed executions.

While Critchell and Allen were each equipped with ankle straps, Pierrepoint carried two sets of wrist straps. For prisoners whom he regarded as exceptional from a criminological point of view, prisoners such as Neville Heath and Josef Kramer, he brought along his own soft calf-leather wrist straps. But he didn't consider Jenkins and Geraghty worthy of special treatment, so they had to make do with the ordinary straps issued by the prison.

Pierrepoint and his colleagues were soon in the corridor outside the condemned cells where they sometimes had to loiter for as long as three minutes. Though he had witnessed the consequences of what Jenkins and Geraghty had done, Pierrepoint made a point of trying not to become emotionally involved in what was about to happen. He felt that there was no sense in passing judgement over the men whom he executed. Irrespective of whether he regarded sentences as fair or unfair, he'd be expected to carry them out. He was, in any event, aware that he didn't possess the education, nor the specialised legal training, nor access to the results of expert police investigation necessary to question the courts' decisions.

Just before 8:00am Sir George Aylwen, Sheriff of London approached. Aylwen—who was there as the King's representative—led a procession comprising the Governor, the Medical Officer, several senior warders and the Reverend J.R. Williams, the Prison Chaplain, dressed in a white surplice. The presence of Aylwen, a stockbroker in his mid-sixties who had lost an eye during the Boer War, demonstrated the prominence of the Antiquis case. Had this been a run-of-the-mill execution, the Under Sheriff would have deputised for him.

Clocks across London were poised to strike as Aylwen gave the signal for the doors to the condemned cells to be unlocked. Wrist strap in hand, Pierrepoint entered one of them. Allen went into the other cell. Pierrepoint would have arranged with the two warders keeping watch over each of the prisoners to make sure that Jenkins and Geraghty were sitting at their tables with their backs to the doors. Both prisoners, who had earlier changed out of their prison clothes and donned suits, may well have been given morphine injections by the Medical Officer.

Taking only a few rapid strides, Pierrepoint was standing over one of the condemned men, ready to tap him on the shoulder and say, 'Follow me'. As the man stood up, Pierrepoint bound his hands behind his back with the wrist strap. To reduce the danger of panicking or enraging the prisoner, Pierrepoint never fastened the strap tightly. He estimated that no more than about one in every hundred executions was preceded by a struggle, yet he did his best to prepare the death watch officers for trouble. Condemned men had been known to escape from their guards or try to jump to safety just as the trapdoors opened. On the other hand, he had observed many prisoners unshaken by the prospect of death. He'd even encountered a man who had said, 'I've always wanted to meet you, but not, of course, under these circumstances.'

In what was known as 'Condemned Cell One', adjoining the execution chamber, the Reverend Williams was, meanwhile, heading for the connecting doors. Buttressed by the death watch officers, the prisoner was shuffling after Williams who was required to declaim the opening part of the official execution service. 'I am the resurrection and the life, saith the Lord. He that believeth in me, though he were dead, yet shall live, and whosoever liveth and believeth in me shall never die…'

At the same time, the other condemned man was escorted through the door that linked the two cells. That door had previously been hidden behind the wardrobes in both bathrooms.

No more than seven paces separated Condemned Cell One from the scaffold. Through the double doors opening onto the adjacent corridor and execution chamber beyond, the nooses were visible. In the presence of the obligatory group of official witnesses, the first of the condemned men was manoeuvred onto the chalk marks by his guards, who stood on the planks placed across the trapdoors. If the guards were new to their grim duty, Pierrepoint would have taught them the grip devised by his uncle. It involved clamping their palms between the condemned man's upper arm and ribcage, enabling them to hold the prisoner on the chalk mark, then let go quickly enough to avoid being dragged into the pit.

As soon as the first prisoner was in position, one of Pierrepoint's assistants, whom he'd trained to work in well-drilled silence, had to sink to his knees and fasten straps round the man's ankles. This was the signal for the chaplain to start reciting the penultimate part of the execution service. 'Remember not, Lord, the offences of these thy servants and not be angry with them forever...'

These words echoing round the execution chamber, Pierrepoint had to take out a white hood, usually kept in the breast-pocket of his jacket like a display-handkerchief. He had to slip the hood over the prisoner's head, then put the noose round the man's neck and tighten it. A rubber washer had to be slid into place to ensure the noose remained under the prisoner's jaw, from where it could rotate, forcing the chin backwards.

When the second of the condemned men reached the trapdoors, Pierrepoint and his other assistant had to repeat the process. Despite the alacrity with which Pierrepoint worked, he liked to ensure that there was a slight lull at this stage, allowing the prisoners to make a last minute expression of guilt. Overzealous clergymen had been known to harangue prisoners into confessing to their crimes, so Pierrepoint insisted on positioning the chaplain well away from them.

Darting to his left, Pierrepoint crouched over the lever controlling the trapdoors. He used one hand to pull the pin from its base, the other to push the lever. There was a loud crack as Jenkins and Geraghty plunged into the pit where they dangled from taut, swaying ropes. Two broken lengths of twine floated down on a more leisurely route through the gaping trapdoors.

At that point Williams embarked on the concluding section of the execution service. 'Into thy hands, Oh Lord we commend the spirit of thy servant,' it began. 'Oh Lord, we beseech thee, mercifully hear our prayers and spare all who confess their sins unto thee...'

To the accompaniment of the chaplain intoning these words, Pierrepoint was accustomed to taking the stairs down to the pit. Beneath the bodies which were hanging from their jawbones, there were pools of excrement, caused by the condemned men's bowels emptying.

Their shirts had to be opened, so that the Medical Officer could use his stethoscope to check that their hearts were no longer beating. If Pierrepoint had done his job properly, they would have died instantly, something that wouldn't have happened if he'd used the American system, employing a standard five feet drop. Pierrepoint, who was appalled by what he regarded as its barbarity, had heard that Field Marshal Keitel, one of the Nazis executed at Nuremburg, had taken the best part of half an hour to die. But even the British system of hanging, which Pierrepoint revered, was far from infallible. A hanged man's heart would sometimes continue functioning for up to twenty minutes. However protracted a condemned man's death was, the Home Office instructed the Governor to tell people that the execution had been 'quick and expeditious'.

Once the Medical Officer had declared the men dead, it was his duty to signal to the Governor in the room above, visible through the open trapdoors. Pierrepoint and the Medical Officer then went back upstairs and joined the exodus from the execution chamber, the entrance to which was locked behind them.

❖

Pierrepoint and his assistants returned to the execution chamber at 9:00am that day. While he knelt beside the open trapdoors, it was the duty of one of his assistants to go down to the pit to help him with a task that, even by his standards, he found distasteful and, more to the point, unnecessary. Regulations dictated that they record the length by which the bodies of Jenkins and Geraghty had stretched. On account of their severed spinal cords, the two friends' necks were grotesquely elongated.

Descending into the pit, Pierrepoint had to strip the hanging bodies. From the scaffold overhead, a spare rope was then lowered and tied round one of the naked corpses which was hoisted a few feet, permitting Pierrepoint to remove the hood and noose. He was strong enough to lift the corpse onto a waiting stretcher. Whenever he handled the bodies of his victims, he tried to treat them with tenderness. He detested the callous attitude of some of his assistants towards the people they'd hanged.

Soon the bare, drooping bodies of Jenkins and Geraghty were both sprawled across stretchers. The corpse of an executed person was, Pierrepoint thought, uniquely broken, whether he was a criminal or Christ.

The stretchers were carried from the pit into the adjacent Post Mortem Room where Sir Bernard Spilsbury was scheduled to conduct immediate autopsies on Jenkins and Geraghty. Their bodies ended up being transferred to a huge, lead-covered slab with a gutter running round it.

Before the post mortem could go ahead, another formality—the identification of the bodies—had to be carried out. The task had been assigned to Bob Higgins, who may well have resented losing time that could have been better spent on his latest murder investigation. This had begun ten days earlier when Rita Green, a thirty-year-old prostitute, had been shot dead in the house on Rupert Street where she took her wealthy clients. Murders of that type were, Higgins recognised, among the most difficult to clear up, due to the absence of an obvious motive. Disapproving though his attitude was towards prostitutes, Higgins believed that everyone was entitled to the law's protection, so he was conducting an investigation as intense and thorough as if she had been a distinguished citizen. He and his colleagues had interviewed the victim's husband, who maintain-

The murdered prostitute, Rita Green, nicknamed 'Black Rita'.

ed that he didn't know she was working as a prostitute. They'd also obtained several hundred statements from people who frequented that part of Soho, but the killer was no closer to being arrested.

When Higgins arrived at Pentonville, its walls wreathed in autumnal fog, he was struck by the grim atmosphere common to all prisons on execution morning. His work had given him a high tolerance of horror, yet he was distressed by the macabre sight of the corpses of Jenkins and Geraghty, young men whose personalities had grown familiar during repeated questioning. The realisation that they were around the same age as his own sons, the eldest of whom was a staunch opponent of capital punishment, amplified the impact.

Never had Higgins been so upset by what he'd seen in the course of his work. Harrowing as the experience was, it didn't make him renounce his support for the death penalty. He regarded it as a valuable deterrent, probably responsible for the comparatively low murder rate in Britain. Most murderers, he thought, deserved their fate and society was better off without them. He was convinced that ardent abolitionists like his eldest son, Ronald, would change their tune if someone near and dear to them was murdered. Too often, in his opinion, the fate of the victim and grieving relatives was forgotten in the blaze of publicity which followed an execution.

For Higgins, there was only one remaining duty before he finished his involvement with the Antiquis case. That morning he joined Fabian, Spilsbury and at least one reporter, plus a jury, all of whom had crowded into the Governor's Office, where an inquest had been convened. The inquest, chaired by W. Bentley Purchase, heard evidence from Spilsbury as well as Higgins and the Governor.

Higgins verified the identity of the hanged men, and the Governor confirmed that the execution had been performed in accordance with prison regulations. Always proficient at conveying detailed medical information in a manner easily understood by laypeople, Spilsbury explained the results of the post mortem.

Purchase, who had chaired many such hearings, had noticed that the spinal columns of hanged men tended to be broken in the same place. He attributed this not to Pierrepoint's expertise but to the sound guidance offered by the *Home Office Table of Drops*.

Presented with conclusive evidence of how Jenkins and Geraghty had died, the jury would not have taken long to arrive at verdicts of 'death by judicial hanging'. Before closing the inquest, Purchase addressed Fabian and Higgins: 'I should like to express on behalf of the public an appreciation of the success of your efforts in this matter. This may act as a deterrent to others who may be like-minded. It is the efforts of you and those who work with you who save the public at large. This is not part of the inquest proceedings but an expression of my own feelings.'

'Thank you, sir,' Fabian replied. 'I was only the captain of a good team.'

❖

A few minutes later, a warder ventured out of the studded prison gates. In front of the waiting crowd which had just been permitted to advance down

The crowd gathers rounds the execution notices placed outside the gates of HM Prison Pentonville on the morning of the execution.

the driveway, he put up three notices. These were displayed in glass-fronted cases, temporarily hooked onto the gates. The notices comprised certificates signed by the Sheriff, the Governor, the Chaplain, the Coroner and the Medical Officer. Above the signatures, one of the certificates stated that 'Judgement of death was executed on Christopher James Geraghty'. Another certificate, issued by the Coroner, provided official confirmation of the death of Charles Henry Jenkins.

Before the crowd had time to disperse, the gates were opened to allow the Reverend Williams to pilot his car slowly down the driveway. On reaching the junction with Caledonian Road, he had to wait for a break in the traffic. Both Jenkins's sister and the reporter from the *Evening News* seized the opportunity and ran over to the chaplain's car. Jenkins's sister asked Williams if her brother had left any messages for his family.

'He sent his love,' Williams replied.

The reporter enquired how Jenkins and Geraghty had reacted to the ordeal.

'They took it very well.'

Jenkins's sister then turned to the reporter and said, ' "Harryboy", as we called him, was always plucky and considerate. He wouldn't like to think that he'd caused his relations more grief than he could help. He wouldn't like to know I'd been here today.'

❖

The dissected and horribly disfigured bodies of hanged prisoners were subject to one final indignity, calculated to punish their families. Instead of allowing a conventional burial, the authorities staged a dismal funeral within the prison walls.

While the surviving inmates were in their cells eating their midday meal, a team of prison officers stood beside a couple of freshly dug graves. Dozens of men had been buried in the prison's improvised cemetery, sometimes making it hard to dig more than a few feet down without striking human remains. Unlike conventional cemeteries, there were no tombstones to commemorate its occupants, among them a cross-section of London's most notorious criminals. There were no mourners either because they were banned from attending.

As the coffins were lowered into the damp soil, the voice of the Chaplain could be heard reciting the burial service. 'In the sweat of thy face shalt thou eat bread, till thou return unto the ground, for out of it wast thou taken, for dust thou are and unto dust thou shall return...'

Oblivious to what was happening behind the prison's giant walls, people in the surrounding streets were carrying on with their normal lives.

Families tucked in to lunches rendered frugal by rationing. Red double-decker buses rumbled past. Hungry queues formed in eel pie houses and fish and chip shops. Customers downed pints of beer in the Caledonian Arms, just across the road from the prison gates, conversation perhaps turning to Denis Compton's record-breaking achievements. The staff at the nearby Mayfair cinema prepared for the next screening of that day's double-bill of the thriller, *Devil's Mask*, and the Technicolor musical, *The Time, the Place and the Girl*. Bookies' runners loitered on street corners taking bets. Newsvendors sold early editions of the *Evening News* which carried the main headline 'JENKINS SENT LOVE FROM THE SCAFFOLD'. And commuters clicked through the turnstiles of the Caledonian Road Underground Station, hair ruffled by the warm breath of passing tube trains.

# EPILOGUE

The Antiquis case has since drifted into comparative obscurity, its victim's hard-to-pronounce surname doubtless playing a part in that, yet it had significant, long-lasting repercussions. These spanned both the public and private spheres.

By fuelling the debate about capital punishment in Britain, the execution of Jenkins and Geraghty contributed to the setting up of a Royal Commission on Capital Punishment just over a year later. The main task of the Commission, on which the novelist Elizabeth Bowen served, was to consider alternatives to the death penalty. Sir Harold Scott was among the witnesses called to give evidence. Arguing in favour of the deterrent effect of capital punishment, he cited the Antiquis case as well as the earlier murder of Captain Binney. 'All the persons concerned in these cases were associates and resided in the Bermondsey district,' Scott declared. 'They had formed themselves into a gang of criminals and, as events have proved, there was no limit to the steps they would take to avoid capture.' Scott went on to assert that the decision not to hang Ronald Hedley, driver of the getaway car that had killed Captain Binney, had encouraged the gang to resume its criminal activities. 'Some of them were arrested and sentenced to varying terms of imprisonment but still they continued living their life of crime. Then came the carrying out of the death sentence on Charles Henry Jenkins and Christopher James Geraghty. Almost immediately, the gang disbanded. They have not been seen in their usual haunts since, and as far as is known, are not engaged in criminal pursuits.'

Scott's evidence was challenged by witnesses from the Howard League for Penal Reform. 'It was suggested that the execution of Geraghty and Jenkins for the murder of Mr de Antiquis broke up a gang which had not been deterred from crime by sentences of imprisonment,' one of their witnesses stated. 'This is a facile explanation and ignores the possibility that it was the removal of the leaders that smashed the gang, and that removal for ten years might have been equally effective.'

Albert Pierrepoint was also summoned to give evidence. Despite his reluctance to discuss his job, he found himself compelled to answer questions formulated to decide whether hanging was a humane method of execution. To that end, Pierrepoint was asked to conduct a demonstration, carried out with the aid of a dummy.

Four and a half years after its creation, the Royal Commission delivered its report. Instead of advocating radical change, it proposed no more than a few minor amendments to the execution process. The report nevertheless provided further impetus to the debate about capital punishment which culminated in its abolition in August 1964. Well before then, however, Pierrepoint had written to the Home Office announcing his decision to resign from his cherished post as Number One Official Executioner. His resignation was prompted by a lucrative contract with a newspaper which wanted to serialise his memoirs. But he would later imply that his early retirement had been motivated by newfound opposition to the death penalty.

'I have carried out the execution of more judicial sentences of death... than any executioner in any British record or archive...,' he wrote in his autobiography. 'The fruit of my experience has this bitter after-taste: that I do not now believe that any one of the hundreds of executions I carried out has in any way acted as a deterrent against future murder. Capital punishment, in my view, achieved nothing except revenge.'

His feelings were lent credence by the continued criminal escapades of thirty-three-year-old Tommy Jenkins, not long released from prison. If deterrence worked, then surely *he*, more than most people, would have been reluctant to risk meeting the same fate as his brother. With the sixth anniversary of his brother's hanging imminent, Jenkins teamed up with two other men—among them an escaped convict named Robert Sanders—who were planning an armed robbery. Their target was the weekly wages consignment delivered to an east London clothing factory. When the factory manager spotted them loitering outside, he rang the police who pursued the gang through the streets of Hackney. Responding to shouts of 'Stop, I am a police officer!', Sanders swivelled round and pointed his revolver at a Detective Constable who was only three yards away.

Sanders shouted back at him, 'Keep away from me, you bastard, or I'll put a bullet through you!'

But the detective refused to obey him. Sanders then fired at him, the bullet passing through the belt that was dangling from his raincoat. A fight ensued and two further shots were fired, neither of them injuring anyone. Jenkins and the rest of the gang were tried at the Central Criminal Court, where they sat in the dock previously occupied by Geraghty, Rolt and Harry Jenkins. Sanders was sentenced to life imprisonment, and Harry Jenkins's brother received a five year gaol term.

The crime for which Sanders and Tommy Jenkins were found guilty echoed the pivotal incident in *The Blue Lamp* (1950), one of the most commercially successful British movies ever. The film hinges on the robbery of a West End cinema, during which a Police Constable is shot dead by a young gunman. Produced by Ealing Studios, a company nowadays more readily associated with amiable comedies such as *The Lavender Hill Mob* (1951), it was inspired by the Antiquis case. In a playful acknowledgment of this, its opening sequence evokes the post-war crimewave with a montage of newspaper front-pages, one of which carries the famous photo of Antiquis lying fatally wounded on the pavement.

Though the film's storyline maximised the drama by making the murder victim a policeman, the parallels between fact and fiction are undeniable. Like the Antiquis case, *The Blue Lamp* takes place against a London backdrop of snack bars, billiard halls, slum housing and bomb-sites, populated by a compendium of urban low-life, ranging from spivs to slouch-hatted bookies. It also features two interconnected robberies, the second of them ending in tragedy when a passer-by intervenes and gets cold-bloodedly gunned down. His killer is a young, masked gang leader who shares many of Harry Jenkins's traits, not least his ruthlessness, arrogance and brilliantined good looks.

Even the police investigation depicted in *The Blue Lamp* bears numerous similarities to the Antiquis case. From real life, the screenwriters plundered ingredients such as the discovery of the murder weapon by a child, the witnesses who fail to pick out the killer at an identification parade, the subsequent surveillance operation, and the way that the culprit is traced via an abandoned mackintosh.

Bernard Lee, an actor who became a familiar presence in the James Bond movies, portrayed the imperturbable Fabian-like CID man, intent on tracking down the gun-toting young tearaways. Dirk Bogarde, then in his late twenties, was cast in the Jenkins role which would propel him towards

*Poster for The Blue Lamp. (Copyright Rank/Granada International plc)*

*Still from* The Blue Lamp, *showing the scene when Dirk Bogarde confronts Jack Warner. Note the poster advertising the spoof film,* Granny Get Your Gun. *(Copyright Rank/Granada International plc)*

international stardom. Patric Doonan, who had appeared alongside Bogarde the previous year in *Once A Jolly Swagman*, took the part of his sidekick. Their victim, the avuncular PC Dixon, was played by Jack Warner. Despite being killed midway through the film, the character was resurrected in *Dixon of Dock Green*, a much-loved BBC television series that continued for more than twenty years after its launch in 1955. Also starring Warner, the series was created by Ted Willis, one of *The Blue Lamp's* screenwriters.

In imitation of much-admired Italian movies such as *Rome: Open City* (1942) and *Ossessione* (1945), *The Blue Lamp* was, unusually among British films of that period, shot on location, providing a patina of dusty, bomb-scarred authenticity. Little else about the film, however, feels authentic, be it the implausible working-class accents, the idealised portrayal of the Met, or the final scene when the underworld boss conspires with the bookies at White City Greyhound Stadium to help the police corner the gang leader. All too many facets of this characteristically sanguine Ealing Studios vision of the world run counter to the much grimmer realities of post-war life.

Thanks to the heavy involvement of Scotland Yard in its production, involvement that was sanctioned by Sir Harold Scott, *The Blue Lamp* has a propagandist flavour. Nowhere is this more evident than the introductory voice-over which blames 'insufficient numbers of police' for the crimewave. The film uses the Antiquis case as a convenient pretext for a reassuring vision of late 1940s London, a city where the police always get their man and where young gangsters are treated as pariahs.

No wonder Scotland Yard was keen to assist with the film by loaning genuine police equipment and personnel, notably Detective Superintendent Fred Cherrill who made a one-line cameo appearance as a fingerprint expert, his voice dubbed by an actor. Police cooperation with the Met even extended to helping to promote the film. Just before a greyhound meeting in Southampton, for example, they supplied a team of officers who re-enacted the film's concluding chase.

The impact of the Charlotte Street shooting could be felt not just in the country's packed cinemas and greyhound stadia but also in the lives of at least nine people whose existences were thrown into turmoil. For the majority of those people, Antiquis's death had predictably negative consequences. Events in North Soho would, however, prove beneficial for one of them. That person could easily have been the journalist, Duncan Webb. Had his editor not maintained such an obstructive attitude, he would have achieved Fleet Street stardom by locating Bill Walsh. As things turned out, Webb's friend, Fabian, was that rare beneficiary of the Antiquis case.

His deservedly celebrated investigation reinforcing his status as Scotland Yard's star detective, he retired from the police. Besides taking a job as a columnist for a national newspaper, the now defunct *Empire News*, he penned his memoirs. Entitled *Fabian of the Yard*, they were first published in 1950, their popularity justifying frequent reprintings. The book, which devoted a section to the Antiquis case, soon served as the basis for a BBC television series. Broadcast in different parts of the country under subtly different titles, the series was billed as *Fabian of Scotland Yard*, *Fabian of the Yard*, or *Inspector Fabian of Scotland Yard*. Creaky though

Bob Fabian and Joslin Bingham, nicknamed 'Frisco', the owner of the International Bar, a West End club favoured by visiting black celebrities, ranging from Joe Louis to the Mills Brothers.

it now seems, it has the distinction of being British television's first hit cop show. It was also groundbreaking in another sense.

Most television drama of that period tended to be broadcast live, but *Fabian of Scotland Yard* bucked the trend by being shot on film, enabling the BBC to sell it to multiple foreign markets, among them America where the CBS network broadcast it under the title of *Patrol Car*. With that in mind, the programme's producers inserted regular travelogue scenes, showing London landmarks such as Nelson's Column and the Houses of Parliament.

The lead role was taken by the debonair Bruce Seton, who had earlier made a fleeting appearance in *The Blue Lamp*. His gentrified portrayal of Fabian would help to earn him a knighthood. So popular was the series, which ran from 1954 until 1956, it generated two spin-off feature films, *Fabian of the Yard* (1954) and *Handcuffs, London* (1955).

Following the short-lived Hollywood vogue for drama-documentaries, each half-hour episode of the series was based on a real case. The episode transmitted on 17 February 1956, presented viewers with a compressed version of the Antiquis investigation. None of the prints of this episode appear to have survived. Like the other programmes in the series, though, it must have featured the same introductory voice-over. 'In the nation's war on crime,' the narrator repeatedly declared, 'Scotland Yard is the brain

*Frontispiece to the American edition of* Fabian of the Yard.

*Still from the episode of* Fabian of Scotland Yard *that was based on the* Antiquis *case.*
*(Copyright: Anthony Beauchamp Productions)*

of Great Britain's man-hunting machine. Routine, detail, science and tenacity, these are the weapons used by squads of highly trained men—men like former Inspector Robert Fabian, hailed by the press as one of England's greatest detectives...'

To add credibility to the drama, Fabian himself appeared at the end of every instalment when he'd talk directly to the audience about what they'd just seen. For all his conversational fluency off-screen, the programme's producers found that he had a regrettable tendency to dry up while the cameras were rolling. Never a natural thespian, he looked and sounded uncomfortable, his flat, nasal voice less in keeping with an action hero than someone doing a bad impersonation of a minor town hall functionary.

Fabian's improbable second career as a television star didn't end there despite his shortcomings as a performer. In 1956, ITV—Britain's first, recently launched commercial television channel—recruited him to join the presentation team on *The 64,000 Question*, a new, nonsensically-titled quiz programme modelled on the American show, *The $64,000 Question*. Any mention of money had been discreetly dropped from the title of the British version because ITV was only offering a basic prize of sixpence per question. Fabian made regular appearances on the programme which remained part of the channel's schedule until 1958. Exploiting his reputation as the broad-shouldered scourge of criminals, he featured as the 'Guardian of the Questions', a gimmicky role that required him to do little else but stand

*Bob Fabian speaking at the end of an episode of Fabian of Scotland Yard. (Copyright: Metropolitan Police Historical Collection)*

guard over the pile of cards on which the questions were written.

Amid the vaguely comical distractions of Fabian's flourishing career, it's easy to forget the many victims of the murder investigation that launched him on that unlikely trajectory. Apart from Antiquis himself, the obvious victims of the Charlotte Street shooting were Mrs de Antiquis and their six children. Far less predictably, the other principal victim was Britain's most famous pathologist.

The post mortem that Spilsbury had performed on the murdered motorcyclist served as a humiliating reminder of the decline in his once remarkable skills. Depressed by his failing powers, their erosion probably hastened by a third stroke soon afterwards, he enacted a sad postscript to an already tragic story.

On the afternoon of Wednesday 17 December 1947, he drove back to Blue Star Garages in Swiss Cottage and parked his car there. He explained to the staff that he wouldn't be needing it over Christmas, so he presented them all with their seasonal tip. Then he went over to University College where he still had a laboratory. It consisted of a tiny room with a fanlight above the door. Inside there was just enough space for a desk on which he kept several card-index cabinets. He worked at a table beneath a window overlooking a courtyard. The window was flanked by a sink, racks of test-tubes and another table, dotted with Bunsen burners. Normally so fastidious, Spilsbury had allowed piles of papers, along with a thick layer of dust, to accumulate, yet he'd refused to allow anyone to clean or even tidy the room.

While he was in his laboratory, he destroyed the papers and notebooks kept there. Before leaving, he completed his report on the autopsy which he had, at the request of W. Bentley Purchase, carried out that morning.

Instead of waiting, as usual, until the following day to deliver the report, he posted it to St Pancras Coroner's Court.

After a solitary dinner at one of his clubs, he approached the hall porter and handed over the key to his locker. Spilsbury told the porter that he wouldn't be needing it in the New Year.

At about 7:30pm, he returned to his laboratory. Forty minutes later, a passing colleague noticed that the light in Spilsbury's room was still on. A pungent odour of gas was emanating from there. The colleague, who knew about his poor sense of smell, tried to alert him, but the door was locked. Pounding on it elicited no reply, so Spilsbury's colleague fetched the nightwatchman who had a key.

When they entered the room, they saw that Spilsbury had gassed himself. The frail old pathologist was barely alive. A succession of emergency phone-calls were made. W. Bentley Purchase was among the people summoned to the laboratory. He got there just as someone was attempting to resuscitate his friend. The attempt failed, and Spilsbury was declared dead at 9:10pm. With his suicide, the sequence of fatalities that had begun one sunny afternoon almost eight months earlier came to a belated end, a single bullet ripping through the lives of so many people.

# Sources

ARCHIVES
British Library Newspaper Archive, British Telecom Group Archives, London Metropolitan Archives, Meteorological Archive, Metropolitan Police Historical Collection, National Film and Television Archive, National Galleries of Justice, Public Record Office, Royal Institute of British Architects Library.

NEWSPAPERS AND MAGAZINES
*Picture Post, Illustrated London News, London Leisure, Daily Express, Daily Graphic, Daily Herald, Daily Mail, Daily Mirror, Daily Telegraph and Morning Post, News Chronicle, Evening News, Evening Standard, Star, News of the World, Observer, People, Sunday Chronicle, Sunday Dispatch, Sunday Express, Sunday Graphic, Sunday Pictorial, Times, Sunday Times, Goole Times, North London Press, Mitcham News and Mercury, Southend Times, Southend-on-Sea and County Pictorial, Kinematograph Weekly, London Police Pensioner, Cinema Theatre Association Newsletter, Picture House, British Journalism Review.*

INTERNET
Times Digital Archive, British Pathé Ltd, British Universities' Newsreel Database.

RADIO
*The Prospect of Hanging*, BBC Radio 4, first broadcast on 16 May 1993.

INTERVIEWS
Alec Vale, Sally Fiber (née Allchild), the late Percy Burgess and the late Tony Van den Bergh.

# Selected Bibliography

Addison, Paul, *Now the War Is Over: A Social History of Britain, 1945-51* (Revised Edition), Pimlico, 1995

Archibald, Sir William Frederick Alphonse, *Metropolitan Police Guide* (HMSO, 1939)

Best, William C.F., *'C' or St James: A History of Policing in the West End of London, 1829-1984* (W.C.F. Best, Kingston-upon-Thames, 1985)

Beattie, James Martin, *Post Mortem Methods* (University Press, Cambridge, 1915)

Bechhofer Smith, C.E., *The Trial of Ley and Smith* (Jarrold, 1947)

Benney, Mark, *Gaol Delivery* (Longmans, Green & Co, 1948)

Beveridge, Peter, *Inside the CID* (Evans Brothers, 1959) *The Borough Men: The Police in Southend-on-Sea, 1840-1969* (Essex Police Museum, no date)

Box, Charles R., *Post Mortem Manual* (J & A Churchill, 1919)

Browne, Douglas and Tullett, E.V., *Bernard Spilsbury: His Life and Times* (George G. Harrap, 1951)

Brutton, C.P. and Studdy, Sir Henry, *A Police Constable's Guide To His Daily Work* (Sir Isaac Pitman and Son, 1940)

Cherrill, Fred, *Cherrill of the Yard* (The Popular Book Club, c.1955)

Cherrill, Fred, *The Fingerprint System at Scotland Yard* (HMSO, 1954)

Clayton, Captain Gerold Fancourt, *The Wall Is Strong: The Life of a Prison Governor* (John Long, 1958)

Dernley, Syd with Newman, David, *The Hangman's Tale: Memoirs of a Public Executioner* (Robert Hale, 1989)

Eyles, Allen and Skone, Keith, *London's West End Cinemas* (Sutton: Premier Bioscope, 1984)

Fabian, Robert, *Fabian of the Yard* (Heirloom Modern World Library, 1955)

Fabian, Robert, *London After Dark* (Naldrett Press, 1954)

Fiber, Sally, *The Fitzroy: the Autbiography of a London Tavern* (Temple House Books, 1995)

Fido, Martin and Skinner, Keith, *The Official Encyclopedia of Scotland Yard* (Virgin Books, 1999)

Fielding, Steve, *Pierrepoint: A Family of Executioners* (John Blake Publishing, 2006)

Firmin, Stanley, *Scotland Yard: The Inside Story* (Hutchinson, c.1950)

Firmin, Stanley, *Crime Man* (Hutchinson, 1950)

Firmin, Stanley, *Murderers in Our Midst* (Hutchinson, 1955)

Gosling, John, *Ghost Squad* (W.H. Allen, 1959)

Gross, Hans, *Criminal Investigation: A Practical Textbook for Magistrates, Police Officers and Lawyers* (Sweet and Maxwell, 1936)

Hamilton, Maurice, *Light and Shade at Scotland Yard* (John Murray, London 1947)

Hastings, MacDonald, *The Other Mr Churchill: A Lifetime of Shooting and Murder* (George Harrap, 1971)

Hatherill, George, *A Detective's Story* (André Deutsch, 1971)

Higgins, Robert, *In the Name of the Law* (John Long Ltd, 1958)

Hoskins, Percy, *No Hiding Place! The Full Authentic Story of Scotland Yard in Action* (A Daily Express Publication, London, 1951)

Jackson, Stanley, *An Indiscreet Guide to Soho* (Muse Arts Ltd, 1947)

Jackson, Stanley, *The Old Bailey* (W.H. Allen, 1978)

Klein, Leonora, *A Very English Hangman: The Life and Times of Albert Pierrepoint* (Corvo, 2006)

Koestler, Arthur, *Reflections on Hanging* (Victor Gollancz, 1956)

Lefebure, Molly, *Evidence For The Crown: Experiences of a Pathologist's Secretary* (William Heinemann, 1954)

Lock, Joan, *Marlborough Street: The Story of a London Court* (Robert Hale, London, 1980)

London Statistics, 1946-1955, Volume II (London County Council, 1958)

*Metropolitan Police Report, 1945* (HMSO, 1946)

*Metropolitan Police Report, 1946* (HMSO, 1947)

*Metropolitan Police Report, 1947* (HMSO, 1948)

Moriarty, Cecil C.H. and Williams, Lieutenant Colonel W.J., *Police Procedure and Administration* (Butterworth and Co., 1944)

Murphy, Robert, *Smash and Grab: Gangsters in the London Underworld* (Faber and Faber, 1993)

O'Donnell, Bernard, *The Old Bailey and Its Trials,* (John Blake Publishing, 1950)

Paul, Philip, *Murder Under The Microscope* (Futura, 1990)

*The Police Code, 1947* (HMSO, 1947)

*Post Office London Street Directory of 1947,* (Kelly's, 1947)

Pierrepoint, Albert, *Executioner Pierrepoint* (George G. Harrap, 1974)

Scott, Sir Harold, *Scotland Yard* (Penguin, 1957)

Scott, Sir Harold, *Your Obedient Servant* (André Deutsch, 1959)

Sandbach, J.B., *This Old Wig* (Hutchinson, 1950)

Saunders, Hilary St. George, *The Middlesex Hospital, 1745-1948* (Max Parrish, London, 1949)

Thomas, Donald, *Villains' Paradise: Britain's Underworld From The Spivs to the Krays* (John Murray, 2005)

Thompson, Laurence, *The Boys' Book of Scotland Yard* (Clerke and Cockeran, 1951)

Webb, Duncan, *Crime Is My Business* (Frederick Muller, 1953)

Webb, Duncan, *Sailor, You've Had It* (W.H. Allen, 1946)

*Life In The Post-War Years: The Photographs of Douglas Whitworth* (Tempus, 2003)

*Who's Who, 1948* (Alfred Otto Dobbs, 1948)

Young, Hugh, *My Forty Years at the Yard* (W.H. Allen, 1955)

Ziegler, Philip, *London at War* (Sinclair-Stevenson 1995)

I  BLOOD ON THE CROSSROADS

See PRO (the Public Record Office) CRIM1/1861 for witness statements describing the robbery. See *An Indiscreet Guide to Soho* for background information about Soho. See *Scotland Yard: The Inside Story, No Hiding Place, Boys' Book of Scotland Yard* and *Fabian of the Yard* for material on Scotland Yard and the Information Room. See *Executioner* for material about Albert Pierrepoint. See *The Fitzroy* for descriptions of the interior of the pub and the Allchilds. Further material was provided by their daughter, Sally Fiber. See *Picture Post* (17 May 1947) for the sections about the reporters covering the police story. See *Middlesex Hospital* and PRO(CRIM1/1861) for the passage about Alec de Antiquis's hospitalisation. See PRO(CRIM1/1861) for the description of the interior of Jay's. See *Daily Mail* (1 May 1947, p.3) for information about the Antiquis family. See *Cherrill of the Yard*, supplemented by interviews with Alec Vale and Percy Burgess, for the portrait of Fred Cherrill.

| | |
|---|---|
| p.11 | 'the only... both sides' (*Indiscreet Guide to Soho*, p.56) |
| p.12 | 'Stop, thief!' (*Daily Mirror*, 30 April 1947, p.12) |
| p.12 | 'Police... them!' (PRO, CRIM1/1861) |
| p.14 | 'Keep off!' (PRO, CRIM1/1861) |
| p.14 | 'They have shot... my best' (*News Chronicle*, 30 April 1947, p.7) |
| p.15 | 'someone had dialled 9-9-9' (*The Boys' Book of Scotland Yard*, p.162, confirmed by Fabian whose foreword states that there are 'no factual errors in the book'.) |
| p.15 | 'Into his decorative... Dartmoor' (PRO,MEPO3/138) |
| p.15 | 'the Yard's switchboard... every hour' (*The Boys' Book of Scotland Yard*, p.49) |
| p.15 | 'Switchboard operators... a call' (*The Boys' Book of Scotland Yard*, p.50) |
| p.16 | 'the nerve... crime' (Voice-over of *Post-War Crime*, Rank Films, 1946, shooting script, PRO, MEPO2/6979) |
| p.17 | 'No more than... the crime' (*Boys' Book of Scotland Yard*, p.141) |
| p.18 | 'When he spotted... by a car' (*Executioner*, p.151) |
| p.18 | 'MY TEN... EXECUTIONER' (*Thomson's Weekly News*, quoted in *Executioner*, p. 27) |
| p.18 | 'What had... cotton-mills' (*Executioner*, p.77) |
| p.18 | 'When I... Official Executioner' (*Executioner*, p. 37) |
| p.18 | 'Death had... at that age' (*Executioner*, p.34) |
| p.18-19 | 'Even so... death sentences' (*Executioner*, p.10) |
| p.19 | 'While several... espoused' (*Executioner*, p.33) |
| p.19-20 | 'top-hat... hanging tassels' (*Executioner*, p.19) |
| p.21 | 'He suspected... comparison' (*In the Name of the Law*, p.38) |
| p.21 | 'To his way of... tidy desk' (*In the Name of the Law*, p.72-73) |
| p.21 | 'In any event... points' (Interview with Percy Burgess) |
| p.21 | 'The thought... administrative job' (*In the Name of the Law*, p.216) |
| p.21 | 'Put those... like amateurs' (*In the Name of the Law*, p.216) |
| p.22 | 'Responsibility was... CID Commander' (*In the Name of the Law*, p.215) |
| p.22 | 'The knowledge... resentment' (*In the Name of the Law*, p.215) |
| p.22 | 'ponces' or 'johnsons' (*London After Dark*, p.54) |
| p.22 | 'scum' (*In the Name of the Law*, p.112) |
| p.23 | 'despicable business' (*In the Name of the Law*, p.181) |
| p.23 | '17,500' (*Evening Standard*, 8 April 1947, p.1) |
| p.24 | 'Higgins felt it ... efficiency' (*In the Name of the Law*, p.214) |
| p.24 | 'Large numbers... elsewhere' (*Scotland Yard*, p.24) |
| p.24 | 'Higgins nevertheless... world' (*In the Name of the Law*, p.15) |
| p.24-5 | 'His colleagues... underworld' (Interview with Percy Burgess) |
| p.26 | 'apples and pears' (Interview with Sally Fiber) |
| p.26 | 'The Allchilds treated... house' (Letter from Albert Pierrepoint to Charlie and Annie Allchild, quoted in *The Fitzroy*, p.54) |
| p.26 | 'ANNIE...BARMAID' (*Fitzroy: Autobiography of a London Tavern*, p.49) |

p.26      'He had admitted... his trade' (*The Fitzroy*, p.53)

p.26      'I am not a showman' (*Executioner*, p.28)

p.27      'These included...Provisions' (*Post Office London Street Directory of 1947*, p.160)

p.28      'For Higgins... attractions' (*In the Name of the Law*, Author's Note)

p.28      'Yet his wife... living' (*In the Name of the Law*, p.74)

p.29      'his job which... in life' (*In the Name of the Law*, p.16)

p.29      'Yard Man's Bible' (*No Hiding Place*, p.38)

p.29      'combining... high speed' (*In the Name of the Law*, p.36)

p.31      '6 AXE... AGED 70' (*Evening Standard*, 25 March 1947, p.1)

p.32      'Much as he... exploitation' (*In the Name of the Law*, p.121)

p.32      'probably beyond human aid' (*In the Name of the Law*, p.124)

p.33      'pathetic bundle' (*In the Name of the Law*, p.124)

p.33      'If Higgins's... becoming a policeman' (*In the Name of the Law*, p.16-17)

p.33      'In no way... might have had' (*In the Name of the Law*, p.212)

p.33-34      'Higgins sensed... again' (*In the Name of the Law*, p.125)

p.36      'Arriving at... *Odd Man Out*' (*Picture Post*, 17 May 1947, p.7-8 & *Daily Mail*, 30 April 1947, p.1)

p.36      'Higgins could have... towards journalists' (*In the Name of the Law*, p.95)

p,36      'He did, however... about it' (*In the Name of the Law*, p.111)

p.38      'On the whole... helpful' (*In the Name of the Law*, p.95)

p.38      'Needless to say... the game' (*In the Name of the Law*, p.96)

p.38      'The case was... years later' (*In the Name of the Law*, p.22)

p.38      'In view of... immediate superior' (*In the Name of the Law*, p.125)

p.39      'Ambitious though... towards Fabian' (Interview with Tony Van den Bergh)

p.39      'Fun and Games' (*Times*, 15 June 1978, p.18)

p.40      'had a reputation... at the Yard' (*Scotland Yard: The Inside Story*, p.20)

p.40      'He liked going... razors' (*Fabian of the Yard*, p.84)

p.41      'He felt... any man' (Fabian's foreword to *Boys' Book of Scotland Yard*, p.10)

p.41      'The fact that... he relished' (Fabian's foreword to *Boys' Book of Scotland Yard*, p.10)

p.41      'He sometimes... rewarded them' (*Fabian of the Yard*, p.10)

p.41      'Feeling as... camp' (*Fabian of the Yard*, p.10)

p.41      'People... interested him' (*Fabian of the Yard*, p.10)

p.41      'Frustrated... drawing office' (*Fabian of the Yard*, p.10-11)

p.42      'A nasty... to die' (*Fabian of the Yard*, p.95)

p.42      'Get the... come in by taxi' (*Fabian of the Yard*, p.95-96)

p.42      'Amid the... about his lunch' (*Fabian of the Yard*, p.95)

p.43      'the West End which... hand' (Fabian's foreword to *Boys' Book of Scotland Yard*, p.11)

p.43      'There was... would surprise him' (*London After Dark*, p.10)

p.45      'As Fabian liked... tears' (Interview with Percy Burgess)

p.45      'Give your eyes a chance' (*Fabian of the Yard*, p.77)

p.47      'Only the... handed over' (Metropolitan Police Report, 1947, 14 February 1946 gun amnesty)

p.48      As Higgins knew... enquiries' (*In the Name of the Law*, p.114)

p.48      'Heavy Mob' (*Scotland Yard: The Inside Story*, p.40)

p.49      'Just two or... promise' (*Star*, 30 April 1947, p.3)

p.51      '173' (*Inside Scotland Yard*, p.91)

p.51      'due to... at 3:15pm' (*Boys' Book of Scotland Yard*, p.140)

p.51      'How he... got older' (Interview with Alec Vale)

p.52      'scene of crime box' (*Boys' Book of Scotland Yard*, p.70)

p.52      'classify... status' (*Scotland Yard: The Inside Story*, p.34)

p.52      'reminded... old-fashioned car horn' (*Fabian of the Yard*, p.192)

II    PERSONS UNKNOWN

See PRO(CRIM1/1861) for Bob Higgins's visit to the mortuary and for the summary of the witness statements. For the section about newsreels, see British Universities' Newsreel Database and unused footage of the crime scene, held by British Pathé Ltd. Details of how Scotland Yard dealt with witnesses were obtained during several interviews with Alec Vale and from *A Detective's Story*. See *No Hiding Place* for details of the Map Room. See *Picture Post* (17 May 1947) for the paragraphs about Sid Brock. See PRO(MEPO9/162) for the layout of Tottenham Court Road Police Station. See *No Hiding Place* and *Scotland Yard: The Inside Story* for the section on the Criminal Record Office and Rogues' Gallery. Further information came from an interview with Alec Vale. See *The Other Mr Churchill* for the portrayal of Robert Churchill. See *Crime Man* for background information about crime reporters. See *Bernard Spilsbury: His Life and Times* for the portrayal of Bernard Spilsbury and his morning ritual. See *Times* (28 September 1961, p.17) for material on Bentley Purchase. See *Scotland Yard, Scotland Yard: The Inside Story* and *Times* (20 October 1969, p.10) for information about Sir Harold Scott. See *Scotland Yard: The Inside Story* and *Times* (1 September 1977, p.16) for information about Sir Ronald Howe. See *Scotland Yard: The Inside Story* and *My Forty Years at the Yard* for information about Hugh Young See London Metropolitan Archive (LCC/MISC.P./41) for description of St. Pancras Mortuary. See PRO(CRIM1/1861) for Donovan de Antiquis's visit to the mortuary. See *Bernard Spilsbury: His Life and Times, In the Name of the Law, Post Mortem Manual* and *Post Mortem Methods* for the reconstruction of the post mortem.

| | |
|---|---|
| p.57 | 'Chief Superintendant... interviewing witnesses' (*A Detective's Story*, p.1) |
| p.58 | 'a prisoner making... actually said' (*Police Code, 1947*, p.32) |
| p.60 | 'Stand back... move' (PRO, CRIM1/1861) |
| p.61 | 'Stand still!' (PRO, CRIM1/1861) |
| p.62 | 'In a cruel... England' (*Daily Mail*, 6 May 1947, p.3) |
| p.62 | 'But Higgins was... contained in them' (*In the Name of the Law*, p.126-127) |
| p.63 | 'three enormous...like blazes' (*Fabian of the Yard*, p.97) |
| p.63 | 'Higgins was beginning... gunmen' (*In the Name of the Law*, p.127) |
| p.63 | 'Nothing on the... either' (*Fabian of the Yard*, p.97) |
| p.65 | 'This is a new era in crime' (*Daily Mail*, 30 April 1947, p.1) |
| p.65 | 'THE AMATEUR KILLER' (*Daily Mail*, 30 April 1947, p.1) |
| p.66 | 'GUN GANG... STICK-UP' (*Star*, 29 April 1947, p.1) |
| p.66 | 'During the Blitz... the rear' (*In the Name of the Law*, p.73) |
| p.66 | 'Well, Chief... all different' (*Fabian of the Yard*, p.97) |
| p.67 | 'Rubberface' (*In the Name of the Law*, p.66) |
| p.68 | 'Mr Fabian?... a clue' (*Fabian of the Yard*, p.97) |
| p.69 | 'He saw himself... of facts' (*Scotland Yard: The Inside Story*, p.7) |
| p.69 | 'Years of probing... he witnessed' (*Crime Man*, p.27) |
| p.69 | 'I did not know him' (*Daily Telegraph*, 30 April 1947, p.6) |
| p.69 | 'Mr Tong... reads your hands' (*Daily Telegraph*, 30 April 1947, p.6) |
| p.70 | 'M.O.' (*Police Procedure and Administration*, p.66) |
| p.70 | 'He'd been... Marylebone Lane' (*Fabian of the Yard*, p.198) |
| p.70 | 'Many of the... twenty years' (*The Boys Book of Scotland Yard*, p.63) |
| p.71 | 'Cummins had what... people' (*In the Name of the Law*, p.60) |
| p.71 | 'Yet he was... career' (*In the Name of the Law*, p.62) |
| p.72 | 'quite dreadful' (*In the Name of the Law*, p.57) |
| p.72 | 'In the average... collaring criminals' (*Fabian of the Yard*, p.19 and interview with Percy Burgess) |
| p.73 | 'Though officers... overtime pay' (Interview with Percy Burgess) |
| p.73 | 'Each morning... company for no one' (*Fabian of the Yard*, p.20) |
| p.73 | 'He sometimes... policeman's equipment' (*Fabian of the Yard*, p.9) |
| p.74 | 'HOLD-UP... IN LONDON' (*Daily Telegraph*, 30 April 1947, p.1) |
| p.74 | 'MURDER, LONDON W.1' (*Daily Express*, 30 April 1947, p.1) |

| | |
|---|---|
| p.74 | 'Scott considered… armoury' (*Scotland Yard*, p.99) |
| p.76 | 'Lieutenant-Colonel Pierrepoint' (*Executioner*, p.152) |
| p,76 | 'He found multiple… as well'(*Executioner*, p.154) |
| p.77 | 'He knew that… officials' (*Executioner*, p.154) |
| p.77 | 'he had a sense… quick death' (*Executioner*, p.155) |
| p.77 | 'Yet Pierrepoint remembered… for them' (*Executioner*, p.143) |
| p.77 | 'He presumed… written on it' (*Executioner*, p.148) |
| p.77 | 'Such was… shooting case' (*The Other Mr Churchill*, p.62) |
| p.79 | 'a very odd… ammunition' (PRO, CRIM1/1861) |
| p.79 | 'Scotland Yard's… news stories' (*Scotland Yard: The Inside Story*, p.8) |
| p.80 | 'Apart from… somewhere else' (*Scotland Yard: The Inside Story*, p.8) |
| p.80 | 'Until recently… criminals themselves' (*Scotland Yard: The Inside Story*, p.9) |
| p.81 | 'Aged 25… dirty raincoat' (Mimeographed Press and Information Deprtment handout) |
| p.81 | 'Somebody somewhere… at large' (*Daily Telegraph*, 1 May, 1947, p.1) |
| p.81 | 'had once led… in London' (Bernard Spilsbury: His Life and *Times*, p.187-188) |
| p.84 | 'Aware that Spilsbury… distant mortuaries' (*Bernard Spilsbury: His Life and Times*, p.400) |
| p.85 | 'He'd assumed… disgrace himself' (*Scotland Yard*, p.11) |
| p.85 | 'Scott had had… post-war crimewave' (*Scotland Yard*, p.12-13) |
| p.85 | 'His initial… undertake the work' (*Scotland Yard*, p.14) |
| p.85 | 'He was concerned… a raid' (*Daily Telegraph and Morning Post*, 29 July 1947, p.1) |
| p.86 | 'Prior to meetings… their minds' (*Scotland Yard*, p.15) |
| p.86 | 'Scott thought… came up' (*Scotland Yard*, p.15) |
| p.87 | 'Even so… curtailed' (*Fabian of the Yard*, p.13) |
| p.88 | 'lived on their wits' (*Times*, 1 May 1947, p.3) |
| p.88 | 'his acrimonious… the killers' (*Crime Is My Business*, p.196 and interview with Percy Burgess) |
| p.89 | 'Great White Chief' (*Bernard Spilsbury: His Life and Times*, p.199) |
| p.91 | 'Higgins always… had happened' (*In the Name of the Law*, p.201) |
| p.91 | 'For all… authority.' (*In the Name of the Law*, p.201) |
| p.91 | 'Whether… and helpful' (*In the Name of the Law*, p.201) |
| p.91 | 'Even so… the greatest detective' (*In the Name of the Law*, p.201) |
| p.92 | 'He appeared… him recoil' (Interview with Percy Burgess) |
| p.92 | 'Unlike other… a question' (*Bernard Spilsbury: His Life and Times*, p.203-204) |
| p.92 | 'He was angered… long periods' (*Bernard Spilsbury: His Life and Times*, p.216) |
| p.92 | 'Spilsbury noticed…surrounding skin' (*Evening News*, 22 July 1947, p.3) |
| p.92 | 'One day he… jurisprudence' (*Bernard Spilsbury: His Life and Times*, p.215) |
| p.92 | 'Higgins got the… index-cards' (*In the Name of the Law*, p.203) |
| p.92-93 | 'Sometimes Higgins… on them' (*In the Name of the Law*, p.203) |
| p.93 | 'For the first… details' (*In the Name of the Law*, p.203) |
| p.93 | 'Regardless… diligence' (*In the Name of the Law*, p.203) |
| p.94 | 'Higgins could see… self' (*In the Name of the Law*, p.208) |
| p.94 | 'Asked… in harness' (*In the Name of the Law*, p.203) |
| p.94 | 'Among Higgins's… cracking up' (*In the Name of the Law*, p.208) |
| p,94 | 'Spilsbury's attention… object' (PRO, CRIM1/1861) |
| p.95 | 'As well as… demise' (PRO, CRIM1/1861) |
| p.95 | 'Spilsbury said… entrance wound' (*In the Name of the Law*, p.208) |
| p.95-96 | 'Lost in thought… to Spilsbury' (*Bernard Spilsbury: His Life and Times*, p.408) |

III    MURDER GUN

See *Fabian of the Yard*, *In the Name of the Law*, and *A Detective's Story* for information about informers. See *Fabian of the Yard*, *In the Name of the Law*, and PRO(CRIM1/1861) for the search of Brook House and the aftermath. See *Fabian of the Yard* for details of police surveillance techniques. See *The Other Mr Churchill* for the account of the test-firing. See *The Fitzroy* for the description of the pub's clientele. Additional information was provided by Sally Fiber. See *Fabian of the Yard* and PRO(CRIM1/1861) for the majority of the material about the Southend leg of the investigation.

| | |
|---|---|
| p.99 | 'He knew they... a gunman' (*Fabian of the Yard*, p.185) |
| p.100 | 'To Detective... From The Boys' (*Fabian of the Yard*, p.82) |
| p.100 | 'Higgins bragged... colleagues' (*In the Name of the Law*, p.216) |
| p.102 | 'Higgins was... lucky break' (*In the Name of the Law*, p.127) |
| p.102 | 'what his friends... green' (*In the Name of the Law*, p.163) |
| p.102 | 'If only... what to do' (*In the Name of the Law*, p.163) |
| p.102 | '4 GUN GANGS ROAM LONDON' (*Evening News*, 30 April 1947, p.1) |
| p.102 | 'SIX GUNMEN ON THE RUN' (*Evening Standard*, 30 April 1947, p.1) |
| p.102-3 | 'to a "guns for hire" gang... armed raid' (*Evening Standard*, 30 April, p.1) |
| p.103 | 'GANG VICTIM'S... POVERTY' (*Star*, 30 April 1947, p.3) |
| p.103 | 'It is all I have... my brothers' (*Star*, 29 April 1947, p.3) |
| p.103-4 | 'Mrs de Antiquis explained... failed in that' (*Daily Mail*, 1 May 1947, p.3) |
| p.104 | 'He did, however... cold water' (*Fabian of the Yard*, p.14) |
| p.104 | 'The raid had... master criminal' (*Daily Telegraph*, 1 May 1947, p.1) |
| p.104-5 | 'A dead man... in our midst today' (*Daily Mail*, 1 May 1947, p.1) |
| p.105 | 'Despite that... be prosecuted' (*Fabian of the Yard*, p.129) |
| p.106 | 'So had a cache... soldiers' (*London After Dark*, p.94) |
| p.107 | 'Fabian's initial optimism... records' (*Fabian of the Yard*, p.96-97 and letter from Albert Pierrepoint to Charlie and Annie Allchild, quoted in *The Fitzroy*, p.54) |
| p.107 | 'He was certain... his face' (Interview with Percy Burgess) |
| p.108 | 'Beau Brummel' (*Times*, 15 June 1978, p.18) |
| p.108 | 'He appeared... to tell it' (*Boys' Book of Scotland Yard*, p.162) |
| p.108 | 'D'you want to... round their chins' (*Fabian of the Yard*, p.98) |
| p.109 | 'Ever since... right moment' (*Fabian of the Yard*, p.12) |
| p.109 | 'MURDERERS SHIELDED' (*Times*, 2 May 1947, p.2) |
| p.110 | 'Ah... 'em all' (*Fabian of the Yard*, p.98) |
| p.110 | 'Try it... Vauxhall' (*Fabian of the Yard*, p.98) |
| p.110 | 'It fits, Chief!' (*Fabian of the Yard*, p.98) |
| p.110-11 | 'He said he'd... next seen him' (PRO, CRIM1/1861) |
| p.112 | 'Mr Williams was in' (*Fabian of the Yard*, p.98) |
| p.112 | 'fawnish... bluish' (PRO, CRIM1/1861) |
| p.112 | 'I think... other labels' (*In the Name of the Law*, p.128) |
| p.113-14 | 'The essence...face value alone' (*Crime Man*, p.35) |
| p.115 | 'There is no doubt...cornered' (*Evening Standard*, 2 May 1947, p.1) |
| p.115 | 'Sorry, sir... in London' (*Fabian of the Yard*, p.99) |
| p.115 | REGRET NO... OR GLOVES' (*Fabian of the Yard*, p.99) |
| p.116 | 'Ah, yes, here we are...' (*Fabian of the Yard*, p.99) |
| p.116 | 'Why, of course... 1946' (*Fabian of the Yard*, p.99-100) |
| p.116 | 'Amos turned out... Kemp Thomas' (*No Hiding Place*, p.129 and *Star* 22 July 1947, p.5) |
| p.117 | 'Fabian disapproved... arms race' (*Fabian of the Yard*, p.18) |
| p.117 | 'Does this...Green Man' (PRO, CRIM1/1861 and *Fabian of the Yard*, p.102-103) |
| p.117 | 'The man... trouble' (*Fabian of the Yard*, p.17) |
| p.118 | 'Its five chambers... .45 cartridges' (PRO, CRIM1/1861) |
| p.119 | 'He spotted... fired in the shop' (PRO, CRIM1/1861) |
| p.121 | 'But experience had... their lesson.' (*In the Name of the Law*, p.37) |

p.121    'most criminals lacked... dishonest life' (*In the Name of the Law*, p.106)
p.121    'Yes, that's mine... Harry Jenkins' (PRO, CRIM1/1861)
p.121    'He could remember... the police' (*Fabian of the Yard*, p.31)
p.122    'It's better... get away' (*Fabian of the Yard*, p.17-18)
p.122    'The present crimewave... a machine' (Voice-over of *Post-War Crime*, Rank Films, 1946, shooting script, PRO, MEPO2/6979)
p.123    'The peerless... business going.' (*Daily Mail*, 3 May 1947, p.3)
p.123    'Both Fabian and... good looks' (*Fabian of the Yard*, p.101 and *In the Name of the Law*, p.129)
p.123    'Higgins discerned... glint' (*In the Name of the Law*, p.129)
p.123    'But I'm not going... Mrs Kemp' (PRO, CRIM1/1861)
p.124    'It looks... serious to me' (PRO, CRIM1/1861)
p.124    'I suppose... any shooting' (PRO, CRIM1/1861)
p.124    'the guvnor... Borstal' (PRO, CRIM1/1861)
p.125-26 'Fabian had strong... blow them up' (*Fabian of the Yard*, p.16-17)
p.126    'Rolt said that... his story' (PRO, CRIM1/1861)
p.127    'Knowing Geraghty's... found himself' (*In the Name of the Law*, p.130)
p.127    'I am enquiring... run down' (PRO, CRIM1/1861)
p.127    'Next to Jenkins... station' (*Fabian of the Yard*, p.102)
p.127-28 'I shouldn't be... stuck up' (PRO, CRIM1/1861)
p.128    'All right... You can go' (*Fabian of the Yard*, p.102)
p.129    'STREET SEALED... NARROWS' (*Star*, 3 May 1947, p.1)
p.129    'the Little Water-Drinker' (*Fabian of the Yard*, p.22)
p.129    'the Fitzroy Tavern which... amazing place' (*London After Dark*, p.80)
p.129    'whom he considered... he knew' (*London After Dark*, p.81)
p.130    'Though he viewed... of the nation' (*London After Dark*, p.4)
p.130    'So inseparable... Macbeth' (*In the Name of the Law*, p.131)
p.130    'Fabian had sometimes... policeman' (*Executioner*, p.151)
p.130    'Grateful for... the case' (*Executioner*, p.152)
p.131    'The station... leaving London' (*Executioner*, p.86)
p.132    'Get in... anything' (*Daily Herald*, 5 May 1947, p.1)
p.132    'considering... HUNTED BY BY YARD' (*Daily Herald*, 5 May 1947, p.1)
p.133    'Fabian hoped... interviewed together' (*Fabian of the Yard*, p.102-103)
p.133    'Let us tell... on the front' (PRO, CRIM1/1861)
p.133    'There was something... Bogart' (*In the Name of the Law*, p.132)
p.133    'Fabian was taken... inform on Walsh' (*Boys' Book of Scotland Yard*, p.168)
p.135    'Higgins got the... in England' (*In the Name of the Law*, p.132)
p.135    'Suddenly Bill Walsh... his revenge' (*Fabian of the Yard*, p.104)
p.135    'Meaningful expressions... the proceeds' (*Fabian of the Yard*, p.104)
p.137    'What's the game?' (PRO, CRIM1/1861)
p.137    'Get out of it' (PRO, CRIM1/1861)
p.140    'He identified it... revolver' (PRO, CRIM1/1861)
p.140    'That's the one... killed Antiquis' (*Fabian of the Yard*, p.100)

## IV ARMED AND DANGEROUS

See *News of the World* (11 May 1947, p.1) for the false confession. See *Evening Standard* (14 May 1947, p.1) for the discovery of the body in the railway tunnel. See *Crime Is My Business* and *Sailor, You've Had It* for the portrayal of Duncan Webb and his involvement in the Antiquis case. See PRO(CRIM1/1861) for the bulk of the scene on Plumstead Common. See *The Other Mr Churchill* for a description of Robert Churchill's routine. See *The Boys' Book of Scotland Yard* for information about 'magnet-dragging'.

p.143    'BANDIT SHOOTS... WITH POLICE' (*Evening Standard* 5 May 1947, p.1)

p.143    'I am sending... same assassins' (*Daily Mail*, 6 May 1947, p.3)

p.143-44    'what official... gallant citizen' (*Hansard*, 8 May 1947, columns 781)

p.144    'I am sure... series of crimes' (*Hansard*, 8 May 1947, columns 781-782)

p.144-45    'Is it not... these illegal weapons' (*Hansard*, 8 May 1947, columns 783-784)

p.146    'Higgins had experienced... genuine affair on him' (*In the Name of the Law*, p.164-165)

p.147    'No, I can't... anymore' (PRO, CRIM1/1861)

p.147    'Arthur Birchall' (For legal reasons, both he and his wife have been assigned pseudonyms.)

p.148    'regarded by the... kill again' (*Evening Standard*, 14 May 1947, p.1)

p.148    'Asked which... were staying' (PRO, CRIM1/1861)

p.149    'I am quite... to Bill Walsh' (PRO, CRIM1/1861)

p.149    'One of the more... her eyes' (*Evening Standard*, 16 May 1947, p.1)

p.150    'Believing that... to them' (*Evening Standard*, 16 May 1947, p.1)

p.150    'It is vitally... protect you' (*Evening Standard*, 16 May 1947, p.1)

p.150    'very blonde' (*Times*, 16 May 1947, p.3)

p.150    'travelling with... dangerous' (*Evening Standard*, 16 May, p.1)

p.152    'Under the influence... respectable newspaper' (*Smash and Grab*, p.105)

p.152-54    'He had heard... you'll get him' (*Crime Is My Business*, p.205)

p.154    'Paper! Paper! *Star, News,* 'n' *Standard!*' (Interview with Tony Van den Bergh)

p.154    'ANTIQUIS... WOMAN' (*Evening Standard*, 15 May 1947, p.1)

p.154-55    'Overnight Webb... in disgust' (*Crime Is My Business*, p.206-207)

p.156    'who had, when... a face' (*Daily Mail*, 17 May 1947, p.1)

p.156    'Hello, chum... going' (PRO, CRIM1/1861)

p.156    'He talked... of Plumstead' (*Daily Mail*, 17 May 1947, p.1)

p.156-57    'This is... any guns' (PRO, CRIM1/1861)

p.157    'What d'you want... other matter' (PRO, CRIM1/1861)

p.157-58    'D'you want to... soon as I could' (*Daily Herald*, 17 May 1947, p.1)

p.158    'she provided... information' (*Evening Standard*, 17 May 1947, p.1)

p.159    'Walsh requested a glass... five years' (PRO, CRIM1/1861)

p.159    'He proceeded to... call all day' (PRO, CRIM1/1861)

p.160    'Walsh described how they'd... wait for me' (PRO, CRIM1/1861)

p.160-61    'He wrote that... Mrs Birchall lived' (PRO, CRIM1/1861)

p.161-62    'Walsh wrote that... back to Wapping' (PRO, CRIM1/1861)

p.162    'Both Fabian... frame Walsh' (*In the Name of the Law*, p.132)

p.162    'I want to say... 23 April' (PRO, CRIM1/1861)

p.162-63    'On examining... Central Police Station' (*Fabian of the Yard*, p.105)

p.163    'We are police... got on me' (PRO, CRIM1/1861)

p.163    'After a... arrested as well' (PRO, CRIM1/1861)

p.163    'I am... the night' (PRO, CRIM1/1861)

p.164    'Despite their youth... around them' (*In the Name of the Law*, p.133)

p.164    'If they arrested... in the chain' (*Fabian of the Yard*, p.105)

p.164    'the police initiated... recent years' (*Evening Standard*, 19 May 1947, p.1)

p.164    'GUNMAN... QUESTIONED' (*Daily Telegraph*, 17 May 1947, p.1)

p.164    'When not out... that stuff?' (*Picture Post*, 17 May 1947, p.29)

V       ECHOES OF A GUNSHOT

See *Marlborough Street* for material about the court and its workings. See *Gaol Delivery* for an account of induction into a prison and the day to day existence of prisoners. See *The Incredible Mrs Van der Elst* for background information about Mrs Van der Elst. See *The Old Bailey* for the description of the building and its history. See *Times* (29 September 1958, p.15) for the portrait of Russell Vick. See *The Trial of Ley and Smith* and *Who's Who* for material on Anthony Hawke. See *Bernard Spilsbury: His Life and Times* for the section about Bernard Spilsbury. See *Executioner* for background information about HM Prison Pentonville and the life of condemned prisoners. See *Executioner* and *The Hangman's Tale* for Albert Pierrepoint's pre-execution routine. See *A Hangman's Tale* for details of Pierrepoint's life as a publican. Additional information was supplied by the late Tony Van den Bergh. See *Executioner* and *A Hangman's Tale* for Albert Pierrepoint's execution day routine. *Reflections on Hanging* was also a useful source.

p.192    'Bill! Bill!' (*Evening Standard*, 20 May 1947, p.12)
p.196    'he declared that... age of sixteen' (*Hansard*, 22 May 1947, column 2531)
p.197    'Higgins entered... 3 June' (*Times*, 28 May 1947, p.2)
p.198    'Crump said... following Friday' (*Times*, 4 June 1947, p.2)
p.198-99    'Through their work... friendship' (*The Other Mr Churchill*, p.9-10, 15-16, 64, 294)
p.199    'Courts were... forceful questioning' (*In the Name of the Law*, p.31)
p.199    'Charles O'Connor began to... with Rolt' (*Evening Standard*, 24 June 1947, p.5)
p.199    'who was... under cross-examination' (*In the Name of the Law*, p.206)
p.199    'agreed that... No, replied Higgins' (*Evening Standard*, 24 June 1947, p.5)
p.199    'He was accustomed... their methods' (*In the Name of the Law*, p.31)
p.199-200    'Did you say... concerned in it' (*Evening Standard*, 24 June 1947, p.5)
p.200    'Did either of you... implicated you in this?' (*Evening Standard*, 24 June 1947, p.5)
p.200    'The truth was... Judges' Rules' (The memoirs of both Higgins and Fabian confirm that Rolt was told about Geraghty's statement, implicating him in the crime. See *Fabian of the Yard*, p.107 and *In the Name of the Law*, p.133.)
p.201    'No' (*Evening Standard*, 24 June 1947, p.5)
p.201    'Geraghty was... quite voluntarily' (*Evening Standard*, 24 June 1947, p.5)
p.201    'Do you wish... call no witnesses' (PRO, CRIM1/1861)
p.202    'Jenkins was... doubtful' (PRO, CRIM1/1861)
p.202    'He was characterised... grab raids' (PRO, CRIM1/1861)
p.202    'By Jove!' (*The Incredible Mrs Van der Elst*, p.30)
p.202    'Doge Cream' (*The Incredible Mrs Van der Elst*, p.22)
p.202    'Marvellous... Restorer' (*The Incredible Mrs Van der Elst*, p.90)
p.203    'legalised murder' (*The Incredible Mrs Van der Elst*, p.45)
p.203    'Pitié Avec Justice' (*The Incredible Mrs Van der Elst*, p.35)
p.204    'Jenkins and Rolt... largesse' (Between 1939 and 1948, Mrs Van der Elst's assistant, Ben Hayes, was sent round 'to arrange for the defence of the accused when necessary'. See *The Incredible Mrs Van der Elst*, p.130)
p.204    'I have interviewed... indictment' (PRO, CRIM1/1861)
p.204    'Since their arrest... en route' (*Times*, 26 May 1947, p.2)
p.205    '145,152,000... OUT!' (*The Old Bailey*, p.121)
p.205    'the genial Cockney judge' (*Daily Mail*, 24 July 1947, p.3)
p.207    'He requested... Vick represents' (*Evening Standard*, 21 July 1947, p.5)
p.207    'His speech... identification' (*Star*, 21 July 1947, p.4)
p.207    'an ordinary... occupation' (*Evening Standard*, 21 July 1947, p.5)
p.207    'Who fired... Antiquis?' (*Times*, 22 July 1947, p.2)
p.207-8    'Hawke read... pulled it' (*Evening Standard*, 21 July 1947, p.5)
p.208    'he told... the gang' (*Times*, 22 July 1947, p.2)
p.208    'very valiant attempt' (*Daily Telegraph*, 22 July 1947, p.5)
p.208    'Grimshaw's reference... shall prevail' (*Daily Mail*, 22 July 1947, p.3)
p.208-9    'Hawke summoned... be recorded' (*News Chronicle*, 23 July 1947, p.3)
p.209    'Higgins then read out... aspects of it' (*News Chronicle*, 23 July 1947, p.3)
p.209    'Hodge confirmed... the Thames' (*Times*, 23 July 1947, p.2)
p.209    'Never mind... Churchill' (*The Other Mr Churchill*, p.9)
p.210    'Hawke questioned... fifty-years-old' (*Evening News*, 22 July 1947, p.3)
p.210    'He disliked... opposing lawyers' (*The Other Mr Churchill*, p.16)
p.210    'Despite finding... defence lawyers' (*The Other Mr Churchill*, p.10 and p.95)
p.210    'He asked... fire each shot' (*Star*, 22 July 1947, p.5)
p.210    'During recent... policy' (*The Other Mr Churchill*, p.11)
p.211    'Questioned by... on Antiquis' (*Evening News*, 22 July 1947, p.3)
p.211    'Spilsbury's courtroom... jury' (*In the Name of the Law*, p.205)
p.211    'began to question... No' (*Evening News*, 22 July 1947, p.3)
p.212    'Shown the... Rotherhithe' (*Star*, 22 July 1947, p.5
p.212    'Hawke also showed... he isn't' (*Evening News*, 22 July 1947, p.3)

p.212    'a white scarf saw him' (PRO, CRIM1/1861)
p.212    'who admired... his job' (Hawke's foreword to *Fabian of the Yard*, p.3)
p.212    'Hawke asked him... the coat' (*Times*, 23 July 1947, p.2)
p.212-14 'Hallett told Fabian... you again' (*Daily Mail*, 23 July 1947, p.3)
p.213    'He remarked... person' (*Times*, 24 July 1947, p.2)
p.213    'Wrightson made... behalf' (*Evening Standard*, 23 July 1947, p.4)
p.214    'O'Sullivan summoned... an alibi' (*Times*, 24 July 1947, p.2)
p.214-15 'Jenkins replied... did not laugh' (*Star*, 24 July 1947, p.4)
p.215    'Mrs Burnham, who... at stake' (*Star*, 24 July 1947, p.4 & *News of the World*, 3 August 1947, p.1)
p.215-16 'Vick delivered... to be obtained' (*Evening Standard*, 25 July 1947, p.5)
p.216    'the judge announced... morning' (*Times*, 25 July 1947, p.2)
p.217    'Hallett asked the ushers... to the case' (*Evening Standard*, 28 July 1947, p.1)
p.217    'It is not... be called?' (*Times*, 29 July 1947, p.2)
p.217-18 'He said... plain lie' (*Evening Standard*, 28 July 1947, p.1 and p.8)
p.218    'Hallett dismissed... heard it, too' (*Star*, 28 July 1947, p.5)
p.218    'You may have... the gunmen' (*Daily Herald*, 29 July 1947, p.1)
p.218    'Hallett warned... intent to rob' (*Times*, 29 July 1947, p.2)
p.218    'Jenkins's sister... outside' (*News of the World*, 3 August 1947, p.1)
p.218    'Members of... We are' (standard wording, culled from *The Trail of Ley and Smith*, p.308)
p.219    'This silence... tears' (*News Chronicle*, 29 July 1947, p.1 and *Daily Mail*, 29 July 1947, p.1)
p.219    'The jury have... known to the law' (*Daily Mail*, 29 July 1947, p.1)
p.219    'Prisoners at the bar... to the (standard wording, culled from *The Trail of Ley and Smith*, p.308)
p.219    'My Lords... King!' (standard wording, culled from *The Trail of Ley and Smith*, p.308)
p.219    'Just then... a death sentence' (*News of the World*, 3 August 1947, p.1)
p.219    'The sentence of... souls' (standard wording, culled from *The Trail of Ley and Smith*, p.308)
p.220    'he was asked... expired' (*Daily Mail*, 29 July 1947, p.1)
p.220    'Hallett said... separately' (*Times*, 29 July 1947, p.2)
p.220    'DEATH FOR... MEN' (*Daily Herald*, 29 July 1947, p.1)
p.220    'Firmin had... pity' (*Crime Man*, p.39)
p.220    'The end of... recent times' (*Daily Telegraph*, 29 July 1947, p.1)
p.222    'the Binney Memorial Medal' (*Evening Standard*, 29 July 1947, p.5)
p.222-24 'a high-spirited... murderer' (*Sunday Pictorial*, 30 August 1947, p.7)
p.225-26 'Speaking on behalf... Antiquis's murder' (*Evening News*, 3 September 1947, p.4)
p.226    'The man was... birthday' (*vening Standard*, 3 September 1947, p.1)
p.226    'If a number... be dismissed' (*Times*, 4 September 1947, p.6)
p.227    'But he still felt... the cheap' (*Executioner*, p.75)
p.227-28 Pierrepoint had noticed... upsetting' (*Executioner*, p.63)
p.228    'Pierrepoint knew from... confusion' (*Executioner*, p.94)
p.228    'Through bitter... trapdoors' (*Executioner*, p.191)
p.228    'Part of the reason... known to the a hanging.' (*Executioner*, p.149)
p.229    'the craft' (*Executioner*, p.9)
p.229    'Old Bill' (*Executioner*, p.89)
p.230    'Our Albert' (*Executioner*, p.91)
p.231    'Pierrepoint was proud... prisoners' (*Executioner*, p.189)
p.231    'Knowledgeable as he... dances' (*Executioner*, p.102)
p.232    'By looking at... to the scaffold' (*Executioner*, p.127)
p.232    'He remembered... for his visit' (*Executioner*, p.181)
p.233    'Despite his... this show' (Interview with Tony Van den Bergh)
p.233-35 'He explained... Love, Jim' (*News of the World*, 21 September 1947, p.1 & *No Hiding Place*, p.134)
p.235-36 'As the hangmen... still warranted mercy' (*Executioner*, p.96)
p.236    'he thought of... be done' (*Executioner*, p.31)
p.236    'STOP CAPITAL... WEAKNESS' (*The Incredible Mrs Van der Elst*, p.43-44)

p.236-37    'The crowd...cigarette' (*Evening Standard*, 19 September 1947, p.1 and p.3 as well as
            *Evening News*, 19 September 1947, p.1)
p.237       'But he didn't... prison' (In his execution diary, Pierrepoint marked the occasions when
            he supplied his own wrist-straps.)
p.237       'He felt that... decisions' (*Executioner*, p.74-75)
p.237-38    'Aylwen, a stockbroker... Boer War' (*Times*, 28 September 1967, p.10)
p.238       'Follow me' (*Executioner*, p.129)
p.238       'he had observed... of death' (*Executioner*, p.111)
p.238       'I've always... circumstances' (*Pierrepoint: A Family of Executioners*, p.194)
p.238       'I am the the resurrection... die' (*Pierrepoint: A Family of Executioners*, p.283-284)
p.239       'Remember not... forever' (*Pierrepoint: A Family of Executioners*, p.283-284)
p.239       'Into thy hands... unto thee' (*Pierrepoint: A Family of Executioners*, p.283-284)
p.240       'Pierrepoint, who was appalled... to die' (*Executioner*, p.182)
p.240       'A hanged man's heart... minutes' (Royal Commission on Capital Punishment, 1949-53,
            Minutes of Evidence, quoted in *Reflections on Hanging*, p.143)
p.240       'However protracted... expeditious' (Royal Commission on Capital Punishment,
            1949-53, Minutes of Evidence, quoted in *Reflections on Hanging*, p.138)
p.240       'Whenever he handled... they'd hung' (*Executioner*, p.130)
p.240       'The corpse... or Christ' (*Executioner*, p.130)
p.241       'Murders of that type... clear up' (*In the Name of the Law*, p.112)
p.241       'Disapproving though... citizen' (*In the Name of the Law*, p.116)
p.241       'the grim atmosphere... morning' (*In the Name of the Law*, p.219)
p.241       'Never had... followed an execution' (*In the Name of the Law*, p.219)
p.242       'Purchase, who... Table of Drops' (*A Very English Hangman*, p.36-37)
p.242       'I should like... team' (*Evening Standard*, 19 September 1947, p.1)
p.243       'Before the crowd... here today' (*Evening News*, 19 September 1947, p.1)
p.244       'JENKINS... SCAFFOLD' (*Evening News*, 19 September 1947, p.1)

## EPILOGUE

See *In the Name of the Law* and *Bernard Spilsbury: His Life and Times* for the section about Bernard
Spilsbury's suicide.

p.247       'All the persons... pursuits' (*Executioner*, p.153-154)
p.247       'It was suggested... effective' (*Executioner*, p.154)
p.248       'I have... revenge" (*Executioner*, p.10)
p.248       'Stop, I am... bullet through you' (*Times*, 24 February 1953, p.3)

# Acknowledgements

I'd like to thank Peter Krämer, John King and Jon Jackson for their countless helpful and morale-boosting comments on various drafts of this book. Further editorial back-up was supplied by Dewi Lewis who had the courage to rescue the project from oblivion. I'm similarly indebted to Virginia Ironside and Marc Glendening who provided me with accommodation in London and, better still, plentiful encouragement and practical assistance over a long period. Thanks are also due to Robert Hastings, Cathi Unsworth, D.J. Taylor, David Collard, Peter Parker and Selina Hastings, all of whom offered much-appreciated support and advice. In addition I'd like to express my gratitude to Alec Vale, Sally Fiber, the late Tony Van den Bergh and the late Percy Burgess for their patience and generosity in answering my often absurdly detailed questions. Other vital information was unearthed with the help of Maggie Bird, Head of the Metropolitan Police Historical Collection; David Capus of the Metropolitan Police Service's Records Management Branch; Rachel Fell of the Home Office; Bev Baker of the National Galleries of Justice; Martin Humphries of the Ronald Grant Archive; David Wall of David Wall Classic Cars; Kirk Laws; Alison Chew of the Royal Institute of British Architects; Paul Duncan, author of a forthcoming biography of Gerald Kersh; Richard Gray of the Cinema Theatre Association for information about London cinemas in 1947; Mike Pentelow and Juliet Brightmore for their help in trying to solve a copyright problem; plus Dr Lawrence Napper and Dr Sheldon Hall, experts on British film history, who sent me a wealth of background information about *The Blue Lamp*. I'm grateful as well to Claire Alexander and Ayeesha Karim of Gillon Aitken Associates for the work they put into finding a publisher for *North Soho 999*. Above all, I want to thank my long-suffering girlfriend, Jo Willingham, who now knows more than she ever wanted to know about 1940s CID work.

Also by Paul Willetts

## FEAR AND LOATHING IN FITZROVIA

The bizarre life of writer, actor, Soho raconteur
Julian Maclaren-Ross

£12.99 softback, 352 pages
ISBN: 978-1-904587-27-9

For a full list of our titles please visit our web sites

www.dewilewispublishing.com

www.dewilewismedia.com

## LONDON BOOKS
flying the flag for free-thinking literature

London Books is an independent publisher specialising in classic London fiction, with a special interest in authors who operated beyond the mainstream, maverick writers with something to say and an exciting way of getting their ideas across.

Mixing substance and style, social concerns with a vibrant use of language, the London Classics series kicks off with three titles. These consist of James Curtis's cult 1930s crime novel *The Gilt Kid*; Gerald Kersh's *Night and the City*, which anticipated the better-known novels of Patrick Hamilton; and, striking a different yet equally resonant note, Alan Sillitoe's *A Start in Life*, published with a new foreword by the author.

For further details and an overview of London literature, please visit www.london-books.co.uk

# THE GORSE TRILOGY
(The West Pier; Mr Stimpson and Mr Gorse; Unknown Assailant)
## Patrick Hamilton

*The Gorse Trilogy* follows the fortunes of a petty swindler and charmer, Earnest Ralph Gorse (based on the real-life con-man and murderer Neville George Heath, executed in 1946). Gorse insinuates himself into the lives of his victims with his good looks and easy confidence, and always with a good story, until he is in a position to turn things to his advantage. The plots are skilfully constructed and developed, the characters' psychology deftly exposed – their naivete, snobbery or greed make them perfect victims – and the books have a brooding menace and sense of terrible inevitability that are entirely Hamilton's own.

Black Spring Press
paperback original
ISBN 978-0-948238-34-5
£9.95, 640 pages

"The entertainment value of this brilliantly told story
could hardly be higher."
— L.P. HARTLEY, SUNDAY TIMES

"Hamilton was a marvellous novelist
who's grossly neglected."
— DORIS LESSING

"A riveting dissector of English life up
to and including the war."
— KEITH WATERHOUSE

"His finest work can easily stand comparison with the
best of his more celebrated contemporaries
George Orwell and Graham Greene."
— SUNDAY TELEGRAPH